AVOCADO DREAMS

Ana Patricia Rodríguez

AVOCADO DREAMS

Remaking Salvadoran Life and Art in the Washington, D.C. Metro Area

THE UNIVERSITY OF
ARIZONA PRESS
TUCSON

The University of Arizona Press
www.uapress.arizona.edu

We respectfully acknowledge the University of Arizona is on the land and territories of Indigenous peoples. Today, Arizona is home to twenty-two federally recognized tribes, with Tucson being home to the O'odham and the Yaqui. The University strives to build sustainable relationships with sovereign Native Nations and Indigenous communities through education offerings, partnerships, and community service.

© 2025 by The Arizona Board of Regents
All rights reserved. Published 2025

ISBN-13: 978-0-8165-4643-5 (hardcover)
ISBN-13: 978-0-8165-4642-8 (paperback)
ISBN-13: 978-0-8165-4644-2 (ebook)

Cover design by Leigh McDonald
Cover art: Awakat Che' picto-glyph by Frida Larios. Awakat Che' picto-glyph depicts an avocado tree with a regenerated Maya hieroglyphics recomposed to create a new meaning. Our Maya ancestors believed that once we died, we resuscitated as fruit trees. The spoken words Awakat Che', Árbol de Aguacate, Avocado Tree, intersect the words: Awakat in Salvadoran Nawat with the word Che' in Classic Maya script and in Maya Ch'orti', a mirror of mixed Indigenous descendancy (mestiza), and just like Awakatero (aguacatero) dog or "chucho" (Shulut in Nawat) was nicknamed that way because of its mestizaje (mixed ancestry).
Typeset by Leigh McDonald in Warnock Pro 10.5/14 and Fenwick (display)

Early versions of chapters 1, 2, and 3 appeared, respectively, in *Constructed Latinx(s) Identities: Racialized Bodies in Visual and Textual Culture*, edited by José I. Lara (Amherst College Press, 2025); in *Washington History* (vol. 28, no. 2, Fall 2016); and in *Imagined Transnationalism: U.S. Latino/a Literature, Culture, and Identity*, edited by Kevin Concannon and colleagues (Palgrave Macmillan, 2009). I have entirely rethought and rewritten these pieces as chapters for this book. I have also gathered and included here bits and pieces from my work throughout the years.

Publication of this book is made possible in part by the proceeds of a permanent endowment created with the assistance of a Challenge Grant from the National Endowment for the Humanities, a federal agency.

Library of Congress Cataloging-in-Publication Data can be found on the last page.

Printed in the United States of America
♾ This paper meets the requirements of ANSI/NISO Z39.48-1992 (Permanence of Paper).

For my father, don Mario Rodríguez Duarte, el gran aguacatero, who was Salvadoran to the core and taught my sisters and me to honor our Salvadoreñidad in diaspora. He nurtured us with his positivity, humor, and storytelling. On February 17, 2023, he became an ancestor.

Until we meet again . . .

CONTENTS

ILLUSTRATIONS

ACKNOWLEDGMENTS

Para comenzar, since *Avocado Dreams* is all about (re)making life and art away from home, I would like to *agradecer* my *familia* for being the shining beacons in my life, always lighting the way back home with their steadfast presence, guidance, and encouragement. To them, I am eternally grateful for planting and sustaining the seeds of my Salvadoreñidad, holding a space for me at the *recinto*, and giving me shelter and *resposo* whenever I have needed it the most. Time and time again, they remind me that home is where the heart is, whether it be San Salvador, Washington, D.C., or San Francisco, California. The *terruño* (homeland) is where you make it, what you make of it, and how you build it with memories, dreams, laughter, and people. Here, I especially thank my family members, whom I carry deep in my heart, mind, and soul, despite the distance and separation: my sisters, Claudia M. Rodríguez, Nancy G. Rodríguez, and Cynthia E. Rodríguez-Oxley; my nephews and niece, Cassius and Caelan Rodríguez-Hayes, and Jaxon and Siena Oxley; my brothers-in-law, Sean Hayes and Mike Oxley; and my cousins, Silvia Ramírez de Lemus, Ana María Figueroa, and Ericka, Kathy, and Sophia Valladares.

While I have been away at work in Washington, D.C., we have lost beloved members of our family, including my father, Mario Rodríguez Duarte, who was the first in our family to immigrate to the United States and who led the way for so many relatives and friends to follow in his footsteps. Originally from Santa Ana, El Salvador, my dad would often repeat a saying that many Santanecos and Santanecas use in reference to their hometown. To them, Santa Ana is the *capital del mundo* (capital of the world) and the *sucursal del cielo* (branch office of heaven). In 2023, my dad passed away before I could return home to see him again. I like to think that he is now in that main headquarters enjoying a *cafecito* with a piece of *quesadilla* (sweet cheese pound cake) and maybe a few *pupusas* (stuffed corn tortillas), in the company of his parents, brothers, and sisters, my mother, and other family members. Thank you, *papi,* for teaching us so many valuable lessons, *consejos,* and sayings, always with such good humor, charm, and gusto. I like to think, too, that my mother, who passed away long ago, when my sisters and I were children, has watched over us and guided us all these years through our many peaks and valleys. *Gracias, mami!*

Through it all, I have found that it is the *amigues del camino,* the constant friends and the happenstance strangers we meet along the way, who make the most difference in our lives, although in different measures. I am grateful to all those faithful friends and fleeting acquaintances who have helped me in some way through the good and bad times. Under the duress of deadlines and all other matters, those loyal friends always seem to come through with a helping hand, attentive ear, and kind word. To paraphrase Roque Dalton's "Poema de amor," these are my *eternos compatriotas* and *hermanes,* my beloved friends, guides, and mentors, whom I carry in my heart, from California to Washington, D.C., and back: Maya Chinchilla, Sergio de la Mora, Martivón Galindo, Angelo J. Gómez and Marina Riquelme, Roxana Guillen, Michelle Habell-Pallán, Vilma Herrera, Millie Lanauze, Victoria-María MacDonald, Carmen Román, Christopher A. Shinn, and Deb Vargas. *Thank you, friends of a lifetime!*

Then, I have to thank my D.C. and DMV (Washington, D.C. metropolitan area) interlocutors, who have shown me how to be Salvadoran in *Wachinton,* starting with Quique Avilés, who has poeticized our D.C. Salvadoran experiences; Mauricio Alarcón, Ricardo Ernesto Campos, Jorge Granados, and Ana Sol Gutiérrez, among others, who came to D.C. with or before the great civil war induced migration and have since offered *sanctuario* and assistance to so many migrants; Olivia Cadaval, who was among the first to record the unfiltered voices of Salvadoreños/as in D.C., writing about us in her groundbreaking work; Dr. Danielle Parada, who has led the way for us to recognize our Salvadoran Blackness in the DMV; Dr. Amelia Tseng, who has been at the forefront of studying the sociolinguistics of Salvadorans in the DMV; Abel Núñez, executive director of the Central American Resource Center (CARECEN) in D.C., and my fellow board members, who are on the front lines of the war on immigration; Mike Balis, National Park Service ranger, who worked with me to design and offer to the general public the D.C. Latino Tour, highlighting Salvadoran landmarks in the nation's capital; and Ranald Woodaman and Patrick D. Scallen, who have opened spaces of representation for Salvadorans at institutions like the Smithsonian and the D.C. History Center. Finally, I am immensely grateful to Dr. Jeannette Noltenius for cofounding and inviting me to be on the board of Casa de la Cultura de El Salvador in Washington, D.C. During the darkest hours of the COVID-19 pandemic lockdown, she established a command center in her home, from which she live streamed hundreds of hours of Salvadoran cultural events via YouTube, literally connecting El Salvador and its diasporas and giving many people a cultural lifeline. She was also only an email, text, or phone call away, whenever I had a query about Salvadoran culture or language. *Gracias, maestra!*

At the University of Maryland, College Park, I have had the privilege to work with colleagues in the Department of Spanish and Portuguese (SPAP) toward our common goal to teach the Spanish language while centering our respective fields and interests. Being in such good company has permitted me to teach at the intersections of Central American and U.S. Latinx studies. Thank you to all my SPAP and School of Languages, Literatures, and Cultures (SLLC) colleagues, but most specially to Ana Acedo García, Evelyn Canabal-Torres, Laura Demaría, Andrea Frisch, Kira Gor, Fatemeh Keshavarz, Manel Lacorte, Chris Lewis, Ryan Long, José Magro, Eyda M. Merediz, Mehl A. Penrose, Professor Emerita Gabi Strauch, and *la mera, mera,* Mel Scullen, SLLC director. I owe a special note of thanks to the people who have helped me do my work in and outside of the university: Gloria Aparicio Blackwell, Chanel A. Briscoe, Nicco Cooper, Barbara Lewis, Charlotte Tai, and Janel M. Brennan-Tillmann, who is ever ready to assist me on Central American–focused projects and programming. Dr. Nancy Raquel Mirabal has been a fearless ally, collaborator, and confidant. I am happy to call her a true friend and *colega,* something that I do not say or treat lightly. *Gracias, amiga!*

To my current and former undergraduate and graduate students who have left a mark on me, thank you for being such good people and making such good trouble in the world, whatever your field or career. Keep on making good trouble *porque ustedes sí son cachimbonxs*: José A. Centeno-Meléndez, Alvi Escobar, Alexa Figueroa, Erica Fuentes, Nery González, José Granados, Arelis R. Hernández, Evelyn López, Ronald Luna, Delmy Liliana Morales Álvarez, Angela Pico Pinto, Laura M. Quijano, Ana Ventura-Molina, and Mariángel Villalobos Benavides. Look at you all, doing great things with passion and *compromiso* in the schools, in the public, private, and nonprofit sectors, and even at the *Washington Post* and the U.S. House of Representatives!

One of the highlights of my career has been to serve as president (2017–19) and ex officio executive council member (2019–23) of the Latina/o Studies Association (LSA). Only a few of us can understand the *angustia*, stress, and joy of organizing a conference on limited funds and watching over an organization that we have nurtured and grown together from inception to the present. A special shout-out, then, goes out my fellow stewards of the LSA: Frances R. Aparicio, Lee Bebout, Marta Caminero-Santangelo, Dolores Inés Casillas, Michael Innis-Jiménez, Ylce Irizarry, Carmen E. Lamas, and Rafael Pérez-Torres.

Another highlight of my academic life has been to help build and elevate Central American studies in the United States. In this book, I honor my *colegas* who have also devoted their lives to this work. May we see the day that we do not have to justify the existence of the important and indisputable field of Central American studies. *Muchísimas gracias* for laying the cornerstones on which we may collectively build Central American futurities: Leisy J. Abrego, Karina Alma, Arturo Arias, Maritza E. Cárdenas, Gloria E. Chacón, Maya Chinchilla, Carlos B. Córdova, Cary Cordova, Kency Cornejo, Beatriz Cortez, Alicia I. Estrada, Valeria Grinberg Pla, Ester E. Hernández, Roberto Lovato, Werner Mackenbach, Julia Medina, Cecilia Menjívar, Yajaira M. Padilla, Suyapa G. Portillo Villeda, Cecilia M. Rivas, Ariana E. Vigil, Ana Yency of the Fundación Afrodescendientes Organizados Salvadoreños (AFROOS), and Karina L. Zelaya. Also, thanks to the brilliant scholars taking Central American studies to new levels and areas: Jennifer A. Cárcamo, José A. Centeno-Meléndez, Manuel Criollo, Jorge E. Cuéllar, Eileen M. Gálvez, José I. Lara, Paul Joseph López Oro, Jeannette Martínez, Alexis N. Meza, Mauricio E. Ramírez, Nicole

Ramsey, and countless others. In her classic poem "Solidarity Baby," Maya Chinchilla does well to remind us to hold the door open for all those who are "coming thru" and who report on "truths untold" about "the silent / who carry this country on their backs!" I would say that is one of the main tenets and goals of Central American studies.

In many ways, Chinchilla, whom I met at the University of California, Santa Cruz, in the 1990s, when I was a graduate student instructor, and have since called a constant friend, planted the seeds for U.S. Central American studies in her 2014 *The Cha Cha Files: A Chapina Poética.* Since then, I have followed the vines and branches that have led me to the artists, writers, poets, and artivists of the DMV, who are the *semilla* or core of *Avocado Dreams.* With their talents, these DMV artists sketch, paint, draw, perform, and imagine worlds and inspire us to materialize those worlds. Infinite thanks go to all the intertwined Salvadoran DMV-based and DMV-allied creatives whose avocado-dreaming work is discussed, or mentioned, in this book: Jorge Argueta, Manlio Argueta, Quique Avilés, Kimberly Benavides, Mario Bencastro, Hilary Binder-Avilés, Aída Esmeralda Campos, Mayamérica Cortez, Lilo González, Lilito González, Muriel Hasbun, Víctor H. Interiano (Dichos de un bicho), Frida Larios, Kiara Aileen Machado, Veronica Meléndez, Sami Miranda, Mauricio Novoa, Carlos Parada-Ayala, Karla "Karlísima" Rodas, Rafael Rodríguez Molina, Claudia Rojas, Ric Salinas and Herbert Siguenza of Culture Clash, Nicolás F. Shi, and Ellie Walton, among others. Because community lies at the heart of community-based work, I would also like to recognize the many community members, including the Central and Latin American immigrant women and children, whom my students and I serve in Prince George's County Public Schools through the Aprendiendo Juntos / Learning Together program. We learn so much more from them than they can ever learn from us. *Gracias, comunidades hispanohablantes!*

Last but definitely not least, I would like to express my utmost gratitude to the folks at the University of Arizona Press for publishing *Avocado Dreams.* I am profoundly grateful to Kristen A. Buckles, editor-in-chief extraordinaire, who has supported this book from our first chance meeting at the 2019 American Studies Association (ASA) conference in Honolulu, Hawai'i, to the book's completion here. I also am grateful to Amanda Krause (editorial, design, and production manager), to Jessica Hinds-Bond of Good Strong Words for her amazing editing prowess, and to all the other personnel who have worked on various aspects of producing this book. Thank you, thank you! To the anonymous reviewers of *Avocado Dreams,* I value every comment and suggestion that you offered for the book's improvement. I can only hope that I have done justice to your assessments of my book. Any and all errors and omissions, of course, are mine.

And finally, thank you, all, for reading *Avocado Dreams.*

AVOCADO DREAMS

INTRODUCTION

THE MISSING PIECES

Salvadorans in Diaspora

For years, I have worked at the intersections of Central American and Latina/o/x studies. I like to think that I came of age as a scholar in pursuit of knowledge about Central America, beginning with my first classes in Central American history, heritage, and literature at San Francisco State University with Professor Carlos Córdova and the Salvadoran writer Manlio Argueta in the mid- to late 1980s, and, years later, completing my dissertation on transnational Central American literatures at the University of California, Santa Cruz, just as Héctor Tobar's *The Tattooed Soldier* and the Archdiocese of Guatemala's *Guatemala Never Again! Recovery of Historical Memory Project* were published in 1998. Before that, I had been homeschooled in the history of the Salvadoran civil war and the stories of the Central American diasporas, of which my family and I are bona fide members. In some small measure, I hope that through the years I have contributed to the formation of Central American studies in the United States with my work on transnational Central American literary and cultural production and my own Salvi (U.S. Salvadoran) story, situated across different translocations of the Salvadoran diaspora, from the San Francisco Bay Area, California, where I grew up, to the Washington, D.C. metropolitan area, where I have worked most of my professional life and put down roots, so to speak, like many Salvadoran immigrants before me. This book, thus, is not only the tale of one of my homes but also an

With my reality, I have won the right to express it and share it.
[Yo, con mi realidad, me he ganado el derecho a expresarla y compartirla].

- Manlio Argueta
Cuzcatlán, donde bate la mar del sur

FIGURE 1. "Cuzcatlán, donde bate la mar del sur," by Víctor H. Interiano (Dichos de un bicho), 2024. Courtesy of Víctor H. Interiano.

exploration into a significant, yet often overlooked, location within the Salvadoran diaspora—the Washington, D.C. metropolitan area, also known as the DMV, encompassing the District of Columbia and surrounding portions of Maryland and Virginia.

Like many other one-and-a-half-generation immigrants, I was brought to the United States as a young child by my parents, who made the ultimate "immigrant bargain," sacrificing their lives and dreams to invest in their children's future and education (Louie). When they emigrated from El Salvador in the late 1960s, they left behind the lives they had known in order to resettle in the San Francisco Bay Area. Growing up in and about San Francisco against the backdrop of the civil rights and immigrant rights movements in the United States and the armed conflicts in Central America in the 1970s, '80s, and '90s, I witnessed the ongoing exodus and the arrival of family members and friends displaced by violence. I remember vividly the media coverage of the assassination of archbishop (and now saint) Óscar A. Romero on March 24, 1980, a watershed event that will, perhaps, forever mark my life, as well as the harrowing stories told by family members fleeing El Salvador at that time. For my family and me, the streets of San Francisco were paved by the comings and goings of loved ones passing through our sanctuary home as they migrated to the United States. The poet Maya Chinchilla has written about growing up as a "Solidarity Baby," witnessing historic events from within her own home and being part of the wider "Central American Underground Railroad" (*Cha Cha* 3–6), which has aided people fleeing war, violence, and persecution, then and now. So, too, my family home served as a sanctuary for many people.

In college and graduate school, like Chinchilla and others, I found my way back home to Central America through my captivated readings of Salvadoran literature, particularly *la literatura comprometida* (engaged literature), resistance texts, and *testimonios*. I remember once reading well into the night the anthology *Poesía de El Salvador*, edited by Argueta, featuring the works of forty-one young poets of the Salvadoran *movimiento revolucionario*, many of whom were eventually killed, disappeared, or forced into exile. One of my cousins in the movement had loaned me the book, which inspired the writing of my very first published essay, "Salvadorean Poetry of Conscience (A Student Term Paper)," for an issue of *Cipactli*, the groundbreaking journal of the then La Raza Studies Department at

San Francisco State University. That raw essay, riddled with writing errors and impassioned claims, by a first-generation college student owes its existence to Central American writers, scholars, intellectuals, activists, and mentors like Dr. Córdova and Argueta, who left their mark on generations of Central American students in and outside of Central America. In that essay, thanks to these mentors, I wrote: "The Central American writer, specifically the Salvadorean poet, writes his [*sic*] poems without money, without privacy, with hunger, by candlelight, in jail, before death, through a voice that is often pained and hoarse, yet hopeful, or else why would s/he write?" (4).

Inspired by the words and *compromiso* (commitment) of so many (unnamed and unrecognized) solidarity workers, I made it my lifelong goal to learn more about Central America and about my own roots and routes as a diasporic Salvadoran.[1] That search would take me to El Salvador in 1989–90, during *la ofensiva final* (the final phase) of the civil war and at the end of my first year of graduate school, to live with family, teach English at the Universidad de El Salvador (UES), and immerse myself in the libraries, archives, and classrooms of the UES and the Universidad Centroamericana José Simeón Cañas. That summer, I also clandestinely attended literature classes and rallies alongside other UES students and, on one occasion, even ran with them across campus as loud booms sounded in the distance. I had come to El Salvador looking for Central American histories and stories constantly beyond my reach, and I found them, again, in the testimonial literature of Argueta, Claribel Alegría, Roque Dalton, Nidia Díaz, Rigoberta Menchú, and others. Central American literature would remain a beacon in my life, illuminating all the questions I have had about my history, culture, and identity and making visible (at least to me) what had been rendered invisible by my own migration to the United States.

Arturo Arias's article "Central American–Americans: Invisibility, Power and Representation in the US Latino World," published in 2003 in the inaugural issue of *Latino Studies*, was, to me, a call to action—a call to confront the intentional speech and visual acts of disappearance committed on all things Central American, including my own family's story (Rodríguez, "Salvadoran Immigrant Acts"). Arias's bold breakthrough publication in Latina/o/x studies inspired me to make visible what has been and continues to be *invisibilized* about Central America/ns and, truth be told, guided my work in Central American studies at a time when the first program in the field had just been established at California State University, Northridge, and when I had only recently, in 1998, begun working at the University of Maryland, College Park.

At that time, U.S. Central American–inspired texts had also just begun to be published as part of a larger U.S. Latina/o literary and cultural boom. For many U.S. Central Americans in the 1990s, such texts as Graciela Limón's *In Search of Bernabé*, Demetria Martínez's *Mother Tongue*, Héctor Tobar's *The Tattooed Soldier*, Francisco Goldman's *The Long Night of White Chickens*, Mario Bencastro's *Odyssey to the North*, and Katherine Cowy Kim and colleagues' *Izote Vos: A Collection of Salvadoran American Writing and Visual Art* were our first exposure to Latina/o/x literature featuring Central American content,[2] although these texts still often told only partial stories and raised even more questions for us about who gets to tell our stories and how they are told (Rodríguez, "Fiction"; Rodríguez, "Refugees"). This nascent U.S. Central American–themed literature, however, began to fill the void left by the missing pieces of our excised history, rarely discussed at home, at school, or in other spaces. With the emergence of U.S. Central American studies, the deep history of Central Americans in the United States and the world began to be uncovered—or rather recovered—and U.S. Latinx and Central American cultural producers, writers, and creatives such as Chinchilla, Leticia Hernández-Linares, and Quique Avilés broke the silence with questions about the Central American diasporas, their histories, and their place in between, or what I have called elsewhere the transisthmus (Rodríguez, *Dividing*; Rodríguez, "Toward a Transisthmian").

Leaving a lasting impact on me, Argueta, who was exiled in San Francisco for part of the civil war, taught me the worth of my Salvadoran story when he had the protagonist of his novel *Cuzcatlán, donde bate la mar del sur* (*Cuzcatlán: Where the Southern Sea Beats*), Lucía (nom de guerre, Ticha) say: "Yo, con mi realidad, me he ganado el derecho a expresarla y compartirla" (With my reality, I have won the right to express it and share it) (211) (figure 1).[3] So too, with this book, *Avocado Dreams: Remaking Salvadoran Life and Art in the Washington, D.C. Metro Area*, I reflect on my journey to and in the Salvadoran diaspora in the Washington, D.C. metropolitan area. Home to the largest Salvadoran immigrant population concentrated in one single area, now almost four generations deep (see

Centeno-Meléndez, *Placemaking*), the DMV has become my Salvadoran home, too. Largely originating in the eastern part of El Salvador, commonly referred to as Oriente, and more specifically in cities and towns like El Triunfo, Intipucá, Usulután, and San Miguel, Salvadorans have made themselves (at) home in the DMV and have transformed the region, contributing their labor, ingenuity, and culture to the making of a thriving but highly neglected and overlooked community. In the process, they have also remade themselves in relation to the cultural, ethnoracial, and sociolinguistic diversity of the DMV and its many communities (most notably Black Washingtonians), developing unique, intergenerational Salvadoreñidades (Salvadoran identities), manifested in particular speech and symbolic acts, ethnoracial embodiments, and local identity formations.

The Makings and Markings of the Salvadoran Diaspora in the DMV

Drawing from my own positionality as a Salvi transplant in D.C. from another translocation of the Salvadoran diaspora (the San Francisco Bay Area), I examine in this book the construction of a unique Salvadoran cultural imaginary in the DMV. Based on readings of works by local writers, performers, artists, and artivists, *Avocado Dreams* delves into the stories of the Salvadoran diaspora from the location of the DMV, which often goes unperceived, despite the fact that, it bears repeating, the largest concentration of Salvadorans in all of the United States resides in this singular region. It is no exaggeration to say that Latinidad is often unwittingly associated with Salvadoran culture in the DMV, given Salvadorans' demographic numbers, their historical presence, and their socioeconomic and cultural impact in the region. Indeed, scholars of the DMV have noted the deep history of Salvadoran migration to the region through the collection and archiving of Salvadoran oral histories and ethnographies (Centeno-Meléndez, *Placemaking*; Repak; Scallen, *Bombs*); the ubiquitous soundscapes of the Salvadoran diaspora heard throughout festivals, streets, restaurants, homes, and mixed musical genres (Cadaval, *Creating*; Villalobos Benavides); and the evolution of new Salvadoran-inflected translanguages intersecting with other U.S. Spanish variants and African American English (Rodríguez "¿Dónde estás vos/z?"; Tseng, *Empanadas*). To this emerging critical literature, I now contribute an analysis of the important role literary and creative texts play in the production of diasporic Salvadoran cultural imaginaries in the DMV. *Avocado Dreams* draws from a wellspring of short stories, novels, artworks, performances, and other cultural texts and practices to shed light on how Salvadorans (re)make themselves and mark their presence in the DMV through literature, storytelling, and cultural productions, understood as evolving sign systems that are not lost in migration and translation, but rather imprint themselves across translocations of the Salvadoran diaspora. In other words, Salvadorans, like other diasporic groups, not only disperse "from an original homeland, often traumatically, to two or more foreign regions," as global diasporas scholar Robin Cohen claims, but also construct collective memories, myths, cultural identities, and "distinctive creative, enriching li[ves] in host countries with a tolerance for pluralism" (17).

In *Signs of the Americas: A Poetics of Pictography, Hieroglyphs, and Khipu*, Edgar García reminds us that "sign systems are living, evolving signifiers, responsive to their circumstances and able to continuously redefine themselves and the nature of the world" (cover). As migrants travel, their sign systems, cultural practices, and social imaginaries also travel, re-creating themselves and transculturating in proximity and in relation to other sign and cultural systems in specific locations such as the DMV. I argue in this book that Salvadorans in the DMV, like Salvadorans in other translocations of the diaspora, travel and migrate to new spaces, in which they transplant sign systems from originating points (although these sign systems are at times unbeknown to them and illegible to others). This book will show how Salvadorans (re)make, mark, and imprint their sign systems and cultures in vivid creative and artistic manifestations across the DMV. To illustrate this process, which I call the makings and markings of the Salvadoran diaspora, I first turn to onetime DMV-based Salvadoran writer and artist Mario Bencastro's short story "Las ilusiones de Juana" / "Juana's Dreams," published in his 2010 collection *Paraíso portátil / Portable Paradise*, which plots the origins of the Salvadoran diaspora in the DMV and inspired my thinking about Salvadoran avocado/ *aguacatero* identity formations in the diaspora. Then, I look at D.C.-based Salvadoran-Nawat-identified graphic artist Frida Larios's marking of public spaces across the Washington, D.C. metropolitan area with her signature Maya-inspired sign system, including avocado imagery. Both Bencastro's and Larios's works are examined at length in later chapters.

The Salvadoran Cultural Imaginary of Avocados and *Aguacates*

Truth be told, this book can trace its origins to my first reading of "Juana's Dreams" / "Las ilusiones de Juana." Most known for his novel *Odyssey to the North* (to date, the first and only novel to document the migration of Salvadorans and Central Americans to the DMV), Bencastro is a legendary figure in the DMV Salvadoran cultural scene, often invited to present his work at public venues, including schools, libraries, and official governmental spaces. In "Juana's Dreams," his protagonist, Juana, represents the iconic figure of the Salvadoran migrant woman, who, upon fleeing the civil war in El Salvador and settling with her family in the DMV, maintains close, transnational ties with her extended family back home. As documented in Terry A. Repak's foundational study of Salvadoran woman-led migration to the Washington, D.C. metropolitan area in the twentieth century, Juana represents the so-called *pioneras* (pioneers) who came to the region to work in the housekeeping, childcare, and hospitality industries, making it possible for family, friends, and other compatriots to migrate later to the DMV. Like her real-life counterparts, Juana sends remittances to her family without fail, communicates regularly with her relatives, and visits her country annually to attend las Fiestas Agostinas, celebrated every August 6 in honor of El Salvador del Mundo, the patron saint of San Salvador. On one such trip, after eating the best *aguacates* (avocados) during her birthday luncheon at her sister's house, Juana decides to return to the United States with smuggled avocado seeds. Upon her return to Virginia, she plants them, only to have them die in the sweltering heat and humidity of the mid-Atlantic summer, a symbolic death that puts an end to her travels to El Salvador and her nostalgic yearnings of returning to the homeland, which, as Svetlana Boym notes, "is a longing for a home that no longer exists or has never existed" (xiii). Indeed, for Boym, like for Juana, "nostalgia is a sentiment of loss and displacement" (xiii), a major theme in Bencastro's story.

Beginning with its title in English, "Juana's Dreams," the story seems to question the American Dream as the driving force behind much of Central American migration to the United States and can be read as an earnest interrogation of the American Dream ideology, which exacts much sacrifice, pain, and even death from migrants, as we know so well.[4] In the Spanish-language title, the word *ilusiones* does not exactly translate as dreams—or illusions, for that matter. The word *ilusiones* alludes to those concepts or images not founded in reality but arising from hopes, desires, and the imagination. What exactly are Juana's dreams and *ilusiones*? The story seems to imply that Juana's dreams (like other migrants' dreams) for material well-being, success, and money to send home in the form of remittances are often guided by *ilusiones*—illusions based on a desire to connect, belong, provide, and be loved. *Ilusiones* do not necessarily represent embodied, lived realities; rather, they represent the aspirations, hopes, and desires of immigrants living away from family, home, and homeland. Hence, scholars talk about nostalgic remittances as part of the *ilusiones* of forging and maintaining affective ties through migrant labor and sacrifice in diaspora.[5] While Juana, living in the United States, enjoys the material comforts of house, job, and trips to El Salvador and sends money to her relatives on a regular basis, she remains far from happy. Based on the title, readers are prompted to ask: Are Juana's dreams fulfilled? What does Juana want in diaspora? Notwithstanding the ability to send remittances home, Juana's *ilusiones* of connecting with her homeland, family, and roots remain suspended and unfulfilled until her fateful encounter with the avocados/*aguacates*. Key to understanding Juana's story, and by extension the story of Salvadorans in diaspora in the DMV, as I posit here, is reading the trope of avocados as part of a larger Salvadoran diasporic sign system, which, once removed from an original soil or source, may fail to take root in the U.S. dirt.[6]

Assuming the significance of the avocado metaphor in Bencastro's story, I ask: Why are avocados—or, rather, *aguacates*—central to the story? What do the avocados/*aguacates* signify? Are avocados simply *aguacates* by another name? Is an avocado still an *aguacate*, regardless of what it is called and where it is planted? To paraphrase William Shakespeare, "What's in a name?" Do *aguacates* known by other names (avocados) "smell as sweet," or retain their essential identitarian qualities even in other contexts? In sum, what makes Salvadorans "Salvadoran" in diaspora, and do they remain "Salvadoran" regardless of where they are located or transplanted? In the aftermath of the death of Juana's would-be avocado trees, Bencastro's story would seem to say that Salvadoran identities may not always take root in diaspora, although some may take new shapes in other soils, as their sign systems and translanguaging may take new forms and expressions in other contexts (E. García; Tseng, *Empanadas*). Thinking closely and deeply for years about Bencastro's story led me to the exploration of what it means, looks, and sounds like to be Salvadoran in a selection of texts by diasporic Salvadoran writers, poets, performers, artists, and artivists in the DMV.

Digging deeper into what it means to signify "Salvadoran" in diaspora, I next turn to the work of D.C.-based Salvadoran-Nawat-identified artist Frida Larios, who, inspired by Indigenous spirituality, thought, and aesthetics, designed the image *Awakat Che' (Awakateros)* for the cover of this book. Based on an ancient Maya glyph representing the avocado and the "Gran abuela K'ANAL-IKAL," or Lady Kanal-Ikal emerging with an avocado tree (see Landon 65; Martin 162), Larios produced an image of a Brown hand rising out of the soil, from which grow avocados in the four directions. As will be examined later in this book, Larios recreates and redeploys ancient Maya glyphs to access the living past in diaspora. Her work falls in line with Edgar García's stricture that Indigenous signifying systems are living and evolving signifiers, responsive to their circumstances (xv, 111), with present (and past) lives that speak to us regardless of the spaces we inhabit or relocate to. Larios, whose modern renderings of Maya glyphs grace such sites as the archaeological museum at Parque Arqueológico Joya de Cerén in western El Salvador and murals throughout the DMV, has developed what she calls a New Maya Language, which she uses to teach pictographic multiliteracy to children and adults in the DMV and elsewhere, as represented in her 2014 graphic book *La Aldea que fue sepultada por un volcán en Erupción / The Village That Was Buried by an Erupting Volcano*. In the image of *Awakat Che' (Awakateros)*, Larios envisions the continuity of the living past and creation of contemporary Salvadoran cultural identities and imaginaries rising from local contexts in diaspora, while Bencastro's short story "Juana's Dreams" represents the death of essentialist notions of Salvadoranness and the creation of new Salvadoreñidades across the translocations of the Salvadoran diaspora. Both artists seem to propose the transformations and transcreations of Salvadoreñidades in diaspora (Rodríguez, "¿Dónde estás vos/z?").

Taken together, these two DMV creatives offer critical visions for the construction of Salvadoran multigenerational, diasporic cultural imaginaries, using similar sociolinguistic and cultural tropes, such as the avocado/*aguacate*, to represent the roots and routes of the Salvadoran diaspora in the DMV. Thus, the avocado/*aguacate* and other cultural, raciolinguistic terms become central to the argument of this book. Drawing from theories of diaspora, worldmaking, and raciolinguistics, as well as my own close readings of texts, I examine the (re)makings and markings of Salvadoran diasporic cultural identities, using the Salvadoran terms *aguacatero/a*, *salvatruco/a*, *salvatrucha*, *cholero/a*, and *cachimbon/a/x*, which originate in Afro-Indigenous and Náhuat languages.[7] To this day, these terms are used, or, at least, are recognized, as colloquial monikers by many Salvadorans both within and outside the country. In this book, I deploy these terms to explore and map out the Salvadoran cultural and ethnoracial diasporic imaginary, with a particular focus on the DMV. I also use these terms as cultural, raciolinguistic tropes that conceptually organize and frame the chapters of this book, through visual memes drawn from the *Salvi Dictionary* of the Los Angeles–based Salvi creative Víctor H. Interiano (Dichos de un Bicho), who is part of the extended Central American diaspora. I identify this work as a cultural and raciolinguistic analysis of the Salvadoran diaspora in the Washington, D.C. metropolitan area and the DMV.

Central American and Salvadoran Diasporic Worldmaking

In her 1999 poem "Central Americanamerican," Maya Chinchilla first gave voice to the Central American (and synecdochally Salvadoran) diasporic subject's existential search for identity, memory, and place in the world, by asking: "Where is the center of América, anyway? / Are there flowers on a volcano? . . . Are there flowers on a volcano? / am I a CENTRAL / American? / Where is the center of America?" The first-person poetic voice here seems to ponder the condition of being and becoming Central American in diaspora. Twice, the poetic voice repeats in circuitous fashion, "Are there flowers on a volcano?" Seemingly, the voice is trying to imagine a homeland in the absence of firsthand memories and experiences and seeking to understand her place in a world where Central Americans (Salvadorans included) are largely racialized as displaced laboring bodies. In *Worldmaking: Race, Performance, and the Work of Creativity,* Dorinne Kondo explains that, among other things, "worldmaking theorizes the production of race—racialized structures of inequality, racialized labor, the racialized aesthetics of genre, racialized subjectivities, racial affect—in theater as an art world" (25). She further claims that the ethnographer, critic, and scholar as artistic collaborator "participates in the work of creativity . . . and a way to remake worlds through engaged participation" (8). Like Chinchilla, Kondo posits the possibility of artistic collaboration that engages in imaginative worldmaking and proposes that through creative cowork communities can remake themselves and mark their presence through artistic representation and expression, as will be discussed later in this book. Indeed, to know how to be/come Central American—or, for that matter, Salvadoran, Guatemalan, Nicaraguan, Honduran, Belizean, Costa Rican, or Panamanian—in diaspora entails circling back to questions of placemaking, art-making, and worldmaking, especially drawing from lived experiences, underlying superstructures and histories, and symbolic and creative practices in order to make meaning of and in the spaces we inhabit.

Chinchilla's poem interrogates, thus, how diverse Central American diasporas become "Central American–American," or Central American in the United States. Her lines capture what global diasporas scholar Robin Cohen identifies as a key feature of diaspora: the process by which diasporic subjects make meaning in diaspora through the construction of "a collective memory and myth about the homeland, including its location, history, suffering, and achievements" (17). To imagine flowers on volcanoes is to draw from the images, texts, stories, and memories re-created and circulated in diaspora. Certainly, however, not all Central Americans come from or identify with regions that experienced outright armed conflict at the end of the twentieth century; hence, Chinchilla's poem traces only one set of migratory roots and routes in the long and various trajectories of displacement and dispersion from the Central American isthmus. We must be clear that certain narratives such as the political narratives of migration often supersede and silence the telling of other diasporic narratives of Central America. As Paul Joseph López Oro reminds us, "in the United States, the invocation of Central America conjures a set of racial and political imaginaries that center mestizos, Indigenous cultures, revolutionary movements, civil wars, and US occupations that eclipse a discussion of race and racism in the region and its diasporas" ("Refashioning" 223). Indeed, Chinchilla's work references and draws from the creative literature produced in response to and often in solidarity with cultural workers and works aligned with left-wing revolutionary movements, factions, and ideologies in northern Central America in the 1950s through the 1990s. At the end of the twentieth century, these cultural narratives contributed, as I have shown in my own grounded intellectual genealogy and positionality, to the construction (worldmaking) of diasporic imaginaries and homeland myths associated particularly with the Salvadoran, Guatemalan, and Nicaraguan period of armed conflict, at the exclusion and expense of other diasporic narratives.

In his book *Global Diasporas*, Cohen presents a typology of diasporas that may prove useful to the project of situating and perhaps decentering the aforementioned centers of diasporic Central American studies. He notes that traumatic historical events are almost always the root cause of the dispersion of peoples. His typology of diasporas identifies enslavement, forced expulsion, induced labor migration, foreign intervention, war, natural and man-made disaster, and religious, political, and other group-based persecution as common root causes of diasporas, especially in the case of "victim diasporas" displaced by "scarring historical calamities" (4). At the same time, Cohen and other diaspora scholars examine the creative ways that diasporic communities resettle, reimagine, and reinvent themselves in their host societies while memorializing their homelands for political, cultural, and economic reasons (Baronian et al.; Braziel and Mannur; Creet; Marschall). Driven violently out of their homelands, exposed to traumatic experiences in migration, and dispersed across continents, Salvadorans, like other "victim diasporas," almost always carry the scars and memories of violence, covered up in intergenerational silences, at the core of their worldmaking. In U.S. Central American studies, these narratives of "victim diasporas" and their traumatic silences have, indeed, "eclipse[d] a discussion of race and racism in the region and its diasporas" (López Oro, "Refashioning" 223), a situation that can only be rectified through the telling of the many worldmaking stories of the diverse Central

American diasporas across locations. This book is about the unsilencing and worldmaking of one location of the Salvadoran diaspora.

In "On Silences: Salvadoran Refugees Then and Now," U.S. Central American studies scholar and sociologist Leisy J. Abrego reflects on "the unspoken rules of silence" that curtail speaking directly and indirectly about past events associated with the civil wars and migration in Central America (75). As Abrego explains, silence has served as a strategy of survival; hence, parents, family members, communities, and others often shelter younger generations born or raised in diaspora from confronting the past. Breaking (with) diasporic silence in his poem "El Salvador At-a-Glance," the Washington-based Salvadoran poet Quique Avilés invites reflection and dialogue about the Salvadoran diaspora in the Washington, D.C. metropolitan area.[8] He says: "El Salvador in Wa*ch*inton [is but a] little question mark / little east of the border / migrant earthquake / wetback volcano / banana eating / tortilla making / mustache holder / funny dressing / forever happy / forever sad / forever Wa*ch*intonian Salvadoran" (emphasis added). His "little question" prompts readers to ask: Who are the Salvadorans who migrate to the Washington, D.C. metropolitan area? What brings them to the region? How do they become Wachintonian? Why are they "forever happy / forever sad"? In other words, what hidden traumas of displacement, migration, and survival do they carry with them? And how do they participate in their own worldmaking in the DMV? Informed by these questions, this book examines Salvadoran diasporic literary and cultural production in the Washington, D.C. metropolitan area, and by extension the DMV, in an effort to understand the signs, expressions, and worldmaking of Salvadoran diasporic communities in this particular translocation. Speaking about Wachintonian Salvadoreñas and Salvadoreños can help us understand what I call the (world)makings and markings of the transnational Salvadoran diaspora in translocal sites, as well as fill in the missing pieces, gaps, and silences produced across migration.

Avocado Dreams: Remaking Salvadoran Life and Art in the Washington, D.C. Metro Area examines, thus, the construction of U.S. Salvadoran diasporic ethnoracial and cultural identities through analyses of literature, popular culture, performance, art, social and digital media, and other texts produced by Salvadorans in the Washington, D.C. metropolitan area and by extension the greater DMV region. The book takes as its point of departure the work of D.C. Salvadoran cultural producers such as Avilés (*The Immigrant Museum*), Larios (Indigenous-inspired images in murals, sidewalk art, Día de los Muertos altars, and other public spaces), Bencastro (*Paraíso Portátil / Portable Paradise*), Culture Clash (*Anthems: Culture Clash in the District*), Lilo González and Los de la Mount Pleasant (*A quien corresponda . . .*), Veronica Meléndez and Kimberly Benavides (*La Horchata Zine*), Rafael Rodríguez Molina (*Madre Inmigrante / Immigrant Mother*), Claudia Rojas (poetry), and this author (creative, community-based collaborations with many of the aforementioned creatives). This book, moreover, seeks to amplify the cultural presence, representation, voices, and internal ethnoracial and cultural differences of Salvadorans in the nation's capital through analyses of various cultural texts and practices of a burgeoning creative scene in the region.

As I have mentioned, Salvadorans in Washington are integral to the economy of the region, providing significant labor capital in the construction, hospitality, health-care, childcare, and domestic labor industries, as examined by Terry A. Repak in *Waiting on Washington: Central American Workers in the Nation's Capital*. However, they remain largely overlooked and their contributions undervalued. They are subject to this gross undervaluation due to their migratory status, labor exploitation, social criminalization, and linguistic, cultural, socioeconomic, and ethnoracial stigmatization (i.e., association with Indigeneity, Blackness, and undocumented immigration). Heightened misconceptions and misrecognitions of Salvadorans reinforce the tropes of invisibility and erasure ascribed to them and alternately produce potential spaces of identification, solidarity, and coalition-building with communities facing similar marginalization. Long before the Trump administration called us out as undesirables from racialized "s*hole countries" requiring removal, Salvadoran migrants were already identified as criminals, gang members, "illegals," disease carriers, and public charges, generally coming to the United States for economic reasons (Abrego and Villalpando; Padilla, *From Threatening Guerrillas*; Rodríguez, "Refugees").

Countless studies have shown how Salvadorans have been denied political asylum in the United States precisely because of the U.S. economic, political, and military interventions that created their conditions for migration (Chomsky; Lovato). Conversely, Salvadorans, through their perceived association with gangs, have come to represent, for the general public in the United States, an imminent "Latino threat" (Chávez), especially in the form of massive caravan, family, and unaccompanied youth migrations. Extreme U.S. immigration deterrent policies have particularly targeted Central American migrants from the northern isthmus through the deployment of the Zero Tolerance Policy (rescinded on January 26, 2021); Asylum Cooperative Agreements or Safe Third Country (terminated on February 6, 2021); the Public Charge Rule (blocked on March 9, 2021); Migrant Protection Protocols (MPP) (ended on June 1, 2021); and Title 42, Public Health and Welfare, of the U.S. Code, used to close borders and restrict migrants from entering the United States under COVID-19 ("Laws"). Repeated attempts have been made to revoke the landmark *Flores* settlement (1997, 2015), which limits the detention of children (regardless of whether they are accompanied by family members) to twenty days and keeps families and children together while detained; to shut down the Deferred Action for Childhood Arrivals (DACA) program; and to rescind Temporary Protected Status (TPS) for Salvadorans, Hondurans, and others.[9] All these laws and executive orders, which were introduced during the first Trump administration and were put on hold or modified during the Biden administration, have been reinstated or reinforced with Donald Trump's return to power, producing heightened conditions of invisibility, "illegality," and marginalization for many Central Americans, particularly Salvadorans, in the United States.

Avocado Dreams positions itself as a discursive response to the stigmatization, racialization, and sociopolitical and economic constructions of Salvadorans as exploitable and disposable human capital produced under transnational neoliberal regimes. It takes as its point of departure Roque Dalton's 1974 "Poema de amor" (Love Poem), an ode to migratory Salvadorans, who, throughout the twentieth and twenty-first centuries, have left their homelands, crossed perilous borders, and suffered incrimination, criminalization, and incarceration, while resurfacing in other lands as a diasporic people. In his oft-cited poem, Dalton describes how Salvadorans have labored in the construction of the Panama Canal, the shipyards of the Pacific Coast, the agricultural and banana zones of the Americas, and the brothels and bars of ports and cities alike. Whatever the destination of Salvadorans in diaspora, no one ever seems to see or know where we come from ("los que nunca sabe nadie de dónde son"). As Dalton would have it, Salvadorans figure in the diasporic imaginary as generic, indistinguishable entities, “los eternos indocumentados, / los hacelotodo, los vendelotodo, los comelotodo” (the eternal undocumented / the do-everything, the sell-everything, the eat-anything); or as a maligned group, “los guanacos hijos de la gran puta” (the *guanacos,* the sons of whores). In Dalton’s final analysis, the Salvadoran *guanaco* national identity is synonymous with the conditions of ethnoracial, cultural, and linguistic stigmatization, economic exploitation, and physical displacement. Although no one knows for certain how the word *guanaco* came to be associated with Salvadoreños/as, sociolinguists have traced it to “la palabra náhuatl *quanaca* . . . [utilizada] para referirse a las personas que eran como gallinas (tontas, bobas, torpes)” (the Náhuatl word *quanaca* . . . [used] to refer to persons who are like chickens [not smart, clumsy]); the word has almost exclusively rural and nonmodern origins (Lemus, “El sorprendente”). Following Dalton’s poem about *guanacos* in diaspora, this book examines the discursive, cultural, and raciolinguistic construction of Salvadorans as demeaned and marginalized diasporic subjects—in short, as *guanacos/as, salvatrucos/as, choleros/as,* and *aguacateros/as.* But, in the end, we can also be heroes and *cachimbonos/as/xs.* These cultural, raciolinguistic terms organize the analyses and chapters of this book on Salvadorans of the DMV diaspora.

Examining the Salvadoran Diasporic Imaginary Through the Lens of Raciolinguistics

In *Global Diasporas,* Robin Cohen identifies nine “strands . . . of a diasporic rope,” or the nine key features or components of diaspora. These include the (1) “dispersal from an original homeland, often traumatically, to two or more foreign regions”; (2) “expansion from a homeland”; (3) preservation of “a collective memory and myth about the homeland”; (4) “idealization of the real or imagined ancestral home”; (5) “development of a return movement to the homeland [even if vicarious]”; (6) evolution of a “strong ethnic group consciousness sustained over a long time and based on a sense of distinctiveness, a common history, the transmission of a common cultural and religious heritage and the belief in a common fate”; (7) emergence of “a troubled relationship with host societies” or fear “that another calamity might befall the group”; and (8) extension of "empathy, and co-responsibility with co-ethnic members in other countries of settlement even where home has become vestigial." Finally, Cohen suggests, "the possibility of [building] a distinctive creative, enriching life in host countries" among diasporic communities (16–17). Assuming most of Cohen's nine key features for the Salvadoran diaspora, this book focuses on how the Salvadoran diaspora is connected by language and culture across extended sites of dispersion, from El Salvador to the Washington, D.C. metropolitan area and beyond. I argue that language, traditions, and cultural practices—in sum, elements of an ethnoracial imaginary—travel with diasporic subjects, are transplanted in other sites, and connect them with notions of homeland and solidarity across vast expanses. Cohen explains that "bonds of language, religion, culture and a sense of a common fate impregnate such a transnational relationship and give to it an affective, intimate quality that formal citizenship or long settlement frequently lack" (7). Language and cultural practices are key to creating, sustaining, and connecting diasporic identities across dispersion sites.

In diaspora, language and other cultural markers and practices serve as threads to connect diasporic subjects to a notion of homeland (Salvadoranness) across dispersed sites, albeit sometimes loosely and tenuously. For Salvadorans dispersed worldwide, the pupusa (corn tortilla stuffed with cheese, pork, beans, and other ingredients), for example, with its Náhuat-derived name (*puxawa*) and its near-native or *típico* (typical) associations, has become one of the primary signifiers of Salvadoran identity (Lemus, "La palabra"). So too has the intentional use of certain linguistic markers such as the *voseo* (informal second-person singular pronoun), characteristically associated with Salvadoran cultural identity and *caliche* (colloquial Salvadoran language that draws from Indigenous Náhuat and African lexical foundations and worldmaking). The chapters of this book are organized around Náhuat-Afro-Salvadoran (*caliche*) terms used to describe or refer to Salvadoran speech acts. To illustrate these terms, I use memes from the *Salvi Dictionary* created by the Los Angeles–based, Salvi graphic artist Víctor H. Interiano, better known online as Dichos de un Bicho. These memes serve as points of entry into critical discussions on Salvadoran ethnoracial and translanguaged identities produced (through migration) in local transnational sites of the Salvadoran diaspora. Although language takes root in dispersion sites and is transformed in situ, the Salvadoran diaspora shares an evolving language that belongs no more to the DMV than it does to Los Angeles or El Salvador but rather can link translocal sites of the diaspora and the home country—hence, my use of the Los Angeles–based creative's work in a D.C. context. Across dispersion sites of the Salvadoran diaspora, Dichos de un Bicho's *Salvi Dictionary* is just as relevant. The memes of the Náhuat-African derived terms *guanaca/o, salvatrucha, salvatruca/o, cholera/o, aguacatera/o,* and *cachimbon/a/x* point to a shared diasporic ethnoracial, cultural, and linguistic imaginary across the Salvadoran diaspora, in and beyond the isthmus.

These Náhuat-Afro-Indigenous-derived terms, moreover, serve here as hermeneutic, raciolinguistic tools to understand how Salvadoran diasporic subjects are ethnoracialized, sexualized, and generally stigmatized "through the lens of language" (Alim 1), even before they become diasporic subjects, in part because of unacknowledged diasporas such as the Black diaspora in El Salvador. *Caliche* is an intersection of Náhuat and African languages uniquely produced in El Salvador, particularly in sites like the rural, eastern Oriente, home to the Salvadoran Afro-Indigenous descendants who have historically migrated to the DMV, as discussed by numerous scholars (Cabrera; Cañas Dinarte; De Burgos; Erquicia Cruz; Parada).

Borrowing from the field of raciolinguistics, this book "interrogate[s] the processes through which Latinos/as/xs [Salvadorans, in this case] become a racially perceivable and linguistically intelligible category" (Rosa 7). It seeks to understand how Salvadoran speech acts like the use of *voseo, caliche,* and, subsequently, Latinx and Black American language code-meshings result in the possible linguistic stigmatization of Salvadorans as less educated, less modern, less "American," and more backcountry—or, as Culture Clash puts it in *Anthems,* as "jinchos," countryfolk from Oriente (201). In his chapter "Salvadoran Spanish in the United States," John M. Lipski notes that "there is little regional variation in the Spanish of El Salvador. The principal differentiating factors are the rural-urban distinction and the level of education" (*Varieties* 157). Measured against prescriptive criteria such as education level, regionalisms, class, race, ethnicity, gender, political affiliation, and even immigration status, speakers of Salvadoran Spanish may be stigmatized by the way they speak, "labelled as more [or less] intelligent, confident, competent, etc." and classified "into social stereotypes" (Ortiz Jiménez 131). Hence, certain speakers of Salvadoran Spanish may be stereotyped as criminals, gang members, "illegals," and "bad" people, as Trump grossly called them at the start of his first presidential campaign. According to Macarena Ortiz Jiménez, the social prestige of a language variety is related not to its intrinsic merits or superiority, or the genuine "traits" of its speakers, but to social norms, power structures, and sociocultural, political, and economic contexts (130). Thus, Lipski suggests "the need to recognize the existence of Central Americans, particularly Salvadorans, as a distinct subset of the Hispanic community in the United States, a subset which has a different background and different needs, and which at the same time will make new contributions to the formation of linguistic patterns of U.S. Spanish" (*Varieties* 163). Salvadoran dialectal Spanish, in sum, is a sign of Salvadoran difference and not a marker or sign of deficiency.

In *Borderlands/La Frontera: The New Mestiza*, Gloria Anzaldúa further reminds us that "language is a homeland" and "ethnic identity is twin skin to linguistic identity" (55, 59). Like other Latinx groups in the United States who retain traces and variations of the Spanish language, Salvadorans are identified by and through language. This book asks readers to ponder: What makes Salvadoran Spanish unique? Why is it stigmatized? What proforma or preestablished schemas contribute to its devaluation on local, national, and transnational levels? How do we begin to understand the ethnoracialization, classing, and *desprestigio* (discrediting) of Salvadorans through language, race, and history in the Latinx and U.S. imperial imaginary and in the specific context of the Washington, D.C. metropolitan area, where Salvadorans are often racialized as a "darker shade of white" (Avilés, qtd. in Walton)? Drawing on the work of raciolinguistics scholars (Alim et al.; Rosa; Rosa and Nelson; Tseng, *Empanadas*), sociolinguists of Salvadoran Spanish (Lara-Martínez; Lipski, *Latin American*; Lipski, *Varieties* 150–64; Martínez Castellón; P. G. Rivas; M. Romero), and scholars studying Salvadoran representation (Abrego and Villalpando; Padilla, *From Threatening Guerrillas*), this book examines how Salvadoran diasporic cultural producers, writers, artists, and creatives in the Washington, D.C. metropolitan area and the DMV challenge the dominant and often weaponized representations of Salvadorans in popular and everyday culture, and resignify Salvadoran words and identities in diaspora.

Decentering U.S. Central American Studies

In recent years, the field of transnational Central American studies has emerged and grown with important works, such as Gloria Elizabeth Chacón and Mónica Albizúrez Gil's compendium *Teaching Central American Literature in a Global Context*; Karina O. Alvarado, Alicia Ivonne Estrada, and Ester E. Hernández's edited collection *U.S. Central Americans: Reconstructing Memories, Struggles, and Communities of Resistance*; Mike Anastario's *Parcels: Memories of Salvadoran Migration*; Arturo Arias's *Taking Their Word: Literature and the Signs of Central America*; Maritza E. Cárdenas's *Constituting Central American–Americans: Transnational Identities and the Politics of Dislocation*; Carlos B. Córdova's *The Salvadoran Americans*; Kency Cornejo's *Visual Disobedience: Art and Decoloniality in Central America*; Robin Maria DeLugan's *Reimagining National Belonging: Post–Civil War El Salvador in a Global Context*; Jennifer Carolina Gómez Menjívar's *Black in Print: Plotting the Coordinates of Blackness in Central America*; Yajaira M. Padilla's *Changing Women, Changing Nation: Female Agency, Nationhood and Identity in Trans-Salvadoran Narratives* and *From Threatening Guerrillas to Forever Illegals: US Central Americans and the Cultural Politics of Non-Belonging*; Cecilia Rivas's *Salvadoran Imaginaries: Mediated Identities and Cultures of Consumption*; and my own *Dividing the Isthmus: Central American Transnational Histories, Literatures, and Cultures.*

Other important works that examine Central American immigration and diasporas include Leisy J. Abrego's *Sacrificing Families: Navigating Laws, Labor, and Love Across Borders*; Beth Baker-Cristales's *Salvadoran Migration to Southern California: Redefining El Hermano Lejano*; Susan Bibler Coutin's *Exiled Home: Salvadoran Transnational Youth in the Aftermath of Violence, Nation of Emigrants: Shifting Boundaries of Citizenship in El Salvador and the United States,* and *Legalizing Moves: Salvadoran Immigrants' Struggle for U.S. Residency*; Nora Hamilton and Norma Stoltz Chinchilla's *Seeking Community in a Global City: Guatemalans and Salvadorans in Los Angeles*; Sarah J. Mahler's *American Dreaming: Immigrant Life on the Margins* and *Salvadorans in Suburbia: Symbiosis and Conflict*; and Cecilia Menjívar's *Fragmented Ties: Salvadoran Immigrant Networks in America.* Most of these foundational works focus on the West Coast, particularly Los Angeles, and center theoretical paradigms of invisibility, illegality, migration, and transnationalism. For example, Arias examines the invisibility and misrecognition of Central Americans vis-à-vis Mexicans (*Taking Their Word*); Cárdenas analyzes the politics of (dis)location of "Central American–Americans" in the context of Southern California; and Padilla discusses constructions of Salvadoran femininity in relation to Chicana icons (*Changing Women*), as well as the general tropes of violence, illegality, and domestic labor "forever" associated with Salvadorans (*From Threatening Guerrillas*).

Exploring other sites of the Salvadoran diaspora, Carmen Molina-Tamacas's *SalviYorkers* and Mahler's *Salvadorans in Suburbia* focus on Salvadoran migration to New York state. To the best of my knowledge, however, only Olivia Cadaval's *Creating a Latino Identity in the Nation's Capital: The Latino Festival*; Judith Noemí Freidenberg's *Contemporary Conversations on Immigration in the United States: The View from Prince George's County, Maryland*; Andrew Friedman's *Covert Capital: Landscapes of Denial and the Making of U.S. Empire in the Suburbs of Northern Virginia*; Gabriella Gahlia Modan's *Turf Wars: Discourse, Diversity, and the Politics of Place*; David E. Pedersen's *American Value: Migrants, Money, and Meaning in El Salvador and the United States*; Terry A. Repak's *Waiting on Washington: Central American Workers in the Nation's Capital*; and Raúl Sánchez Molina and Lucy M. Cohen's *Latinas Crossing Borders and Building Communities in Greater Washington* shed light on Central American and Salvadoran migration to Washington and the DMV. To date, there have been no book-length studies of diasporic Central American or Salvadoran cultural and literary production in this region. Nor has there been a critical examination of the ways that U.S. Central American studies is centered on *mestizaje*, whiteness, and diasporas largely originating in the northern region of the isthmus—and its consequential invisibilization of Blackness and Indigeneity. At this juncture, López Oro does well to remind us that "the absence of Black Central Americans in Latinx studies and Central American studies is an epistemological violence inherited from Latin American *mestizaje*" ("Refashioning" 225).

As López Oro rightly argues, "within Central American *mestizaje*, Blackness is relegated, alienated, and ascribed to the Caribbean coast erasing centuries of Black folks in the interior and Pacific coasts. By ascribing Blackness and Black people to Central America's Caribbean coasts, *mestizaje* constructs its imaginary in opposition and in negation to Blackness, especially when the Caribbean coast is understood to be removed from the national public spaces of mestizo governance, i.e., Managua or Tegucigalpa." Blackness is seen as a foreign element "coming from elsewhere and not already always present prior to the formation of the Republic" ("Refashioning" 223). Case in point, the Salvadoran state could deny its Blackness and Indigeneity on the basis of its geography (El Salvador has no Caribbean coast), its use of eugenic discourses (El Salvador has no Afro-descendants), its implementation of scientific instruments like census counts (there are no records of nonmestizos), and its execution of outright state violence and terror such as the genocide or La Matanza of 1932. Through discourse and action, the Salvadoran state could thus claim the racial myth that there were no Indians in the country and that "*nunca llegaron negros*" (Blacks never came) to El Salvador (Parada [original emphasis]). Shaped by the historical and ideological forces represented by the racial myth of *mestizaje*, Salvadorans in diaspora, thus, often carry and reproduce anti-Blackness and anti-Indigeneity in other sites. This book seeks to challenge the racial myth of mestizo Salvadoran cultural identities and to explore how Salvadoran ethnoracial identities transform in diaspora, whether by recognition of our own Blackness, "already always present prior to the formation of the Republic[s]" (López Oro, "Refashioning" 223), or by proximity to other racialized groups like Black Americans, African and Caribbean migrants, Afro-Latinxs, and Afro-Centroamericanos/as in sites like the greater DMV. As López Oro, moreover, tells us, we should be "vexed about the absence of Black Central Americans in the emerging scholarship of US Central Americans" ("Garifunizando" 211). This book is a small attempt to trouble the question of U.S. Salvadoran identities and to acknowledge that we have been complicit in the erasure of Blackness in U.S. Central American and Salvadoran studies.

Project *Avocado Dreams*

Avocado Dreams converses, thus, with the aforementioned critical works on and from the translocation of the U.S. mid-Atlantic, a blind spot in the critical literature on the Salvadoran diaspora. Although focusing on Salvadoran cultural and artistic production in the Washington, D.C. metropolitan area and the DMV, I do not purport to re/present the story or history of the Salvadoran migration in the region or to offer in this book a tell-all or cover-all project. Moreover, this is not an oral history of Salvadorans in and of the region. The valuable telling and writing of those stories are left to other scholars (Centeno-Meléndez, *Placemaking*; Scallen, *Bombs*). Rather, *Avocado Dreams* serves as an entry point into discussions about the representation and ethnoracial, sociolinguistic, and cultural formations of Salvadorans in the region up until the time of this writing. This book is a reflection on U.S. Salvadoran diasporic cultural production in the Washington, D.C. metropolitan region, as shaped by race and language through raciolinguistic and cultural studies lenses.

Avocado Dreams took a long time to conceive and write because it grew out of and alongside the emerging work of writers, artists, and creatives in the region. I have witnessed the flourishing of Salvadoran cultural and artistic production in the DMV and often attended, supported, participated in, and even hosted at my institution countless poetry readings, art exhibitions, book presentations, film screenings, and spoken performances. A San Francisco Bay Area transplant in Washington, D.C., where I have now lived for the greater part of my life, I learned to be Wachintonian from my fellow diasporic Salvi communities, activists, artists, writers, and creatives, whom I honor here in no small measure. For that reason, readers will notice that the D.C.-based Salvadoran poet, artist, and activist Quique Avilés and his oeuvre play an especially pronounced role in my work. Throughout my years in the region, my students and I have collaborated with Avilés on various projects documenting the Salvadoran diaspora in the Washington, D.C. metropolitan area, from the 2010 performance piece *Los Treinta* (Thirty Years), produced on the thirtieth anniversary of the Salvadoran civil war, to the 2024 film *Las muertes más bellas del mundo* (The Most Beautiful Deaths in the World), representing his artistic journey alongside many of the artists whose work is discussed in this book. I make no excuse for the central role Avilés plays in this book, for though he is little known beyond the Salvadoran and DMV communities, he is one of the most important Salvadoran cultural producers of the greater metropolitan region. Much like how it is unbeknown to many that Salvadorans are the third-largest Latinx population in the United States and that the DMV area comprises the largest concentration of Salvadorans in one region of the country, Avilés asks readers: Why don't you know more about Salvadorans in the DMV? Indeed, why don't we know more about

Avilés's work in U.S. Latina/o/x and U.S. Central American studies? This book fills that gap by examining Avilés's work about the multigenerational Salvadoran diaspora in the Washington, D.C. metropolitan area.

In the end, *Avocado Dreams* is my ode to the artists, writers, and creatives who have become part of my community in the region. As a project, this book began to germinate in papers presented at the forty-second annual conference on D.C. Historical Studies (November 2015); the "Expanding Latinidades: Emerging Diasporic Communities in Latino USA" symposium at Northwestern University in Evanston, Illinois (May 2016); and the Central American Cultural Studies Conference at the University of Central America, Managua, Nicaragua (July 2017). At the start of the COVID-19 pandemic, in 2020, I tested out ideas for this project on my then Twitter account (@aprodrig77). Casting an imaginary avocado into the Twittersphere, I tweeted about using the metaphor of the avocado and the term *aguacatera/o* to resignify Salvadoran hybrid identities in diaspora. From afar, María Elena Cepeda (@mecepeda), then chair and professor of Latina/o studies at Williams College, and author of *Musical ImagiNation: U.S. Colombian Identity and the Latin Music Boom*, tweeted in response that the term "has both Salvi-specific as well as broader Latinx applications," and that she was "truly *fascinada* and [couldn't] wait to read this!" My hope is that this book will find more such engaged readers and critics.

Filling in the Missing Pieces: Chapter by Chapter

Chapter 1, "'Darker Shade of White': Salvadorans in the Chocolate City," provides a brief genealogy of the narratives of *mestizaje*, anti-Blackness, and ethnoracialization that shape the Salvadoran diaspora in the Washington metropolitan area. Settling in the hyperdiversity of the region, which comprises the historical presence of African American residents, as well as immigrants, refugees, and asylees from around the world and transplants from across the United States, Salvadorans have not only transformed the region with their migration but also left their mark in the nation's capital. This chapter explores the intersections of race, ethnicity, language, and placemaking in the discursive construction of Salvadoreñidades in the District of Columbia, as represented in the everyday spoken word poetics and *we-is-placemaking* of Quique Avilés's and Sami Miranda's poetry, and Ellie Walton's documentary film *La Manplesa: An Uprising Remembered.*

Chapter 2, "*Aguacateras/os*: Remaking Identities and Dreams in the DMV," discusses the hybridizing cultural practices of the Salvadoran diaspora in the DMV. In the wake of the great migration of Salvadorans fleeing the civil war (1980–92) and their subsequent transmigrations to the region, this chapter seeks to understand how Salvadorans make home in the DMV, or what I identify as their *aguacatera/o* identities and avocado dreams, following a short story by onetime DMV resident Mario Bencastro. The avocado, or *aguacate* in Spanish, is used here, in the context of El Salvador, as a metaphor of hybrid identities, diasporic subjectivities, and the process of becoming *típico* in transnational contexts. Following work in raciolinguistics by H. Samy Alim, Jonathan Rosa, and Nelson Flores, and Salvadoran sociolinguists Matías Romero and Pedro Geoffroy Rivas, I use the term *aguacatera/o* to examine the construction of diasporic ethnoracial Salvadoreñidades. Special attention is paid to Bencastro's work as well as local D.C. graphic artist Frida Larios's murals, children's storybook, and cover art for this volume, *Awakat Che' (Awakateros).*

Chapter 3, "*Salvatrucas/os*: Finding Voice and *Voz/s* in the District," recounts the story of when the renowned Los Angeles–based Latinx theater/comedy troupe Culture Clash came to Washington to create a site-specific performance piece based on D.C.'s multiethnic and multiracial communities, including the Salvadoran diaspora. After a series of interviews with community members, artists, and activists in fall 2002—on the first anniversary of 9/11, and amid what came to be known as the D.C. sniper attacks, a spree of shootings across the DMV by John Allen Muhammad and Lee Boyd Malvo (October 2–24, 2002)—Culture Clash produced and performed *Anthems: Culture Clash in the District* at the Arena Stage. *Anthems* not only reconstructed the "multicultural story" of a racially, politically, and socioeconomically stratified Washington, D.C., but also brought into focus the transnational narrative of Salvadorans in the district. By virtue of its title, *Anthems* provided a platform to discuss the post-9/11 state of the union. This chapter further deconstructs the classic American Dream through Culture Clash's representation of the arrival of Salvadoran refugees in the racially divided city of Washington in the 1980s. Grounded in this potential contact zone, this chapter explores what sociolinguist Vershawn Ashanti Young calls the "code-meshing" or absorption of Black English and other cultural practices and identities by Salvadoran/Latinx youth in Washington, as represented in *Anthems* and in Lilo González's tribute to Black/Brown youth struggles and solidarities in the district.

Chapter 4, "*Choleras/os*: Documenting Histories in Wachinton," discusses the more than three decades of the Salvadoran diaspora in the District of Columbia, from the official start of the Salvadoran civil war in 1980 until the year 2010, when the artist, poet, and activist Quique Avilés produced *Los Treinta*. Consisting of *testimonios*, popular anecdotes, and oral histories of the Salvadoran diaspora of the 1980s, *Los Treinta* sought to challenge the invisibilizing of Salvadorans in the historical record by bringing their stories to life in Avilés's embodied performance. Through what I call a cultural, raciolinguistic analysis of the Náhuat-derived term *cholera/o*, often used pejoratively by Salvadorans to refer to people who work as servants or in poorly remunerated jobs (P. G. Rivas; M. Romero), this chapter also contemplates why Salvadorans are forever imagined, in the words of Roque Dalton, as "los eternos indocumentados, / los hacelotodo, los vendelotodo, los comelotodo" (the eternal undocumented / the do-everything, the sell-everything, the eat-anything) ("Poema")—in sum, as disposable or expendable subjects, or *choleras/os*.

The epilogue, "*Cachimbonxs*: Curating Cultural Resistances for a New Era," closes the book with a discussion of zines, social media, artwork and art exhibitions, concrete spoken word poetry, and other multimodal practices in the production of Salvadoran and Central American diasporic imaginaries in the DMV. It reflects on the work of diasporic Salvadoran *cachimbonxs* (courageous artists and scholars) who challenge and deconstruct dominant narratives of Salvadoranness and create new intersectional diasporic imaginaries and identities through their work and social media presence. The epilogue looks at diasporic narratives featured in the multivolume *La Horchata Zine*, co-edited by Veronica Meléndez and Kimberly Benavides; the exhibition *Connected Diaspora: Central American Visuality in the Age of Social Media*, curated by Meléndez at the University of Maryland, College Park; and the writing and artwork of DMV Salvadoran creatives Rafael Rodríguez Molina and Claudia Rojas. The epilogue, moreover, reflects on the value of public humanities scholarship and community-engaged scholarly work. I discuss my own digital storytelling projects *Entre Mundos / Between Worlds* and *Home*

Stories, which document Salvadoran diasporic stories in the DMV and which were developed in collaboration with my students throughout the years. These projects capture and archive moments in the lives of migrants, neighborhoods, and local histories through digital storytelling. Examples of digital stories include "Amor a la distancia" (Ashley Escobar, 2018), "La Mount Pleasant" (Sheyla Alpach, Julia Blindon, and Caroline Nugent, 2015), and "Los 30" (Marissa Lang, 2010). With this epilogue, the book opens a window on new media representations and practices of Central Americans and Salvadorans in the Washington metropolitan area, the DMV, and the United States at large.

1

"DARKER SHADE OF WHITE"

Salvadorans in the Chocolate City

In 2011, Salvadorans became the third-largest Latino/a/x demographic group in the United States, after Mexicans and Puerto Ricans (Brown and Patten; Moslimani et al.), as well as consolidated their long-standing status as the largest immigrant, foreign-born, and Latinx ethnic group in the DMV (Singer et al.; see also "American Community"). Ronald Luna, a DMV-based demographer of Salvadoran descent, has noted that from 1990 to 2000, there was a 62 percent nationwide increase in the number of Salvadorans, with an increase of 130 percent in D.C., 118 percent in Maryland, and 132 percent in Virginia, percentages that have continued to grow in successive census counts. In 2019, the U.S. Census Bureau estimated that Salvadorans accounted for 2.8 percent of the population of Washington, D.C.; 3.2 percent of the population of Maryland; and 2.1 percent of the population in Virginia. At that time, approximately 19,984 Salvadorans resided in the District of Columbia, 198,863 in Maryland, and 179,437 in Virginia. Overall, 328,477 of these Salvadorans lived just in the D.C. metropolitan area ("B03001").[1] Although the Salvadoran population count in the region is somewhat imprecise due to the large number of undercounted, undocumented, and newly arrived or arriving immigrants, what is certain is that the number of Salvadorans in the Washington, D.C. metropolitan area will continue to increase.

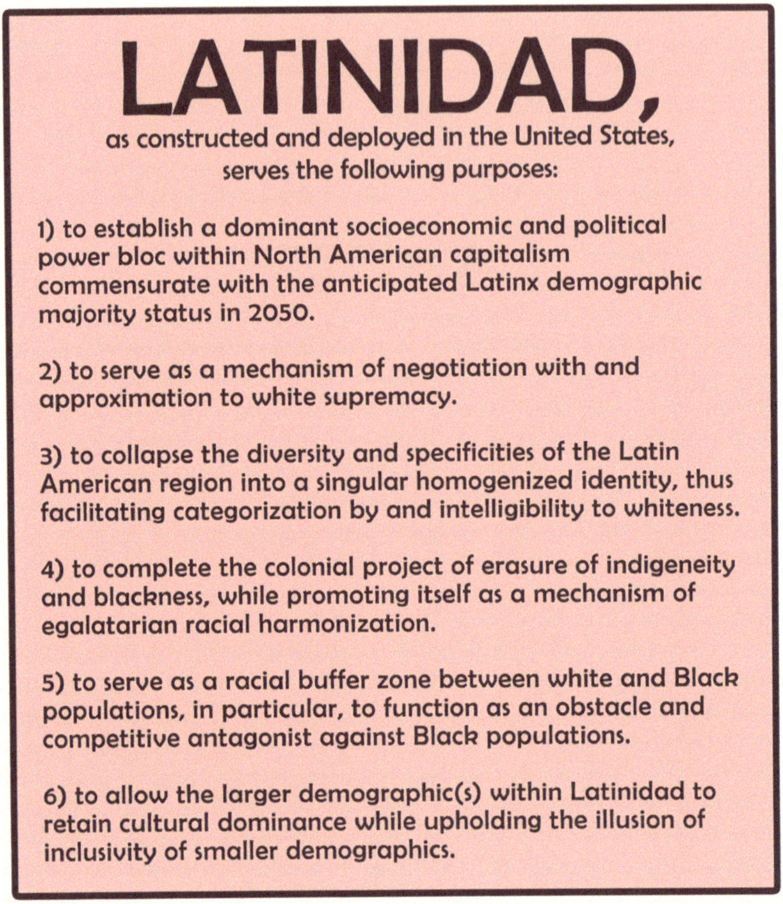

LATINIDAD,

as constructed and deployed in the United States, serves the following purposes:

1) to establish a dominant socioeconomic and political power bloc within North American capitalism commensurate with the anticipated Latinx demographic majority status in 2050.

2) to serve as a mechanism of negotiation with and approximation to white supremacy.

3) to collapse the diversity and specificities of the Latin American region into a singular homogenized identity, thus facilitating categorization by and intelligibility to whiteness.

4) to complete the colonial project of erasure of indigeneity and blackness, while promoting itself as a mechanism of egalatarian racial harmonization.

5) to serve as a racial buffer zone between white and Black populations, in particular, to function as an obstacle and competitive antagonist against Black populations.

6) to allow the larger demographic(s) within Latinidad to retain cultural dominance while upholding the illusion of inclusivity of smaller demographics.

FIGURE 2. "Latinidad," by Víctor H. Interiano (Dichos de un bicho), 2020. Courtesy of Víctor H. Interiano.

In contrast to California and the Southwest, where a majority of Latinxs are of Mexican heritage, or the Northeast and Southeast, where Latinxs of Caribbean or other descents predominate, the DMV is home to the largest concentration of Salvadorans in one region of the United States (Singer; Singer et al.). As such, according to DMV-based sociolinguist Amelia Tseng, Salvadorans serve as the premier Latinx referential group, standing in for Latinidad in the Washington, D.C. metropolitan area ("Advancing"; *Empanadas*) (figure 2). They make up a great part of the labor force not only in the District of Columbia but also in Maryland and northern Virginia and contribute greatly to the local economy and cultural scene. For these reasons, there is a need to understand how Salvadorans make home in the Washington, D.C. metropolitan area, or the DMV, transform it, and shape it through their significant socioeconomic and cultural contributions, as well as how, in turn, they are transformed by the people, communities, and histories of the Chocolate City, as the District of Columbia is known for its historically Black communities (Asch and Musgrove). This chapter examines how Salvadoran ethnoracial identities are shaped and transformed in diaspora and in proximity to other racialized groups like Black Americans, African and Caribbean migrants, Afro-Latinxs, and Afro-Centroamericanos/as in sites like the greater DMV. Special attention is paid to the work of D.C. Latino poets Quique Avilés and Sami Miranda and filmmaker Ellie Walton (*La Manplesa: An Uprising Remembered*), who represent the everyday places, exchanges, and code-meshings of intersecting communities sharing spaces, precarities, and struggles, or what I call the we-is-placemaking of the DMV. Indeed, D.C. is made not by its monuments but by the diverse people and communities that call it home.

Blackness in El Salvador and the DMV

According to Virginia-based Afro-Indigenous Salvadoran activist and scholar Danielle Parada, in her piece titled "Learning About My Blackness: Afrodescendencia in El Salvador,"[2]

> The Washington D.C. metropolitan area (or "DMV" for locals) is one, if not the only, region in the U.S. where Salvadoran culture is found at every turn and the people work in every industry imaginable. For a U.S. raised Salvadoran like me, this meant being immersed in a unique culture that was equally just as Salvadoran as it was American. Bakeries dedicated to Salvadoran baked goods, grocery stores filled with jocotes, nances, and mamones in the vegetable aisles, and pupuserias [can be found] in every town in the DMV.
>
> It is common to see American folks learn Caliche [Salvadoran dialectal] words before any other dialects of Spanish. Many refer to our area as

> "Little Central America" because of how connected we are to our culture and home countries. This created a bubble of Salvadoranness for many of us raised in the U.S. When folks asked about our race or identities, it was not uncommon to hear "Salvadoran" as an answer rather than an actual racial category. However, our education and understanding of the world came from an American perspective. This meant learning about history through the perspective of the U.S., the enslavement of African people, and the modern legacy of slavery on African Americans, but left us clueless to our own histories in El Salvador.

As Parada points out, the DMV is a unique "bubble of Salvadoranness," not only because of the notable presence of Salvadoran restaurants, grocery stores, and foods, among other things, but more significantly, as mentioned in the introduction, because Salvadoran migrants in the DMV tend to come from Oriente, the eastern region of the country, bringing with them particular language idioms, rural Indigenous lived experiences, and distinct Afro-Salvadoran identities, which have been historically rejected, negated, discriminated against, and violated in El Salvador and within Salvadoran communities both inside and outside the isthmus.

For Parada, "learning about the brutal, and often violent, history of race in the U.S. during my K–12 education initiated my quest to learn more about Afro-Salvadoran history," even when her parents insisted that "*nunca llegaron negros*" (Blacks never came) to El Salvador (original emphasis). With these words, her parents reiterated the national myth of *mestizaje* in El Salvador, a myth institutionalized by laws, traditions, popular beliefs, and the denial and erasure of Blackness, whose presence is only now being recognized by Salvadoran scholars and others (Cabrera; Cañas Dinarte; De Burgos; Erquicia Cruz). According to José Heriberto Erquicia Cruz, in "'¡Aquí no hay negros!': La negación de la raíz africana en la sociedad salvadoreña" ("There Are No Blacks Here!": The Denial of Black Roots in Salvadoran Society) the official state discourse of *mestizaje* not only provided the language to homogenize the nation as mestizo but also denied the existence of Afro-Salvadoreños: "a diferencia de otros grupos o comunidades étnico-culturales que se invisibilizaron; estos peor aún, se negaron" (while other ethnocultural groups or communities were invisiblized, they [Afro-Salvadoreños] were denied existence) (143). Today, however, Afro-Salvadorans trace their histories, lineage, and ethnoracial identities to

Spanish colonization and settler colonialism (1524–1821), which destroyed, displaced, and dispossessed the diverse Indigenous peoples who lived in the region before and after the Conquista. Europeans not only enslaved Indigenous survivors but also forcibly brought enslaved Black people to work in the production of *añil* (indigo), cacao, sugarcane, and other monocultural crops, as well as in gold and silver mining, livestock herding, and militia defense against seventeenth- and eighteenth-century buccaneers and other invading forces, especially in the eastern part of El Salvador (Cabrera; Erquicia Cruz). With the independence of the country and the briefly existing Central American Federation or United Provinces of Central America (1823–40), emancipation came to enslaved Afro-Salvadorans in 1824–25, but their exclusion and erasure continue to this day.

Yohalmo Cabrera, cofounder of the collective AFROOS (Fundación Afrodescendientes Organizados Salvadoreños [Organized Salvadoran Afrodescendants Foundation]), which "works for the constitutional recognition of the Afro-descendant population in El Salvador and the diaspora" and seeks "to eliminate racism and discrimination in all its forms" (AFROOS), affirms that legal emancipation of Salvadoran Afro-descendants came to them, "por medio de estrategias basadas en lazos matrimoniales, servicios militares, involucramiento en comercio, cimarronaje y manusión, que en algunos casos les ayudo a ascender socialmente" (through marriage, military service, participation in commerce, cimarronage, and manumission, which led, in some cases, to social mobility) (Cabrera 41). State ideology, however, in the words of Salvadoran scholar David J. Guzmán, cast Afro-descendants as "el prototipo de la estupidez, de la abyección, de la miseria y de la ignorancia" (the prototype of stupidity, abjection, misery, and ignorance) (qtd. in Cabrera 41).

A leading nineteenth- and early twentieth-century intellectual, eugenicist, and member of the coffee-producing ruling class in El Salvador, Guzmán not only was the founding director of the National Museum of Anthropology in San Salvador, which carries his name to this day, but also shaped Salvadoran racial thought and the national myth of *mestizaje* or *blancamiento* for decades to come. In "Población y área, Razas y costumbres" (Population and Area, Race and Customs), Guzmán proposes that "los mestizos forman la clase que más fraterniza con los elementos blancos de nuestra sociedad, cuando éstos, que forman el núcleo civilizado del país, se inspiran en los nobles propósitos del engrandecimiento de la patria" (the mestizos comprise the class that most agrees with the white elements of our society, when these, which are the civilized nucleus of the country, are inspired by the greatness of the nation) (196). For Guzmán, a positivist, the progress and modernization of the country could only be achieved by racial fusion and whitening. He postulates, "el elemento dirigente de la sociedad es el blanco o criollo, el cual tiende, con medidas de previsión y altruismo, a igualar todas las clases, dictando leyes como la Constitución de 1871 y la del 86, que hacen desaparecer las desigualdades de raza, y tienden a elevar a la raza desheredada al nivel de ciudadanos de la República liberal y progresista" (the white or criollo ruling class, with its forethought and altruism, tends to equalize all classes, dictating laws like the Constitution of 1871 and the one of '86, which erase racial inequalities, and to elevate the indigent race to the level of citizens of the liberal and progressive Republic) (197). From its inception, thus, the Salvadoran state all but erased Afro-Salvadorans, Indigenous first peoples, and other racialized groups from the national imaginary and, by the 1930s, institutionalized the myth of mestizaje, omitting ethnoracial classifications from official records, including census surveys (Tilley 170). Along these lines, in *Black in Print: Plotting the Coordinates of Blackness in Central America*, Jennifer Carolina Gómez Menjívar asserts, "in all isthmian countries with the exception of Belize, the collapse of Blackness into mestizaje was held as an indicator of parity among men and republican civility" (18).

According to Virginia Q. Tilley, in *Seeing Indians: A Study of Race, Nation, and Power in El Salvador*, "the last national census to attempt any count of ethnic identity [in El Salvador], [the 1930 census] reported a national indigenous total of only 5.6 percent, concentrated entirely in the western departments and especially Ahuachapan and Sonsonate" (173). Before that, the Civil Registry, which recorded births and deaths in municipalities beginning in the 1860s, had already begun to use informal and inconsistent language that blurred the racial lines between the categories of ladino/a and *indígena*,[3] as well as, though "much more rarely [used], mulata (mixed African-ladina or African-Indian) or negra (Black, i.e., Afro-Latino). In the 1930s (notably, starting before the Matanza), the term mestizo was introduced" (Tilley 178). Indigenous people, Black Salvadorans, and other racialized groups were, thus, systematically erased from the face of the country via the elimination of its recording apparatus, reifying the mestizo anti-Black and anti-Indigenous ideology and narrative which the state sought to implant in the national imaginary. There would be no *indios*, *negros*, or immigrants from undesirable foreign countries in El Salvador. In the context of the continued appropriation of Indigenous lands by the state, capitalistic extraction by national and international forces, and the global economic crisis of the 1930s, Tilley affirms that state ideologies of *mestizaje* swept Central American countries; *mestizaje* "obtained an aura of objective truth and moral authority, able to recast any indigenous movement that challenged it not only as retrogressive but as divisive to the nation—even seditious" (188).

Indeed, in the wake of the Indigenous rebellion of January 22–25, 1932, the military dictator Maximiliano Hernández Martínez carried out La Matanza, killing almost thirty thousand Indigenous people and communist-branded campesinos, along with their leader, Agustín Farabundo Martí. Earlier, in 1928 and 1930, the National Legislative Assembly of El Salvador had passed legislation (Decree no. 65) that restricted the entry and "settlement in the country of individuals originating in Turkey, Arabia, Syria, Palestine, [Lebanon], etc., known in the Republic by the name of 'Turks'" (National Legislative Assembly; see also Rivas Montoya). As early as 1897, in fact, El Salvador had passed a law modeled on the U.S. Chinese Exclusion Act (1882), "defining Chinese as 'pernicious foreigners' (*extranjeros perniciosos*), and prohibiting any further settlement" (Tilley 211). Although, contrary to popular belief, the 1950 Constitution of El Salvador did not actually prohibit Black people from entering, settling in, and becoming citizens of the country, the official Salvadoran national narrative, to this day, "rejects any historical presence of negros" and asserts that "Salvadoran mestizaje is a Black-free mestizaje" (Tilley 208, 210–11). Despite the state's imperative to stamp out ethnoracial categories and identities from the nation, the living signs of Salvadoran Blackness, Indigeneity, and immigrant plurality—as seen, for example, in the rise and recognition of Palestinians in the nation (Rivas Montoya 201)—can be found in the Salvadoran language, music, place names, foodways, cultural practices, stories, anecdotes, and records in municipal archives, among other contexts. Signs of Blackness, for example, include the everyday reference to *la sopa de pata* (cow's feet soup), horchata, marimba music, and dances like "El Baile de la Negra Sebastiana" (Black Sebastiana's Dance), as well as the use of dialectal words such as *cachimba* (angry face, sexual organs, house, etc.), *encachimbado* (numerous in quantity), and *mucama* (maid)

(Cabrera; Cañas Dinarte; Parada; M. Romero), within El Salvador and diasporic sites such as the Washington, D.C. metropolitan area.

Given this Salvadoran sociocultural, linguistic, and historical context, one must ask: how, then, does a people who have been shaped by anti-Blackness and who often negate their own Blackness negotiate their ethnoracial identities and settle in(to) a city that has been home to predominantly Black communities as well as other immigrants and transplants from around the world, including Europe, Asia, the Middle East, and the rest of the Americas?

Salvadoreñidades in the Hyperdiverse Washington Metropolitan Area

In "Advancing A Sociolinguistics of Complexity: Spanish-Speaking Identities in Washington, D.C.," the sociolinguist Amelia Tseng describes the city and region as a "global metropolitan area and immigrant gateway" (330). With its "international flows of people, commerce, and communication" (331), as well as ties to the global economy and politics, the nation's capital is a hyperdiverse urban site, historically home to a large population of African American residents and now home to transplants from across the United States, and immigrants, refugees, and asylum seekers from around the world. Today, D.C. is a hyperdiverse city, one in which "(1) at least 9.5% of the total population is foreign-born, (2) no one country of origin accounts for 25% or more of the immigrant stock, and (3) immigrants come from all regions of the world" (Price and Benton-Short 112, cited in Tseng, "Advancing" 331). However, the largest number of immigrants in D.C. are of Latin American and Caribbean descent (Tseng 332), particularly Salvadoran. According to Audrey Singer of the Brookings Institute, the Latino/a/x population grew approximately 600 percent between 1980 and 2006, with a large number of them being of Salvadoran descent (cited in Tseng 348n3).

In 2023, Latinos/as/xs accounted for 11.5 percent of the city's population (not counting the large number of undocumented residents), representing all the countries of Latin America, the Caribbean, Spain, and beyond. Within the Latino/a/x demographic, Salvadorans are the largest group (2.8 percent of the total population), followed by Dominicans

(1.3 percent), Mexicans (1.3 percent), and Puerto Ricans (1.2 percent), making the D.C. area distinct for its Salvadoran presence and concentration ("American Community"). Noting the area's hyperdiversity, Quique Avilés, in his poem "Latinhood," ponders the discursive construction of Latinidades and Salvadoreñidades, almost echoing the deconstruction of Latinidad in the meme by Dichos de un Bicho (figure 2). Avilés asks: "How does it do what it does? / What is it that makes it happen / in the way that it happens? . . . Who are you in this crazy web of latins? . . . Are we related?" Avilés, like Dichos de un Bicho, troubles essentializing and normalizing constructions of Latinidad—constructions embedded in exclusive ideologies of nationalism, whiteness, and anti-Blackness—and pushes readers to think of Latinidades and Salvadoreñidades in relation to the hyperdiversity of Washington, D.C.

As cultural anthropologist, folklife specialist, and longtime collaborator and mentor of Avilés Olivia Cadaval explains, "at the heart of Quique's [critical inquiry] is the emergence of a new American identity that he describes as 'rooted in an East Coast experience and by a 'lower,' 'new' breed of Mesoamericans, *los salvatrucos,* Mexican tortilla cousins (not Mexicans, not Puerto Ricans, not Cubans [but Salvadorans])'" ("My Tongue" 113). For Cadaval, Avilés is a chronicler and autoethnographer of the Salvadoran diaspora in Washington, D.C. as he arrived with other migrants fleeing the civil war in El Salvador in 1980 and writes from the positionality of "his experience as a Latino [Salvadoran] immigrant in a Black city" (111). According to Cadaval, D.C. was for him,

> a new and unknown territory. His experience of African Americans in El Salvador was limited to the music celebrities of the 1960s–'70s that he encountered in mainstream television programs broadcast in El Salvador—Stevie Wonder and Aretha Franklin; Black boxers—Muhammad Ali, Fraser [*sic*], Foreman—and the famous fights. But now living in a Black neighborhood, he discovers that Blacks [*sic*] are mothers, children, and families like other ordinary people. He attends their schools, they become his friends and his assailants, and they model what "American" is. He learns their language. He describes his earliest experiences: "Nobody told us there were Black folks in the U.S. and a lot of Blacks did not know who or what Salvadoran was. Out there in the streets, there was a lot of ignorance, a lot of violence." (118)

In other words, Avilés learned to be "American" and diasporic "Salvadoran" in relation to Black people in Washington, D.C., by living in the Mount Pleasant barrio, which bordered, absorbed, and in many cases pushed out Black neighbors, attending Black and immigrant schools, hanging out with his Black neighbors and friends, and creating artistically with Black and other creative peers ("Story Circle"). Throughout his years producing poetry and spoken word, and engaging in artivism, Avilés has attempted "to understand what it means to be a rural Salvadoran immigrant in urban Washington, D.C." and has participated in the creation of "new multiethnic generations" (Cadaval, "My Tongue" 113), shaped in relation to Black American identities, histories, and communities and the wider racial and ethnic diversity of the Washington, D.C. metropolitan area. In his work, Avilés recognizes that Washington, D.C., perhaps like no other immigrant reception site in the United States, has provided Salvadorans and others with the opportunity to be "informed and strengthened by the spaces created by the original civil rights movement, the Black Struggle" (Cadaval 113). While D.C. sits on territory that was taken from the Piscataway and other First Peoples, occupied by Europeans, and worked by enslaved Black peoples, newcomers today often reside in neighborhoods where descendants of those same Black Washingtonians are being pushed out by development, gentrification, and new waves of migration, embedded in systemic racist structures as old as the nation itself.

According to Avilés, in the 1970s and '80s, Salvadorans arrived in a "city, divided by DuBois's 'color line'" (Cadaval, "My Tongue" 118), whose racial dynamic and complexity they may not have fully understood, often resulting in anti-Black perceptions and practices that prevail to this day and contributing to what Avilés calls the Salvadoran racial identification with a "darker shade of white," as analyzed later in this chapter. Avilés explains that upon arriving in the Chocolate City (whether in the 1980s or the present), Salvadorans become "outsiders squeezing themselves [into] the already established White vs. Black dynamic." Understanding the "color line" as such permits Avilés to talk about racialization in, of, and across Washington, D.C., beyond a racial binary or "duality." He explains: "This makes me think not of a duality but of triplicity," into which migrants, asylum seekers, refugees, and others insert themselves, often opting for proximity to whiteness and reproducing anti-Blackness in situ (Cadaval 118). In this context, Latina/o/x and other identities produced *in place* are shaped in relation to Blackness as well as ideologies of *mestizaje*, whiteness, nativism, and nationalism, which may exacerbate immigrant and Latino/a/x anti-Blackness embedded in preconceived notions of unity, community, *familia*, and other essentialist markers of Latinidad (Beltrán). Thus, Avilés posits that constructions of Latinidad must remain in question, in situ, and in relation to other groups, recalling lines from his poem "Latinhood": "How does it do what it does? / What is it that makes it happen / in the way that it happens? . . . Who are you in this crazy web of Latins? . . . Are we related?"

Given that Salvadorans make up the largest Latino/a/x group in the region, Salvadoran Latinidades perhaps "pass" as the wider Latinidad in the Washington, D.C. metropolitan area—from Salvadoran-dominated labor markets, pupusa eateries, and regional idioms and vernaculars heard in the streets, to Salvadoran-inflected poetry, art, and music, incorporating Black cultural and linguistic elements and "code-meshings" (V. A. Young et al.), discussed later in this chapter. According to Tseng, "due to their strong local presence, Salvadorans have a special referential role in local Latino identity" ("Advancing" 334). It is not surprising, then, that Avilés, who immigrated to the region at the age of fifteen, in 1980 (at the start of the Salvadoran civil war), would write about *salvatrucans* or *salvatrucos/as* in relation to Black, Latino/a/x, and other racial, ethnic, and diasporic groups in the area. From his collaborative work with LatiNegro, Sol & Soul, Spoken Word Resistance, Para eso la Palabra, Paso Nuevo at the GALA Hispanic Theatre, and the community documentary *La Manplesa*; to his solo performances of *Latinhood, Chaos Standing, Caminata: A Walk Through Immigrant America, Rehab*, and *The Children of Latinia*; his published poetry collection *The Immigrant Museum*; and his film *Las muertes más bellas del mundo: A Film About Salvadorean Artists in Washington, D.C.*, Avilés has represented the Salvadoran community and identity formations in process, in relation to other groups, and in the context of Washington, D.C., albeit in connection to transnational and global migration (Rodríguez, "Becoming"; Rodríguez, "Departamento 15"; Rodríguez, *Dividing*).

Indeed, in his poem "El Salvador At-a-Glance," Avilés describes Washington as yet another translocation of the Salvadoran diaspora, "San Wachinton, D.C." as another city of El Salvador, Salvadoran immigrant laborers (e.g., "city builders, busboys, waiters, poets") as yet another export commodity of the country, and D.C. Salvadorans as new "Wachintonians" (see also

Rodríguez, “Becoming”). In “Barrio,” his ode to the Mount Pleasant–Columbia Heights–Adams Morgan neighborhoods known as the historical epicenter of Salvadoran migration, Avilés alludes to Salvadorans as “last call ripe avocados”: they are part of D.C.’s rich cultural hyperdiversity, but their communities are often overlooked, underappreciated, and disenfranchised, “in this arrogant time / in this arrogant place / this place of slanted eyes / corn rows / this place of last call ripe avocados.” In the poem, the metaphor of “last call ripe avocados” serves as commentary on the neglect experienced by marginalized, racialized communities in the District of Columbia. As a poet of the everyday, mundane, and unseen of D.C., Avilés tries “to write things about this place / to say it right / to put it down.” So, too, does Sami Miranda, who has collaborated with Avilés on numerous D.C. poetic enactments, slams, and performances, including the documentary *La Manplesa*.

Like Avilés, Miranda—a Nuyorican transplant, public high school educator, spoken word poet, and frequent Avilés artistic collaborator—writes about his everyday encounters with people in the streets and neighborhoods of D.C. He writes about D.C. Salvadorans by proximity and positions his readers as adjacent to Salvadoran experiences. In “The Waffle Shop,” for example, Miranda recalls that “on the corner of 14th and park / by the payless / thick fingered / salvadoran women / ball up masa / . . . to fill an order / of pupusas revueltas for the intipuqueño / whose hands are scarred / and calloused / from building homes / for people who pay him poorly / and support the laws / that would send him home / where he belongs.” This poem appears in his poetry collection *Protection from Erasure*, which, like his earlier *We Is*, focuses on migrants fleeing violence, unaccompanied minors seeking refuge, and families and individuals displaced from their homes by gentrification, as longtime Black residents and others are pushed out of Washington, D.C. Forming an affinity with the displaced, Miranda asks: “What does it mean to be told / you are, or are not / of a place / you have always been from, / not from a dirt that knows your blood / not from a place whose soil is fertilized / with your ancestors, / that you must flee the home / that once held you to its chest” (“ILL Legal”). Miranda seems to voice the sense of unbelonging often experienced by Salvadoran immigrants and others, drawing from shared affinities and affects related to exclusion and erasure, as the title of his poetry collection signals. Like Avilés, Miranda offers new ways to construct identities out of shared situations and in situ lived experiences rather than from worn notions of unity, community, and identity markers, fraught with contradictions and exclusions. Both Miranda and Avilés suggest that immigrants and longtime residents—like Salvadorans and Black Washingtonians—living side by side, share similar conditions of displacement, whether global or local, which have become part of their everyday, mundane, and unseen humanity. Along these lines, in "Home," Miranda writes of home as a series of arrivals and departures: "When it's time to leave it all behind: / discard, button, bead, or bauble / leave all things unfamiliar / be sure not to miss the boat. / People are moving, quietly / migratory water birds in flight. / Many immigrants land / in a city of so many places, everyone / sooner or later finds one special / they name, home." In the poem, home is composed of places left behind and perhaps remade in Washington, D.C. People seem to share a common "boat" in movement or diaspora, "moving quietly," like "migratory water birds in flight" looking for a home. Indeed, in "ILL Legal," Miranda asks: "What does it mean to be home—/ less?" whether for those arriving or those departing. Both Miranda's and Avilés's works suggest that in mundane, everyday situations, people come together for affinity, protection, and resistance in erstwhile Black and Brown D.C. neighborhoods like Adams Morgan, Columbia Heights, and Mount Pleasant, otherwise known by the Latinx Spanish-speaking community as La Manplesa, the subject of a film production in which Avilés, Miranda, and other community members are featured.

"Darker Shade of White": Salvadorans in *La Manplesa*

Drawing from interviews with Avilés, Miranda, and other D.C. artists and community members, as well as news footage and artworks, local D.C. filmmaker Ellie Walton directed *La Manplesa: An Uprising Remembered* in 2021. The documentary tells the story of the Mount Pleasant uprising of May 5–7, 1991. Screened across the United States, especially in locations where Salvadorans reside, the film has not only informed the world about this historic but little-known uprising in Washington, D.C., but also generated conversations about racial struggles in the greater Washington metropolitan area. Both Miranda and Avilés serve as narrators in the film, and their poetry is used to frame episodes, reconstructing events leading up to and after the uprising. Piecing together scenes from multiple perspectives, the film uses testimonials to describe how, on the evening of Cinco de Mayo, after a day of festivities in the barrio, officers of the Metropolitan Police Department were called to the intersection of Mount Pleasant and Lamont Streets NW to respond to reports of a man acting disorderly, under the influence of alcohol. Subsequently, the man—a Salvadoran immigrant by the name of Daniel Enrique Gómez—was shot by a Black woman police officer for resisting arrest (Scallen, "1991"). As depicted in the film, the shooting set off days of violence, looting, and confrontations between the authorities and people in the streets. Fueled by years of neglect, abuse, and wide economic disparities, Latinxs, African Americans, and others joined in the uprising, which extended into the surrounding neighborhoods of Columbia Heights and Adams Morgan (Escobar). For many Salvadoran immigrants and residents of the district, the uprising triggered memories of persecution, war, and state violence, now re-created in the streets of Washington, D.C.

More than representing the historical event of the 1991 uprising, *La Manplesa* tells the hidden-in-plain-sight stories of long-disenfranchised Washington neighborhoods in which Black Americans, Salvadorans, and others share everyday conditions of economic neglect, police violence, and systemic racism. Longtime residents, neighbors, and protagonists of the uprising—including Avilés, Pepe González, Lilo González, Ronald Chacón, Rick Reinhard, Pedro Avilés, Lori Kaplan, Lupi Quinteros-Grady, Arturo Griffiths, Roland Roebuck, Jackie Reyes-Yanes, Butch Chappell, Felix Dilone, Haydee Vanegas, and others featured in the film—give voice to past and present struggles of Latino/a/x and Black communities in La Manplesa. Filmed in the streets and in homes, on porches and door stoops of the neighborhood, these memory-keepers re-create scenes of the uprising and recall its aftermath for a new generation—those living in the time of Black Lives Matter activism, heightened inequities, and the COVID-19 pandemic, as seen in background scenes of mask-wearing protestors at neighborhood vigils and demonstrations. The documentary is infused with images of the struggle for racial and social justice in Washington, D.C., as narrators connect the dots between old and new struggles against policing, gentrification, and displacement.

Connecting present and past memories of La Manplesa, spoken and visual *testimonios* of the narrators and memory-keepers are stitched together with stop-motion animated scenes of the shooting of Gómez and captioned stanzas from Avilés's poem "Barrio." Lines from this poem serve as transitions between film segments, connecting the images, words, and struggles of the narrators in 1991 and 2020. Photos and news footage of narrators participating in the uprising and reflecting on it in the face of COVID-19 and Black Lives Matter create particularly poignant memorial spaces in which poets, artists, artivists, and spectators are called to take stock of the slow arc of social justice and the resilient role of the artist. As Avilés reminds us in a key monologue, "Things get lost. Memory is erased. The role of the artist is to create a file of memory." This line recalls another of Avilés's poems, "Let the Poems Run the Country," in which he declares: "I say let the poets run the country / we'll be better off with books and pens / instead of the misery of weapons . . . they'll give out poetic justice / they will listen to us who want to speak." The interspersed lines from "Barrio," too, remind spectators that words can fail or elude us, for "trying to write things about this place . . . is difficult, very difficult," but words can also be acts of resistance.

In a key scene in the documentary, Avilés recites another of his poems, provisionally titled "Darker Shade of White," announcing that the day of reckoning has come, perhaps, for both Salvadorans and others in the District of Columbia: "The skies are cloudy. / The storm is near." He recites:

> Today is not a good day to be a darker shade of white.
> The skies are cloudy.
> The storm is near.
> The most unwanted have understood that they are not wanted.
> "I'm sorry, sir, but today is not a good day to be a darker shade of white.
> You will go to jail.
> You will be deported.
> Just thank God that you're alive today because honestly, sir,
> Today you chose the wrong day to be a slightly darker shade of white."[4]

To be a "darker shade of white" marks the referential subject (Salvadoran?) in the poem as nonwhite and "unwanted," subject to incarceration, deportation, and exclusion. Categorically positioned as neither white nor Black, but as something different or off-white—or, perhaps, Brown, belonging to what José Esteban Muñoz calls the "Brown commons" of identities (and elements) formed under "duress and pressure" that, nonetheless, struggle and persist (2)—Salvadorans are racialized as a "darker shade of white." According to Muñoz, "They [these identities] are brown in part because they have been devalued by the world outside their commons" (2), much like Salvadorans have been discounted, devalued, and pushed into invisibility in the district. In a foreboding warning, the poetic voice in Avilés's poem seems to allude to impending violence targeting all those who are identified as this "darker shade of white": as part of the "unwanted," their day has come to be incarcerated, deported, and ultimately eliminated from the body politic. The voice of authority in the poem declares: "I'm sorry, sir, but today is not a good day to be a darker shade of white." Near whiteness, then, offers no protection to the unwanted in the poem. Reading in between the lines of Avilés's poem, however, offers the subject in question another option—the possibility of identifying, aligning, and joining forces with all those of a "darker shade of white," as part of what Muñoz identifies as the "Brown commons" and what Avilés calls the "triplicity" or "multiplicity," challenging racial binaries. In the end, Avilés's poem seems to suggest that we can choose to stand with those in the commons of the "darker shade of white." In other words, we can build (on) commonalities, aligning in antiracist solidarity and rejecting white racial identifications and converged interests. It is telling that this poem, centered in the documentary, calls Salvadorans and others to antiracist identification, action, and solidarity with Black struggles.

In *La Manplesa*, Avilés, Miranda, and the other memory-keepers tell their personal stories of having been "there," in the struggle within the "commons," as tear gas rained down on them and the police turned their weapons and batons on the people, as they do again in the final scenes of the documentary, but this time against Black Lives Matter demonstrators in the streets of D.C. in 2020 and 2021. Connecting past and present struggles for racial justice, the narrators of *La Manplesa*, thus, call on spectators to witness and stand with the Black Lives Matter demonstrations that erupted in the nation's capital following the killing of George Floyd, Breonna

Taylor, and other Black and Brown Americans. What is made clear in the film is that police forces have turned their firepower on protestors in the past and may do so again, for, as memory-keeper Roland Roebuck says, some will always be "more loyal to the concept of Blue" than to "the red of our common humanity" (Walton). At that point in the documentary, *La Manplesa* seems to invoke the words of Salvadoran revolutionary poet Roque Dalton, who made the same call to action and resistance in his poem "The Cops and the Guards." Dalton writes: "They always saw the people / as a mass of backs running away / as a field on which their clubs fell with hatred / . . . They too were once people / but with the excuse of hunger and unemployment / they accepted a weapon a club a monthly salary / to defend the makers of hunger and unemployment" (23). Set during the Salvadoran civil war, Dalton's poem recalls the moment that the people, tired of authorities firing on them, finally turned the tables and fired back at the police. So, too, Walton's film captures the moment that Salvadorans and their allies in the Mount Pleasant barrio rebelled against the D.C. Metropolitan Police and the inequities and violence that have been heaped on Black and Brown communities for decades. In the end, Dalton's poem and Walton's *La Manplesa*, alike, ask spectators to "think about that a while . . . decide whether it's too late / to seek the people's side" (Dalton, "Cops" 27). Indeed, in *La Manplesa*, the poets, artists, and community members are called to stand with the "darker shade of white" and to align themselves with the resistance of communities, barrios, and Blackness across the Americas.

We-Is-Placemaking

In her concluding chapter to *The Trouble with Unity*, titled "Latino Is a Verb: Democracy, *Latinidad*, and the Creation of the Political," Cristina Beltrán reminds us that "Latinidad must always remain a question" (162), in much the same way that Avilés casts Latino/a/x identities in Washington as a series of questions in his poem "Latinhood." Cuing us to the Latino/a/x diversity of the D.C. region (the result of the dispersion and intersection of countless global diasporas), Avilés marks the specificities (e.g., Salvadoreñidades) and indeterminacies of Latinidades ("How do you know that you are a latin? / that you are not / a russian imposter with a peruvian accent?"). He signals Latinidad as an entangled "web" of differences of languages, phenotypes, races, ethnicities, and last names, or what Beltrán calls Latinidad's rhizomatic, "unexpected assemblages that are created from its connections" (167). Avilés shows D.C. Latinidades and Salvadoreñidades, hence, to be assemblages of differences, always in question, in process, and in relation to other groups (long-residing Black Washingtonians, immigrants, refugees, asylum seekers, newcomers, and transplants from every part of the world and the United States, who bring their own specificities to the demographic mix of the region). Avilés ponders: "What language does it like to speak? / cachitquel / spanish / náhuatl / creole / or english? . . . What color is this latinhood of mine? / is it black latin / brown latin / indio latin / white latin / latin latin / italian latin via buenos aires / latin with a tinge of whiteness / mestizo latin with korean roots?/ . . . Is it mexican latin / salvatrucan latin / patagonian latin / latin with an american passport?" He asks, "Who are you in this crazy web of latins? / are you a jimenez, an escobar / a maravilla, a scapini, a molina / a well of broken wishes / Who are you? / did I meet your moustache / somewhere else? are we related?"

Dovetailing with the work of Avilés, Miranda, and Walton, Beltrán reminds us that "Latino political [and cultural] identity can also be understood in terms of collective creation and fugitive enactments" (161). Poetry, as a "fugitive" or ephemeral enactment of identity, positionality, and alignment, can express the many ways that Latinxs and other affinity groups such as African Americans connect, relate, and engage beyond essentialist narratives of nationalism, community, unity, and common interests, which have historically informed and coalesced into identity formations for Chicanos and Puerto Ricans, the two case studies examined by Beltrán in her book. Beltrán suggests that ephemeral affinities, sensibilities, and what she calls "shared practice[s] of acting and speaking together" (170) can activate seemingly collective identities in and for specific moments and contexts. So, when Sami Miranda, in his poem "We Is," begins every stanza with the first-person plural pronoun *we*, he assembles a collective identity that is yet differentiated and differential, in a site (Washington, D.C.) where hyperdiverse communities form solidarities based on their "darker shade[s] of white" and Black and Brown commonalities, as Muñoz would have it.

Centering African American English and claiming Black code-meshing (blending and mixing) as a collective speech act (V. A. Young et al. 1–11), Miranda repeats the phrase "we is": "We is the crowd . . . We is the dance . . . We is the traffic . . . We is the song of migration." Miranda closes the poem by saying, "We is home / carried into conversation, / about a crowing rooster, / a ritual, dancing and medicine / to cure what ails us." In a first-person plural pronoun collective voice and speech act, "we is" marks an assemblage of shared situations and lived experiences of people hearing a city rooster crow, "shimming" to salsa in the local market, rushing in traffic, and searching for medicine that "can heal the wounds of our entrances or exits." Finally, with the phrase "we is home," Miranda recalls his poem "Home," in which he lays claim to the possibility of forging collective identity, forming community, and making home, "in a city of so many places, [where] everyone / sooner or later finds one special / they name, home." Like Avilés, Miranda seems to say that it is this assemblage of "fugitive," everyday, mundane situations and lived experiences that makes possible community formation and home making amid the hyperdiversity of the Washington, D.C. metropolitan area and DMV.

Conclusion

Indeed, Beltrán suggests that we look at "Latinidad as a moment when diverse and even disparate subjects claim identification [and place] with one another" (168), through shared spaces, languages, and struggles. As I hope to have shown through my reading of the work of Quique Avilés, Sami Miranda, and Ellie Walton, it is precisely this in-flux assemblage of everyday, mundane, and often ephemeral situations, affiliations, affects, sensibilities, and positionalities that shapes Latinidades and Salvadoreñidades in relation to other groups (e.g., Black Americans) in urban spaces like Washington, D.C. It is in the everyday, mundane reimaginings of D.C. that artists and creatives see the ever-evolving, transitive "we-is" home making of the city, which Miranda identifies as the "unfamiliar space, one where I am the unfamiliar . . . where I am from" ("We Is"). It is here that "we is home" amid the hyperdiversity, where Salvadorans and others make home by positioning themselves with a "darker shade of white," unlearning their anti-Blackness, and adopting cultural and linguistic code-meshings produced on-site with Black communities (V. A. Young et al.). In this instance, the "we is" of Latinidades and Salvadoreñidades is an active and transitive process of relating, aligning, and acting with others. It is in this in-flux space that the Salvadoran diaspora has made the Washington, D.C. metropolitan area its home.

2

AGUACATERAS/OS

Remaking Identities and Dreams in the DMV

Any person in the DMV will tell you that they know (of), work with, or have had some contact with "El Salvadorans," who fill every niche of the labor market in the area. Salvadorans are students, teachers, professors, doctors, engineers, scientists, entrepreneurs, writers, artists, performers, activists, and specialists in the nonprofit, construction, hospitality, health-care, home-care, daycare, and security industries, among other fields. Indeed, in his "Poema de amor" (Love Poem), the Salvadoran revolutionary writer Roque Dalton describes Salvadorans as a can-do-everything (*hacelotodo*), resilient people who, despite experiencing great repression, violence, and hardships in their homeland and elsewhere, persevere and prevail in and outside of their country. They create belonging, home, and cultural and ethnoracial identities wherever they settle in their extended diaspora.

In this chapter, I discuss the social incorporation of Salvadorans in the DMV and their growing demographic and hybridizing cultural presence in the United States. First, I provide a historical overview of Salvadoran migration to the Washington metropolitan area. Second, I discuss the culturalscape of Salvadorans in the DMV, as represented in a growing corpus of cultural texts (e.g., narratives, memories, sounds, and images) by Salvadoran artists, writers, and creatives in the region. In the wake of the Salvadoran great migration associated with the civil war (1980–92)

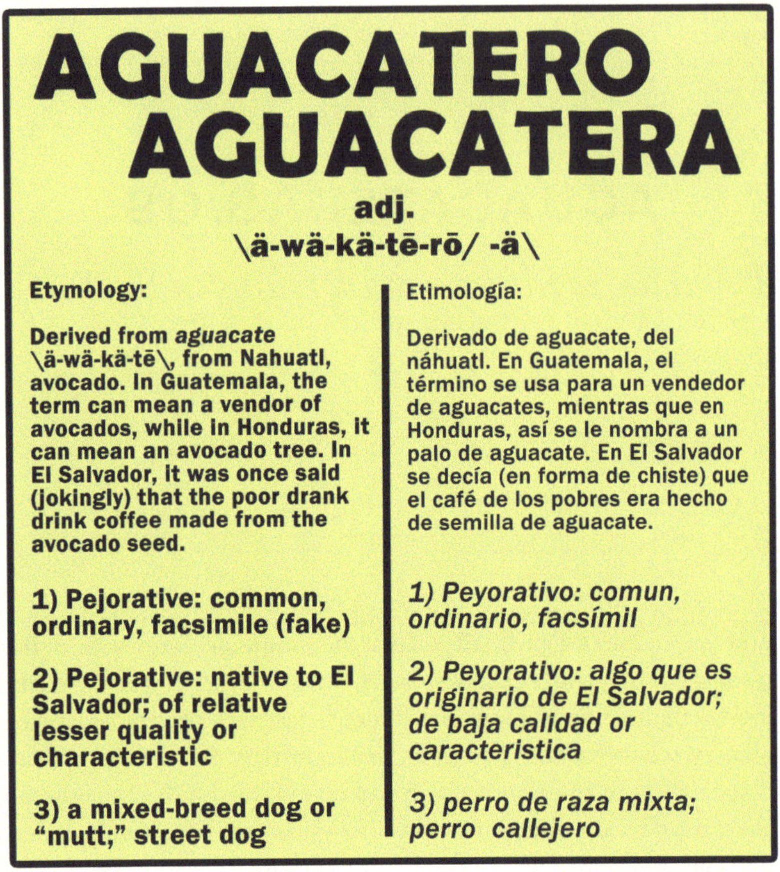

AGUACATERO
AGUACATERA
adj.
\ä-wä-kä-tē-rō/ -ä\

Etymology:

Derived from *aguacate* \ä-wä-kä-tē\, from Nahuatl, avocado. In Guatemala, the term can mean a vendor of avocados, while in Honduras, it can mean an avocado tree. In El Salvador, it was once said (jokingly) that the poor drank drink coffee made from the avocado seed.

1) Pejorative: common, ordinary, facsimile (fake)

2) Pejorative: native to El Salvador; of relative lesser quality or characteristic

3) a mixed-breed dog or "mutt;" street dog

Etimología:

Derivado de aguacate, del náhuatl. En Guatemala, el término se usa para un vendedor de aguacates, mientras que en Honduras, así se le nombra a un palo de aguacate. En El Salvador se decía (en forma de chiste) que el café de los pobres era hecho de semilla de aguacate.

1) Peyorativo: comun, ordinario, facsímil

2) Peyorativo: algo que es originario de El Salvador; de baja calidad or caracteristica

3) perro de raza mixta; perro callejero

FIGURE 3. "Aguacatero/Aguacatera," by Víctor H. Interiano (Dichos de un bicho), 2020. Courtesy of Víctor H. Interiano.

and Salvadorans' subsequent back-and-forth transmigrations to the Washington metropolitan area, there is a need to understand how migration to and between translocal sites such as the DMV affects and transforms traditional constructs of Salvadoran cultural and ethnoracial identity—or what I call their diasporic *aguacatero* identities—following the short story by onetime D.C.-based Salvadoran writer Mario Bencastro, "Las ilusiones de Juana" / "Juana's Dreams," discussed in the introduction and later in this chapter.

The trope of the avocado, or *aguacate* in Spanish, is used here not as a gratuitous folkloric motif, but, in the context of El Salvador, as a metaphor of cultural (hybrid) identities, diaspora, and community formation, or the process of becoming *típico* (typical) in national, transnational, and translocal sites in any given historical context. The term *aguacatero* signifies "native [or indigenous] to El Salvador," as the meme by Dichos de un Bicho in figure 3 states, and can be read as a raciolinguistic and ethnoracial trope of cultural formation and resistance. According to the Salvadoran social linguist Pedro Geoffroy Rivas, in *La lengua salvadoreña* (The Salvadoran Language), Náhuatismos like *aguacatero/a* are not merely colloquial words, but signs of the resistant and resilient cultural character and practices of a people who have survived waves of conquest, colonization, settler colonialism, imperialism, genocide, ethnogenocide, wars, displacements, dispersions, and diasporas. Náhuatismos like *aguacatero/a* carry the traces of the silenced and hidden histories, memories, and traumas that lie at the base of Salvadoran social, racial, cultural, trans/national, and diasporic identity formations. Following the work of Rivas, words like *aguacatero/a* come to signify the layered hybridity of Salvadoran identities produced in and outside of the nation-state and founded on settler colonialist and imperialist interventions that often repeat in Central American history. Moreover, following the work of Benedict Anderson, Robin Maria DeLugan, and others, the nation and the homeland are understood here to be imagined communities constructed through shared texts, images, metaphors, and signs of *agucatero/a*-alterity (Salvadoran) in diaspora.

In this light, I turn to the creative works of diasporic Salvadorans—both immigrant foreign-born and U.S.-born or U.S.-raised Salvadorans of the D.C. area—to explore how *aguacatero/a* identities take shape, and how they shape the intersections of race, ethnicity, class, gender, sexuality, religion, language, age, migration status, and generation in the District of Columbia and the DMV. In this book, I differentiate between immigrant, foreign-born Salvadorans and U.S.-born or U.S.-raised Salvadorans, who together forge "El Salvador in Wachinton" and become "Wachintonians" (Washingtonians of Salvadoran descent), as local D.C. Salvadoran performance artist, poet, and activist Quique Avilés calls Salvadorans in his poem "El Salvador At-a-Glance." Here, I mostly concentrate on the voluntary and forced cultural and ethnoracial adaptations of Salvadoran migrants, who construct new *aguacatera/o* identities in the Washington metropolitan area and the DMV.

Salvadoran Arrivals in the Washington Metropolitan Area

Salvadoran and Central American migration to the D.C. area dates back to at least the late nineteenth and early twentieth centuries, when government business brought diplomatic émigrés and sojourners from around the world to the U.S. capital. In fact, Central American intellectuals like Salvadoran Jacinto Castellanos, Guatemalan Máximo Soto Hall, Nicaraguan Salomón de la Selva, and Costa Rican Roberto Brenes Mesén often traveled to Washington as part of diplomatic delegations and as cultural ambassadors, to use a term coined by literary critic Kirsten Silva Gruesz in the context of New Orleans. From October 1889 to April 1890, Dr. Castellanos, for example, represented El Salvador at the First Pan-American Conference, also known as the First International Conference of American States and subsequently as the Summit of the Americas, which was held in Washington, D.C. (Karras 84). More than a century later, in 2003, his granddaughter Ana Sol Gutiérrez would become the first Latina and Salvadoran delegate elected to the Maryland General Assembly, representing District 18 in Montgomery County. In the early to mid-twentieth century, artistic sojourners such as Salvadoran writers Salvador Salazar Arrué (Salarrué) and Claribel Alegría also lived in Washington, D.C. Best known for his 1933 *Cuentos de barro* (Tales of Clay) and his 1943 *Cuentos de cipotes* (Children's Stories), Salarrué trained as a painter at the Corcoran School of Art between 1916 and 1919, while Alegría, author of more than forty books of poetry, short stories, and *testimonios*, earned a bachelor of arts in philosophy and letters at the George Washington University in 1948. These writers were followed by dissident exiles and others who gravitated to Washington, D.C., planting the seeds of burgeoning Salvadoran sociopolitical and cultural enclaves.

Like their Central American compatriots, Salvadoran embassy personnel and staff also began to travel regularly to or settle in the District of Columbia in the twentieth century, taking up "residence near present day Adams Morgan and Mt. Pleasant" (Cadaval, *Creating* 56). Salvadoran migrants, however, did not arrive in large numbers until the 1960s and '70s, when U.S. and home country diplomats, government employees, and international agency personnel sponsored Central American women, including Salvadorans, for employment in domestic work, childcare assistance, and other industries (Córdova 77). As Terry A. Repak explains in *Waiting on Washington: Central American Workers in the Nation's Capital*, women "pioneered the migration in the 1960s and 1970s" to the Washington metropolitan area, providing immigrant labor in the care, domestic, hospitality, service, and construction industries (2, 59–60). Focusing on gender-based migration, labor recruitment, and social networks, Repak further describes the establishment of a primarily Salvadoran enclave in the neighborhoods of Mount Pleasant, Adams Morgan, and Columbia Heights. In the 1970s and 1980s, somewhat affordable housing, access to immigrant service agencies, and viable commutes to jobs in the District of Columbia and nearby suburbs in Maryland and Virginia drew Salvadorans to the area, just as at the civil war erupted between El Salvador's right-wing government and various left-wing organizations (these would coalesce into the Farabundo Martí National Liberation Front in 1980). As U.S. military and economic aid to El Salvador increased and the war intensified during the 1980s, so did the migration of Salvadoran refugees and asylum seekers to places like Washington, D.C. These migrants, especially women, would remain in the shadows of legalization for decades to come (Córdova 69–89; Friedman 238–40).

In *Covert Capital: Landscapes of Denial and the Making of U.S. Empire in the Suburbs of Northern Virginia*, Andrew Friedman examines the ties that bind the Washington, D.C. metropolitan area to Central America, focusing on how the military and security industries transformed the built environment of northern Virginia, created great wealth for top-level corporate personnel, and attracted immigrants precisely from the countries where the United States intervened militarily, politically, and economically in the twentieth century. According to Friedman, northern Virginia, with its ubiquitous military-industrial complex extending across a wide network of security, technology, and contractual businesses, is closely tied to some of the most notorious interventions in Central America, such as the procurement of weapons used in the overthrow of President Jacobo Árbenz Guzmán in Guatemala in 1954; the exchange of arms for money in the Iran-Contra scandal and the CIA training of Contra-revolutionary forces to defeat the Sandinista government of Nicaragua in the 1980s; and the support of right-wing death squad leaders such as Salvadoran Roberto D'Aubuisson, "who himself spent time in D.C. and Virginia as a trainee at U.S. AID's International Police Academy" in the 1970s (237–38). D'Aubuisson would go on to found the Nationalist Republican Alliance (ARENA), the right-wing party of El Salvador, as well as the brutal death squads responsible for countless disappearances and assassinations such as that of Archbishop (San) Óscar A. Romero on March 24, 1980. It is worth recalling, as Friedman writes, that "the United States sent some $6 billion in military and other aid to El Salvador in the 1980s, making the tiny country, with its population only five-and-a-half times the size of Fairfax County's [in northern Virginia], the globe's third largest recipient of U.S. military aid" (238). By the end of the war, more than seventy-five thousand Salvadorans were dead, and over 25 percent of the Salvadoran population was displaced (Gammage). Many Salvadorans immigrated to the Washington metropolitan area.

In *American Value: Migrants, Money, and Meaning in El Salvador and the United States*, David E. Pedersen explains how the robust job market in the Washington, D.C. metropolitan area, including the ever-expanding U.S. military-industrial complex, attracted Salvadoran immigrant workers to D.C., Maryland, and especially northern Virginia. High-tech industry workers engaged in research and development, telecommunications, transportation, defense, and international finance, as well as individuals employed in legal, governmental, and diplomatic services, having flocked to the region, in turn required the services of immigrant workers. In time, Salvadorans gravitated to the region and built enclaves, social networks, and hometown associations linking their diasporic communities to El Salvador (see also Friedman). As a site of economic opportunity, political activity, and activism, the Washington, D.C. metropolitan area thus drew a wide range of Salvadoran migrants (Cadaval, *Creating* 56; Ferris 121; Sánchez Molina, *Mandar* 74–76; Sánchez Molina, *Proceso*). They established primarily Salvadoran enclaves within the increasingly Latino neighborhoods of Mount Pleasant, Adams Morgan, and Columbia Heights in northwest Washington, D.C., especially along the Columbia Road and Mount Pleasant Street corridors. Tomás Guevara and Hugo Salinas, in their 2008 documentary *Intipucá: 40 años de emigración hacia los Estados Unidos* (Intipucá: 40 Years of Emigration to the United States), tell the stories of the so-called *pioneros* (pioneers) who emigrated in the late 1960s from the easternmost parts of El Salvador, including the Department of La Unión, to the Mount Pleasant neighborhood, where they established businesses, homes, immigrant boardinghouses, communities, and foundations to provide mutual aid to Intipucá City in El Salvador. To provide necessary services to the newly arrived migrants, a number of church-affiliated refugee centers, solidarity networks, service providers, artistic venues, businesses, stores, and restaurants concentrated in the area. By the early 1990s, Salvadorans and other Latino/a/x immigrants had settled in D.C.'s Ward 1, amid mounting racial tensions, economic disparities, police brutality, and what has been called the "willful neglect" of the Latino/a/x community by local and national governmental agencies (Yzaguirre and Aponte), all of which would reach a breaking point with the Salvadoran-led Mount Pleasant uprising of May 5–7, 1991 (Jennings and Lusane).

Known also as the "Mount Pleasant Riots," these disturbances were set off when a D.C. Metropolitan Police officer, a Black woman, shot a Salvadoran man, Daniel Enrique Gómez, who was allegedly drunk and arrested for disorderly conduct after the Cinco de Mayo celebration in Adams Morgan (Jennings and Lusane 65–67). Almost thirty years later, the story of this little-known uprising was told through the voices of multiple participants and witnesses interviewed in Ellie Walton's 2021 documentary *La Manplesa*, as discussed in chapter 1. To recall, over a three-day period, Latino/a/x and African American youths confronted police, damaging buildings, breaking into stores and businesses, blocking traffic, and setting fire to police cars and buses (Nnamdi). To stop the violence, Sharon Pratt Dixon, then mayor of Washington, D.C., declared a state of emergency and imposed a 7:00 p.m. curfew in the Mount Pleasant, Adams Morgan, and Columbia Heights neighborhoods. In a show of force, one thousand police officers were deployed to patrol the largely poor Central American, Latino/a/x, and Black neighborhoods, where residents had long experienced increasing racial tensions, discrimination, police violence, and crime, as well as ever-encroaching gentrification, threatening to displace residents (Nnamdi). In the aftermath of the uprising, the *Mount Pleasant Report* was drafted. It found that Latinxs experienced abuse at the hands of the D.C. Metropolitan Police Department as well as neglect by the D.C. government, which failed to recognize the growing Latino/a/x population and to provide adequate social services to Latinxs

(Pratt 2011). As a consequence of the uprising, a Latino Civil Rights Task Force, headed by longtime D.C. resident and community leader Pedro Avilés, was established to study the state of Latinxs in the city and to make recommendations for improved community relations. This led to the creation of a bilingual police unit and the support of various nonprofit organizations serving Latinxs in the district.

Unfortunately, throughout the 1990s and early 2000s, the D.C. area's Salvadoran population continued to experience willful neglect, if not systemic violence and racism, while newly arrived Salvadoran immigrants continued to fill regional employment demands. During the 1970s and '80s, Salvadorans had gravitated to jobs held or formerly held by African Americans, who historically supplied labor for various job markets in the region. After September 11, 2001, the newly created Department of Homeland Security generated new jobs for employees directly or peripherally attached to the Washington area's military and security sectors. Entwined and offshoot industries produced employment not only for highly skilled attorneys, engineers, architects, and bureaucrats, but also for workers in landscaping, construction, housekeeping, childcare, hospitality, and other service jobs (Pedersen, *American Value* 149; Repak 73–124). Drawn to these jobs, Salvadorans have continuously made important contributions to the economy, community, culture, and lifestyle of the region. They have brought to the region their rich culture, their unique language, and their lively music, as well as their foodways, including the pupusa (cornmeal tortilla stuffed with cheese, beans, pork, and other items), which in 2000 was declared a *comida típica* (local food) of Washington, D.C. (Peterson). In 2017, D.C. mayor Muriel Bowser even made a trip to El Salvador to sign an accord with then mayor (and future president) Nayib Bukele, making San Salvador and the District of Columbia sister cities, and she was photographed making and eating pupusas by the national and international press. Without a doubt, Salvadorans are an important socioeconomic and cultural component of the local labor force and the U.S. economy, paying sales and income taxes (often using government-issued individual taxpayer identification numbers [TINs]), as well as contributing more than $8 billion annually in remittances to the Salvadoran economy as of 2023 (Harris and Maldonado).

In the first quarter of the twenty-first century, the D.C. metropolitan area began receiving another influx of migrant families, women, and children from the so-called Northern Triangle of Central America (El Salvador, Guatemala, and Honduras), all seeking refuge from conditions of extreme poverty, scarcity, and social and political violence. In 2014–15, Maryland and Virginia each admitted almost five thousand unaccompanied immigrant minors, and D.C. almost four hundred youth migrants, figures that do not accurately account for migrant youths who arrived alone and undetected by immigration services, then and thereafter ("Children"; Krogstad and González-Barrera). To date, many continue to struggle to regularize their migratory status, adding to the backlog of immigration cases. From 2008 to 2010, the U.S. government denied 90 percent of all Salvadoran political asylum cases, much like it did for asylum seekers fleeing the Salvadoran civil war in the 1980s (Peralta). Hoping to reunite with relatives and find better living conditions in the D.C. area, but without the foreseeable possibility of attaining legal resident status, many Salvadorans have remained undocumented or under Temporary Protected Status (TPS), the renewable U.S. Citizenship and Immigration Services permit that allows qualifying immigrants to live and work in the United States while conditions of armed conflict, environmental disaster, epidemic, or other extraordinary and temporary conditions persist in their home country (see "Temporary Protected Status"). Salvadorans were first granted TPS on March 9, 2001, in response to a series of devastating earthquakes, and, since then, have been able to renew their permits every eighteen months, upon payment of fees and program reauthorization.

Despite their growing number and their significant contributions to the economy and culture of the D.C. area, Salvadorans have generally lacked political representation and participation in local D.C. politics and government. As of 2025, there were no Salvadorans on the City Council and Salvadorans had little representation on D.C. governmental committees and boards, including those of education, business, planning, parks, and other public services. Likewise, in the local suburbs of Virginia and Maryland, Salvadoran political representation has been minimal, although Democrats Ana Sol Gutiérrez and Victor Ramírez have served in the Maryland General Assembly, and Republican Yesli Vega served on the Board of Supervisors in Prince William County, Virginia. Despite such representation, the cultural critic Arturo Arias has rightly argued that Central Americans, including Salvadorans, are "nearly invisible within the imaginary confines of what constitutes the multicultural landscape of the United States" (*Taking Their Word* 185). Although they have been one of the largest immigrant and foreign-born groups in the Washington metropolitan area since the 1980s, Salvadorans have remained politically invisible and underrepresented for multiple reasons, not least of which is the white/Black racial binary structuring D.C. politics and many of its neighborhoods and communities (Jennings and Lusane 65–67). In response to these mechanisms and to their own experiences of violence, trauma, forced migration, and lack of legal resident status, Salvadorans in the region have adopted strategies of invisibility, as Arias has argued (*Taking Their Word*). They have used artistic and cultural representation as a means of preserving and refashioning their culture, traditions, and customs, and of making their presence, needs, and struggles known.

Though relatively invisible in local politics, Salvadorans in the Washington area have actively engaged in various forms of "cultural citizenship," which political scientist William V. Flores and oral historian Rina Benmayor define as "a broad range of activities of everyday life through which Latinos and other groups claim space in society and eventually claim rights" (15). The back cover to their book explains further that "Latino cultural citizenship" may be understood as "the use of cultural expression to claim political rights in the larger culture while maintaining vibrant local identity." Indeed, Salvadorans in the D.C. metropolitan area, up until the COVID-19 era, not only built vibrant economic niches, exemplified by restaurants, supermarkets, money transfer centers, and other informal markets, but also elaborated local cultural identities through media, music, sports, performances, artwork, festivals, customs, traditions, and other cultural practices that re-create elements of their homeland and speak to migration flows of Salvadorans to the United States. Artists such as musician Lilo González; photographer Muriel Hasbun; graphic artist Frida Larios; painter Karla Rodas (Karlísima); writers Quique Avilés, Mario Bencastro, Mayamérica Cortez, Daniel Joya, José Vladimir Monge, Carlos Parada-Ayala, and Grego Pineda; and a host of creatives like Veronica Meléndez and Kimberly Benavides of *La Horchata Zine*, not only represent the living history of Salvadorans but also embody, document, and mark their presence in the Washington metropolitan area (see Ambroggio and Parada-Ayala; Ambroggio et al.; Cortez; Joya; Monge, *Pasajeros*; Monge, *Voces*; Pineda). Through their artistic and cultural productions, they have sought to represent the lives of Salvadoran "Wachintonians."

The Art of Being "Wachintonian"

Among the most notable Salvadoran artists to represent how Salvadorans have made D.C. home and become "Wachintonians" is Quique Avilés: poet, performer, cultural activist, and graduate of the Duke Ellington School of the Arts (figure 4). Avilés arrived in D.C. from El Salvador at the age of fifteen, in 1980, along with others fleeing the civil war. He soon began to write, in English, Spanish, and Spanglish, about his own experiences and observations as a Salvadoran immigrant, and to give public performances with other artists about life in the "Latino barrio" of Mount Pleasant, making visible a community that went largely unperceived by the general population. He cofounded, directed, or participated in a number of art collectives, including LatiNegro, Sol & Soul, Para eso la Palabra, and the youth program Paso Nuevo at the GALA Hispanic Theatre, bringing his wry satire to bear on social issues such as racism, war, migration, identity, and gentrification. His performances have included *Latinhood, Chaos Standing, Caminata: A Walk Through Immigrant America, The Children of Latinia, Los Treinta,* and the documentaries *La Manplesa* and *Las muertes más bellas del mundo,* as well as his published poetry collection *The Immigrant Museum.* His work is analyzed throughout chapters of this book and runs like an *hilo conductor,* a connecting thread, through many of my discussions of Salvadoran cultural production and representation in the Washington, D.C. metropolitan area.

Longtime D.C. resident, one-and-a-half-generation Salvadoran immigrant, and painter Karla Rodas (Karlísima) captures, throughout her work, moments in the migration of Salvadorans, especially women, to the region. Her painting *Indigenous Lament II* (*Lamento indígena II*) (figure 5), which I have examined extensively elsewhere (Rodríguez, "Becoming"; Rodríguez, "Departamento 15"; Rodríguez, *Dividing*), is based on a poem of the same title written by her mother, the poet Mayamérica Cortez. Karlísima's painting majestically represents the liminal passage of Salvadoran women into Washington, D.C. Caught midstep in between her homeland and the gray city of Washington, the Indigenous woman-queen (a self-portrait of Karlísima), dressed in regal garments and headpiece, looks back at her native land with grief or perhaps ambivalence. She is shown in motion, one foot in a sandal, the other in a high heel shoe, moving into unknown territory. While the painting suggests that the woman is moving

FIGURE 4. Quique Avilés and friends performing *Here Comes the Funky Wagon / Aquí viene el carretón* on Eleventh Street NW in Columbia Heights, October 2014, in protest of gentrification in the Latino neighborhoods of D.C. Photo courtesy of author.

FIGURE 5. *Indigenous Lament II (Lamento indígena II)*, by Karlísima, 2005. Photo courtesy of author.

toward the point of no return—into what, with its monumental federal buildings, is clearly Washington, D.C.—it also represents an imaginary, almost surreal home/land populated by colorful, larger-than-life images of fruits, palm trees, and crystal-clear lakes, which exist, perhaps, only in nostalgic memory (Boym xiii).

Framed by borders featuring motifs associated with Fernando Llort's popular art of La Palma, which circulates hugely in the diaspora and solidarity movements (Rodríguez, "Tan cerca"), the painting is divided into two panels. In the left panel, the painting captures D.C. as modern, urban, and stately; in the right panel, El Salvador figures as primitive, rural, and natural. As the migrant woman (read: mestiza) leaves behind her rural homeland and moves into the modern city, her progression can be read as one of assimilation into the cultural, social, and economic values of her new homeland. After all, she represents the thousands of laboring women who migrate to the DMV to find work and to send remittances home. Her movement west can also be read as a process of deracialization as she enters the modern flexible economy, for, as the Salvadoran anthropologist José Heriberto Erquicia Cruz notes in his study of Blackness in El Salvador, "la vision fundamental era para modernizarse y 'avanzar' hay que dejar de ser indio, negro y mulato y pasar a ser mestizo" (the fundamental vision was that in order to modernize and 'advance,' one had to cease to be Indian, Black, and mulatto and become mestizo) (135). In crossing over into the United States, the migrant woman seems to move away from her former ethnoracial and cultural identities and step into other structures of race, ethnicity, gender, sexuality, and class, which will henceforth remake and mark her as an immigrant laborer. Rodas's painting, thus, can be read as a commentary on how Salvadoran migrant women navigate, translate, and embody various positionalities, from migrants, border-crossers, and "illegals" (Padilla, *From Threatening Guerrillas*), to labor migrants and "jinchos/as" (countryfolk) in the process of becoming "Wachintonians," as we will see in my analysis of the Los Angeles–based Cultural Clash's production of *Anthems*, examined in chapter 3.

FIGURE 6. Musician, educator, and activist Lilo González with writer Carlos Parada-Ayala at Don Jaime Restaurant on Mount Pleasant Street NW, October 2014. Photo courtesy of author.

Like Rodas and Avilés, the D.C.-based Salvadoran musician Lilo González represents the Salvadoran diaspora in Washington through his artistry (figure 6). A guitarist, songwriter, and educator, González migrated with his family to the D.C. area in the 1980s and worked as a dishwasher while studying at the Carlos Rosario International Public Charter School (then called the Gordon Center) in Columbia Heights. For years, he has composed music and lyrics about the life of Salvadoran immigrants in the area. In 1989, he won the Organización de Televisión Iberoamérica (Iberoamerican Television Organization) prize for his song "Amor sin papeles" (Love Without Papers), and, in 1994, he released his first CD, *A quien corresponda . . .* (To Whom It May Concern) ("Student Success Stories"). The CD cover features folkloric, La Palma–like images overlaid on landmarks of Mount Pleasant; the CD, recorded with his band, Los de la Mount Pleasant, offers a compilation of songs, mostly in Spanish, about Salvadoran life in D.C. Songs describe mothers forced to migrate without their children ("The Border Crossed My Land"), undocumented residents living in fear of deportation ("No Human Being Is Illegal," "Love Without Papers"), and the difficulties of immigrant adaptation and the consequences of cultural assimilation ("Mount Pleasant Street").

Once a resident of the DMV, Mario Bencastro (figure 7) has written a number of novels and short story collections, many of which have been translated into French, German, and English, including *A Shot in the Cathedral, The Tree of Life: Stories of Civil War, Odyssey to the North, A Promise to Keep, Paraíso portátil / Portable Paradise, La Mansión del Olvido,* and *El vuelo de la alondra.* His monologue *Vato Guanaco Loco: Rap en Caliche,* written in the 1990s and published by Casa de la Cultura El Salvador in Washington, D.C. in 2019, reproduces the sounds of Afro-Indigenous, Náhuat-inflected *caliche* slang. The monologue has been performed by youths in local schools, in an effort to bring Salvadoran culture to the schools and diasporic communities of Washington. All of Bencastro's works are set against the backdrop of Salvadoran history, from the start of the twentieth century through the civil war and the postwar era, following the signing of the Salvadoran Peace Accords in 1992, and including the migration of Salvadorans across the world. His novel *Odyssey to the North,* in particular, focuses on Salvadoran migration to D.C. through the telling of the story of a migrant named Calixto, who flees the violence in El Salvador, makes the perilous voyage through Mexico, and resettles

FIGURE 7. Writer Mario Bencastro presenting his book *La Mansión del Olvido* at the Embassy of El Salvador on Sixteenth Street NW, June 5, 2015. Photo courtesy of author.

and works in neighborhoods near Mount Pleasant and Adams Morgan in the 1980s. There, he witnesses the death of a fellow migrant cleaning windows in a high-rise building near the National Zoo in Woodley Park, a place far from home in countless ways.

In his short story collection *Paraíso portátil / Portable Paradise*, Bencastro writes about transnational Salvadoran lives in the DMV and across the world. In "From Australia with Love," a young massacre survivor living in Melbourne, Australia, meets her family's killer in an internet chat room called Tierra Linda (Beautiful Land). The virtual chance encounter between victim and victimizer reveals the ghosts of past traumas, which have made the transnational passage into diasporic sites and now lurk in the dark corners of the web. In other stories from the same collection, migrants conjure up memories of an ideal(ized) country that simply does not exist and perhaps never did, while some return to a country disfigured by a culture of impunity that has purposefully failed to bring war criminals to justice. Now, former death squad leaders and guerilla fighters are government officials, next-door neighbors, caretakers, and *wachimans* (watchmen) of houses owned by migrants living abroad. Like other texts of the Central American diasporas, Bencastro's stories are populated with victims, perpetrators, and ghosts of past and present violence.

Finally, Frida Larios, whose image *Awakat Che' (Awakateros)* graces the cover of this book, is a typographic artist from El Salvador. She identifies as mixed Indigenous Nawat-Maya-Ch'orti', resides in Washington, D.C., and has taught visual literacy and design at the London College of Fashion, Camberwell College of Arts, American University, and the University of the District of Columbia. A onetime volleyball gold medalist, Larios was selected as art director of the Team ESA (Team El Salvador) uniforms for the 2019 Pan American Games in Lima, Peru, and as codesigner of the award-winning Team ESA uniforms for the opening ceremony of the 2015 Pan American Games in Toronto, Canada, all of which used Indigenous motifs and symbology (Larios, artist website). For years, she has worked on graphic design, conducted research on Indigenous cosmologies and practices, and participated in community-based, cultural revitalization initiatives, resulting in her creation of a "New Maya (visual) language coding methodology," or, simply, a New Maya Language ("Meet the Author").

In the Washington, D.C. metropolitan area, Larios has collaborated with artists on the production of murals, altars for Día de los Muertos,

FIGURE 8. Frida Larios with Quique Avilés at the unveiling of the mural *Our Seeds Will Be Millions* at Marie Reed Aquatic Center on Eighteenth Street NW, November 20, 2021. Photo courtesy of author.

and other public art, honoring the ancestors and celebrating local communities. The mural *Our Seeds Will Be Millions* (figure 8), coproduced with Musah Swallah, Etai Rogers, and community members, is inspired by the Honduran-Salvadoran proverb "blood of martyrs, seed of freedom" (Larios, "Our Seeds"). It depicts the Yáaxche (Ceiba) tree of life, which rises from the sea to the skies and branches into human hands, encasing the four directions (representing life forces) and uplifting a Black child dressed in yellow. In another mural collaboration with Swallah, this one painted on the wall of the Panam Grocery on Fourteenth Street NW in Columbia Heights, Larios pays tribute to the U.S. Army soldier Vanessa Guillén, murdered on the grounds of Fort Hood in Texas on April 22, 2020. In solidarity and remembrance, Larios and Swallah depict Guillén's image framed by Larios's characteristic imagery of hands around her heart (Meneray). Larios has also produced chalk art using her signature imagery with community members at street festivals, and Día de los Muertos altars honoring fallen migrants at the border and women leaders like the Honduran Indigenous Lenca environmental activist and water defender Berta Cáceres, assassinated on March 3, 2016, in her homeland.

Inspired by the hieroglyphic writing systems of the Classic Maya (250–900 CE) and their living descendants—the Maya-Ch'orti', Nawat, Cacaopera, Lenca, and other Indigenous peoples of El Salvador—Larios has created a visual writing system of *pictoglyphs* (pictograms + hieroglyphics), which makes no claim to authenticity, but pays homage to the First Peoples of El Salvador by attempting to preserve, re-create, and reengage with ancient imaginaries in the twenty-first century. Larios's reinvented system of pictographic writing, featured in her children's book *The Village That Was Buried by an Erupting Volcano*, "was published with guidance of Iniciativa Portadores del Náhuat and Central de Organizaciones Indígenas Campesinas Ch'orti' Nuevo Día, with a foreword by Payson Sheets, Ph.D., principal researcher of Joya de Cerén of UC Boulder" (Larios, artist website). Written in Spanish, English, and what Larios calls a "New Maya (visual) language," her book tells the story of the Green Child, whose home and community lie buried beneath the UNESCO-recognized World Heritage Site of Joya de Cerén in western El Salvador, at the southernmost tip of the Maya Empire in the Preclassic to Classic eras. The story imagines day-to-day scenes in the life of the Green Child using elements of Larios's New Maya Language, whose pictoglyphs readers learn to read alongside

FIGURE 9. *La familia en la casa de adobe*, by Frida Larios, 2014. Courtesy of Frida Larios.

English and Spanish translations, making for a multilingual, multisensory, and multilayered reading experience. Larios describes pictoglyphs as "logo-legos," which like LEGO pieces can stand alone or be combined in compositions (figure 9). As graphic designer Ellen Shapiro explains, with reference to a quote from Larios, her pictoglyphs are "constructed from two or more parts 'that are strong individually, but become even more meaningful conjugated as a whole.'"

Larios's book *The Village That Was Buried by an Erupting Volcano* begins with the story of the Green Child living and working in community in his village and participating in the "fire ceremony" at the temple of San Andrés in honor of his grandfather. One day, Loma Caldera, on the outskirts of his village, erupts, hurling lava bombs all around, depicted in Larios's narration by pictoglyphs. Based on archaeological findings at Joya de Cerén, Larios depicts the Green Child "eating tamales and beans with his mother and brother from ceramic vessels they made themselves." Although the village is soon "devoured in smoke," the Green Child and his family escape the eruption of Loma Caldera, and his village is preserved under the lava ash and uncovered 1,400 years later by "an American archaeologist called Payson." Through her pictoglyphs, also presented in a glossary at the end of the book and available for viewing at her artist website, Larios represents elements of the artifacts preserved to this day at Joya de Cerén: utensils, beans, ruins of houses, and even the remains of a mouse, all evidence of Indigenous life and foodways. Indeed, Larios cites the archaeological findings at Joya de Cerén ("the Pompeii of the New World")—so well documented in Payson D. Sheets's book *Before the Volcano Erupted: The Ancient Cerén Village in Central America*—to illustrate in her book how Maya peoples of the region might have "harvested corn, manioc, and chocolate; and what a day in the life of the Green Child was like."

On the twentieth anniversary of the recognition of Joya de Cerén as a UNESCO World Heritage Site, Larios was commissioned to paint a mural at the site, using her New Maya Language to represent scenes from the volcano eruption that buried Joya de Cerén. Her work has been exhibited at the Smithsonian National Museum of the American Indian, the Smithsonian National Museum of American History, the Peale Museum in Baltimore, and the Museo de Arte de El Salvador, among others (Larios, artist website). Her work has been described as "bridging the stories from Indigenous peoples and lands to contemporary reflection and appreciation, through her award-winning New Maya (Visual) Language coding methodology" ("Meet the Author"). In *Signs of the Americas: A Poetics of Pictography, Hieroglyphs, and Khipu*, Edgar García comments on the conversion of ancient sign systems and their incorporation into new writing to produce a continuation of mythic history in the present, a project in which Larios thoroughly engages through her revitalization of Maya writing.

For the cover of *Avocado Dreams*, Larios designed the pictoglyph *Awakat Che' (Awakateros)* (figure 10), which recalls the Classic Maya iconography of the "gran abuela K'ANAL-IKAL," or "Lady Kanal-Ikal emerging with

FIGURE 10. *Awakat Che' (Awakateros)*, by Frida Larios, 2023. Courtesy of Frida Larios.

an avocado tree on the side of Janaab-Pacal's sarcophagus," built in 650 CE in Palenque, Chiapas, Mexico (Landon 65; see also Martin 162).[1] In Larios's iteration, an avocado tree emerges from the nurturing Brown hand of Mother Earth. The hand holds up a tree from which sprout four green avocados flanked by four green leaves on four quadrants, representing the four corners and four cardinal points and directions—north, south, east, and west—from which emanate all life forces. In Maya cosmology, green signifies life and rebirth. The two and three (not a bar signifying five) yellow seeds in the trunk of the tree seem to signify the cycle of life and death followed by regeneration or harvest, while the magenta-red half circle at the bottom of the hand signifies earth, which nurtures life, crops, and the avocados. For me, Larios's composition in pictoglyphs aptly captures the essence of this book. In diaspora, Central Americans and Salvadorans travel with their avocado dreams, seedlings of hope, and roots of homeland. Replanted in other soils, with a nurturing hand, persistent dream, sense of direction, knowledge of history, and memory of origins and connections, Central Americans and Salvadorans can reemerge, strong like the "gran abuela K'ANAL-IKAL," in other soils. With this philosophy of worldmaking, bridging the ancestral and the diasporic, *Awakatero Dreams*, or *Avocado Dreams*, invites readers to reimagine the place- and worldmaking, constructions, and transformations of Salvadoreñidades in diaspora.

This brief overview of some of the D.C.-based writers, artists, and artivists of the Salvadoran diaspora spotlighted in this book brings to light how Salvadorans reimagine, remake, and transplant themselves, their identities, and their crafts in the DMV. Drawing from their histories, memories, hopes, and dreams, Salvadoran cultural producers and everyday folks transplant their avocado life force and build hybrid transnational and diasporic identities. With the work of the artists and creatives highlighted here, we can begin to examine the (re)making of traditional constructs of Salvadoran cultural and ethnoracial identities in situ.

Aguacatero Diasporas

In the urban dictionary of El Salvador, if there were one, the avocado or *aguacate* would signify Salvadoran cultural identity. While the avocado has become the wonder health food, even called one of the world's healthiest foods for its high content of healthy fats, nutrients, and vitamins, it has, with its four hundred varieties, long been a staple in the Salvadoran diet and culture. No Salvadoran meal or home is complete without the avocado—avocado with the breakfast beans, the midday soup, the dinner meal, and the in-between snacking. One scoops it out of its skin with a tortilla at any time of day, and, hence, it has been the go-to food for many Salvadoran families of different socioeconomic classes and means. In El Salvador, there is a saying that if there is an avocado, then there is a meal. Indeed, the avocado is linked to Salvadoran cultural identity, as it is a world fruit indigenous not only to Africa but also to Mesoamerica and northern South America, as noted in the first natural histories and reports written by Spanish missionaries, cultural translators, and others (Galindo-Tovar et al.; Zentmyer et al.).

According to one of its many origin stories, the avocado seems to have originated in Africa and migrated to Europe, Asia, and the Americas; it "has been consumed in Mesoamerica by human groups since prehistoric times [and] grown [in the Supe Valley of South America] . . . at least since 1200 BC" (Galindo-Tovar et al. 326). In what is now Mexico, the Aztec referred to the fruit as *ahuacatl* in Náhuatl, and it was used as a tribute exchanged among groups (Galindo-Tovar et al. 329; Landon 65). The Maya venerated the avocado as part of their creation story in the *Popol Vuh*. For the Maya, the avocado held great significance, represented by the glyph associated with the fourteenth month and inscribed in King Pacal's tomb in Palenque, Chiapas, Mexico, where Pacal's mother, Lady Kanal-Ikal, is represented rising with an avocado tree (Landon 65). According to María Elena Galindo-Tovar and colleagues, the Maya believed that "their ancestors were reborn as trees" and that the avocado held great medicinal and spiritual value. Thus, "understanding the naming and significance of [the] avocado is the first step in understanding the cultural perceptions that various groups had of [the] avocado; and two or more names for a single species represented a greater cultural significance" before and after the arrival of Europeans in the Americas (327, 329).

In 1519, Martín Fernández de Enciso makes first mention of the "maravilloso" (marvelous) avocado in *La suma de geografía* (Bárcenas Ortega 434); in 1526, the Spanish natural historian Gonzalo Fernández de Oviedo, in *Sumario de la natural historia de las Indias*, describes it as "being like a pear but better" (Galindo-Tovar et al. 328); in 1550, Pedro de Cieza de León documents his sighting of the fruit called *palta*, in the region now known as Panama and Colombia (Bárcenas Ortega 434); Francisco Cervantes de Salazar notes how well the *aguacate* sold at the market in Tenochtitlan in 1554; and José de Acosta gives a comprehensive description of the fruit in his *Historia natural y moral de las Indias* in 1590. Bernardino de Sahagún describes different types of avocados in his *Historia general de las cosas de la Nueva España*, while, in 1605, the poet and historian Inca Garcilaso de la Vega (known as El Inca) traces the Incan voyage, between 1450 and 1475, of the avocado from Palta in Ecuador to Peru (Bárcenas Ortega; Galindo-Tovar et al.; García Trejo 21–44; "History of Avocados"; Zentmyer et al.). Indeed, "The Spanish liked the avocado so much that they distributed it to their other colonies in the Americas, in the eastern hemisphere, and to Europe. [. . .] In Europe, the first introduced avocado was the West Indian type. [. . .] Avocado was introduced to Indonesia by 1750, to the Philippines in 1890, and to Brazil in 1809" (Galindo-Tovar et al. 329). Later, the avocado would travel to the Caribbean and other places, where it was always deemed a marvel. As of the twenty-first century, avocado horticulture and production extend across the world (e.g., Australia, Brazil, Chile, Dominican Republic, Guatemala, Israel, Mexico, South America, and the United States), making it a well-traveled and vastly transplanted fruit as well as an apt metaphor of transculturation and diaspora (Zentmyer et al.).

In another story of voyage, the California avocado—the gold standard of avocados—figures as a transplant, brought from Antigua, Guatemala, to the West Coast of the United States by American expatriates F. Wilson and Dorothy Popenoe in the early twentieth century. In his early career, F. Wilson Popenoe (1892–1975) worked for the National Geographic Society, the U.S. Department of Agriculture, and, as chief agronomist of the United Fruit Company. Between 1916 and 1924, he traveled throughout Latin America looking for new strains of avocados, which he eventually transplanted to California. In *The Avocado in Guatemala*, Popenoe traces the roots of the avocado to Central America, associating the fruit with the native, Indigenous, and local people. He writes, "bananas are grown mainly for export, while the entire avocado crop is consumed locally. [. . .] An avocado, four or five tortillas (small round cakes of coarsely ground maize), and a cup of coffee—by many Indians these are considered the constituents of a good meal" (1–2). While he identifies the avocado with the Indigenous population and local consumption patterns, he goes on to promote the production of the avocado outside of its native lands and for mass consumption in the United States. An NPR article reports that "until the early 1900s, the ahuacate had never been grown commercially in the United States. By 1914, however, hotels in Los Angeles and San Francisco were ordering as many of the fruits as they could and paying as much as $12 for a dozen" (Yoon). By 1935, another California and Florida smash hit, the Hass avocado, was patented in the United States; it remains one of the most popular brands of avocado to this day. Today, California accounts for 90 percent of avocados grown in the United States, while the state of Michoacán in Mexico is the largest supplier of avocados to the country, producing eight out of ten avocados consumed in the United States—and resulting in a number of environmental, social, and criminal issues in Mexico, thus dispelling the myth of avocados as "clean eating" (Bárcenas Ortega 442; Lourentzatos). The avocado is, indeed, a product of colonization, settler colonialism, extractive capitalism, U.S. imperialism, and migration, with its roots originating in Mesoamerica and neocolonial and imperialist forces transporting it to northern territories. Circuitously, it may be read as a metaphor of diaspora, representing the Salvadoran diaspora and, perhaps, the larger Central and Latin American diasporas.

In the context of El Salvador, the avocado has ethnoracial and raciolinguistic connotations for national identity. To be *aguacatero/a*, or "native to El Salvador," as stated in the meme in figure 3, means to be typically Salvadoran, as defined by certain essentialist, nationalist markers like language, history, racial and ethnic composition, socioeconomic class, and popular social behaviors. The *Diccionario de salvadoreñismos*, compiled by Matías Romero, defines *aguacatero/a* as something or someone that is common, base, and originally from the country, like naturally grown avocados or free-range *chuchos* (street dogs), which feed off of avocados naturally falling from trees. In El Salvador, free-roaming street dogs or mutts are commonly called *chuchos aguacateros*. There is a nomadic quality to *chuchos aguacateros* as they live in and off the streets. Further, the *Diccionario de salvadoreñismos* defines *aguacatero/a* as follows: "1. Común, bajero. 2. Que no tiene calidad especial, que es del país. 3. 'chucho aguacatero': Perro que no es 'de raza.' 4. Aguacates. 5. Aficionado a comer aguacates. 6. Apodo de los de Corinto, Morazán. 7. Apodo de los de San Luis de la Reina, San Miguel. . . . *Aguacatero quiere decir: del país*" (1. Common, lowly. 2. Not having special quality, being from the country. 3. "Street dog": mutt without breed. 4. Avocados. 5. Fan of eating avocados. 6. Nickname of people from Corinto, Morazán. 7. Nickname of people from San Luis de la Reina, San Miguel. . . . *Aguacatero means: from the country*) (M. Romero 57 [emphasis added]). In *La lengua salvadoreña*, the eminent Salvadoran sociolinguist and poet Pedro Geoffroy Rivas notes that the word *aguacate* is also associated with the word *tonto* (dumb, stupid) (40). For Salvadorans, hence, the term *aguacatero/a* carries national, ethnoracial, classed, and gendered meaning, with implications of nomadism, nonbelonging, and exclusion, produced within racist structures of power and against the national racial ideologies of whiteness, hybridity, and *mestizaje*. In the raciolinguistic ideology of El Salvador, *aguacatero/a*, hence, may be associated with Black, Indigenous, mixed, and nonwhite people (including nonwhite immigrants), who are often viewed as inferior, impure, and base and have been largely erased and excised from the history books, official records, and imagined community (Tilley).

Indeed, internalizing racism rooted in a colonial caste system, Salvadorans have historically denied, negated, and denigrated Blackness in El Salvador, seeking also to stamp out their Indigeneity through racial and cultural genocide, most notably enacted on the killing fields of General Maximiliano Hernández Martínez's massacre of almost thirty thousand Indigenous people in 1932, otherwise known as La Matanza. At the same time and throughout the twentieth century, Salvadoran immigration laws (borrowed almost wholesale from U.S. immigration laws) have sought to bar Black, Chinese, and Middle Eastern peoples on the basis of "seguridad interior" (national security) and "higiene social" (social hygiene) ("Decreto"; "Ley"; "Registro"). The infamous Decree no. 65, approved by the National Legislative Assembly of the Republic of El Salvador in 1928 and ratified in 1930, explicitly restricted "the settlement in the country of individuals originating in Turkey, Arabia, Syria, Palestine, [Lebanon], etc. known in the Republic by the name 'Turks'" (National Legislative Assembly). In this racial order, associated with Spanish coloniality, *mestizaje* was adopted as the premier racial identifier of the nation, while Blackness, Indigeneity, and foreignness (encompassing distinct immigrants) were rejected and erased through the national racial ideology. *Mestizaje* served not only as a synecdoche of the nation but also as a symbol of near whiteness in a country of mostly nonwhite people. In this context, Salvadoran *mestizaje* may be read as a sign of neocolonial desire for near whiteness (R. J. C. Young), a common shared identity, or *lo típico* (typical) mestizo, which comes to be codified by the signifier *aguacatero/a.*

I suggest here, then, that the racial sign of *aguacatero/a* supplants identifications of Blackness and Indigeneity and stands in as a ubiquitous and popular form of local hybridity, *mestizaje,* or what I call near or faux nativeness or *aguacatero*-alterity in El Salvador. In the most common, ordinary, or base sense (to recall the definition of *aguacatero/a* in figure 3), Salvadoran street dogs are called *chuchos aguacateros* (i.e., mutts). Salvadorans (regardless of class, race, gender, sexual identification, or birthplace, if they are of the diaspora) who identify with popular lore, everyday idioms, and common or essentialist notions of Salvadoranness may be identified or self-identify as *aguacateras/os.* In diaspora, Salvadorans often adopt and repeat the tropes of being *aguacatero/a* to identify as Salvadoran near natives despite their transplantation in other lands. (Recall that one of the features of *chuchos aguacateros* is that they are nomadic, mobile, and thus diasporic.) It is possible to disperse, transplant, and produce roots in other soils, yet still be Salvadoran at the core, through the retention or performance of Salvadoran popular (essentialist) idioms, customs, traditions, and cultural practices. In the diaspora, to be *aguacatero/a*, thus, is to be *típico*, near native (mestizo/a), or Salvadoran-identified with the home/land, but not Indigenous or Black. To identify as *aguacatero/a* may be read as sign of hyper–cultural nationalism, often aligned with national markers of Salvadoranness, which are heightened and preserved away from home and in nostalgia, especially for a people wrenched by war from their native soil. The image of the border-crossing, near-native woman in typical dress in Rodas's painting *Lamento indígena II*, for example, captures an *aguacatera* nostalgic moment as she looks back at the magical realist fruits of her homeland, as discussed in the previous section.

To be *aguacatero* or *aguacatera* may further serve as a point of identification (re)activated as people migrate, adapt, transplant themselves in other lands, and become diasporic, as is the case of Salvadorans in the United States. To identify as *aguacatera/o* in diaspora is to preserve certain essentialist (and often nationalist) cultural and linguistic identifiers like the hyper-, metareflexive usage of the *voseo*, eating of pupusas, or use of raciolinguistic terms such as *aguacatero/a, salvatrucha, cholera/o*, among other lexical markers of transnational, ethnoracial Salvadoran identity. To deconstruct an essentialist notion of *aguacatero/a*, hence, is to question the very essence of what it means to be Salvadoran in the nation-state and in diaspora, especially when those essential(ist) markers of identity are unmoored and displaced. Questions that bear asking at this juncture are: Can an avocado or *aguacatera/o* take root in other distant soils and preserve the same elements and features of Salvadoran nationals? Until what point in time and distance will Salvadorans, or any diasporic people, continue to be identified with their homelands and identity constructs? What makes a Salvadoran "Salvadoran"? These questions lie at the heart of Bencastro's short story "Las ilusiones de Juana" / "Juana's Dreams" from his book *Paraíso portátil / Portable Paradise*, a compilation of stories of Salvadorans in diaspora.

The Life and Death of Avocado Dreams

In the story "Juana's Dreams," Bencastro brings to life a character named Juana, a Salvadoran woman who immigrates to northern Virginia in the 1980s after fleeing the violence of the civil war. She is "Salvadoran by birth and resident of the United States" (176). Every year, she travels to El Salvador during las Fiestas Agostinas (August Festivals) to see her family, whom she supports financially by regularly sending remittances. On one of her annual visits to San Salvador, she celebrates her birthday at her sister's house over a sumptuous lunch of *comida típica*, including "an overflowing pot of fragrant *gallo en chicha* . . . surrounded by a steaming rice with *chipilines*, *rellenos de huisquil*, *crema*, cheese, *flor de izote* with eggs, tortillas, and tamarind drink" (176 [translanguaging in original text]). But, on that visit, three luscious, oversize avocados at the center of the table capture her attention and trigger her yearnings for her homeland: "Juana looked at the slice of avocado for a second. Immediately, she cut a piece, sprinkled it with salt and put it in her mouth. She savored it, taking her time, and when she experienced the pleasure of the creamy, vegetable meatiness, she closed her eyes and exclaimed, '¡Dios mío! How delicious! It's the best avocado I've ever eaten!'" (177). To everyone else seated at the table, the avocado is merely a dietary staple, a typical part of their daily routines, norms, rituals, and meals—in sum, a sign of their everyday, homegrown cultural identity. At this table, the avocado may be read as an everyday symbol of the family's Salvadoranness. Observing their aunt's fixation on an ordinary avocado, "they didn't understand why Juana was so excited about that fruit that for them was something as normal as day and night" (177).

For Juana, however, the *aguacate* has become an object of desire, signifying a yearning for her faraway homeland (Boym). Associated with all things Salvadoran, the giant avocado acquires a heightened sense of value, filtered through her nostalgia and desire, living in northern Virginia as an *hermana lejana* (distant sister), as diasporic Salvadorans are sometimes called in El Salvador. Indeed, the woman crossing over in Rodas's *Lamento indígena II* looks back at the surreal, oversize images of mangoes, melons, and bananas of her homeland with similar nostalgia and yearning. While Juana has distanced herself from her homeland, family, language, history, and traditions because of her migration, she also feels increasingly drawn to the enchanting *aguacates* of El Salvador, which she purchases from an Indigenous woman in the marketplace. Packing them, the market woman "put them into a plastic bag with a certain sense of ceremony as she murmured something" over the avocados (178). Infused with "something" (magic, dreams, memories, nostalgia), the traveling *aguacates* metonymically represent the homeland in diaspora. This scene, thus, seems to suggest that Juana and the Salvadoran diaspora remain connected to their homeland by forces that pull them back—that is, by their *aguacatero*-alterity, or nomadic Salvadoranness. Indeed, while Juana feels her difference as a Salvadoreña in and from Virginia and grapples with degrees of alienation, she cannot help but feel mesmerized by the hidden signs of her own Indigeneity buried deep in the avocado seeds, which she smuggles to the United States and transplants into a pot full of American soil.

Truth be told, Juana cannot see beyond the ideologies of Salvadoran deracialized national identity. To Juana, now living abroad in diaspora, far away from her family, the avocado plant becomes a symbol of her unquestioned Salvadoran mestiza identity and an exotic object, tied to her desire for homeland, family, and connections, or lack thereof in her northern Virginia home. She invests affective meaning in the avocado plant as she ponders the sacrifices she has made in pursuit of her dreams, her husband and U.S.-born and -raised children having long since deserted her. It is through the deconstruction of Juana's illusions of a diasporic deracialized Salvadoranness that we can finally begin to articulate a critique of the color blindness that permeates this story, Bencastro's oeuvre, and much of the Salvadoran and Salvadoran diasporic literature published to date.[2] In "Juana's Dreams," the avocado calls on readers to question the very essence of Salvadoran ethnoracial, cultural, and national identity. The avocado serves as a metaphor not only of Salvadoran identity, origins, and roots, so to speak, but also of the ways that Salvadoran identities translocate along diasporic routes and take root (or make home) in other places. Like the *aguacate* of Juana's dreams, Salvadoran immigrants migrate, resettle, reroot, and adapt in other soils, often transporting and transforming their *aguacatero/a* identities—associated with Salvadoran popular idioms, customs, traditions, "native" costumes, and cultural practices—to the exclusion or detriment of Indigenous and Black identifications. But the fact of the matter is that Salvadoran diasporic identities, like others, can be produced in other sites, contexts, and soils, and with different cultural materials, much like the avocado seeds that were successfully rehomed in California to produce the California avocado. But the soil must be nurturing and provide the right conditions for transplants to take root, as we shall see with what happens to Juana's avocado plant in Virginia. Will it take root? Will it survive and thrive in the Virginia soil and environment? What conditions are necessary for diasporic identities to be fruitful? How will it be shaped by its surroundings and in situ elements?

For Juana, the avocado symbolizes memory, family, homeland, and, perhaps, near whiteness, as understood within the racial mestizo ideology of El Salvador. In the United States, she has lost status as she becomes one of the many Salvadoran expendable laborers in the DMV (figure 11). She believes—if only implicitly—that she has sacrificed her Salvadoranness by moving to the United States, where she has worked many years as a *cholera* (servant), cleaning other people's houses and raising other people's

FIGURE 11. Salvadoran folkloric dancers in the Fiesta DC Parade, Mount Pleasant Street NW, September 25, 2011. Photo courtesy of author.

children. Although she has acquired a level of comfort and number of material goods in the United States, she has also lost her family, friends, community, and (national) status to become an *hermana lejana*, who can only go home during las Fiestas Agostinas. Like the woman crossing over into D.C. in Rodas's painting, Juana has lost her footing in her homeland and attempts to find her bearings and worth in a new land. So, it is no surprise that during her return to the United States, Juana tries to bring a bit of home by smuggling the seeds of three clandestine (undocumented) avocados to be savored and transplanted in Virginia, in the hopes of restoring her Salvadoreñidad and preserving her *aguacateridad* in the diaspora.

Once back in Virginia, Juana takes meticulous care of her transplanted avocado seedlings. In an act of rehoming her seedlings, which have been displaced from their Salvadoran soil and are now dispersed in American dirt, Juana tells them stories of El Salvador, revealing how her two eldest children were killed in the civil war, one serving in the army, the other in the guerrilla forces. She recalls how she, her husband, and her surviving daughter fled to the United States and settled in Washington, D.C. with the help of friends. Like many immigrants, she and her husband worked countless hours to provide for their family, as their U.S.-born kids grew up, married, and moved away. Eventually, her husband also leaves her, for another woman. Juana feels abandoned, unable to return to El Salvador, "to our family, to our roots," and destined to remain "forever in this strange country" (179). By the end of the story, she is stripped of the hopes and dreams that had brought her to the United States in the first place.

Although the avocado seedlings flourish indoors in a pot, once Juana replants them in the yard in the heat of the Virginian summer, they begin to die. Outdoors, alone, without strong roots, in foreign dirt, assaulted by the inhospitable climate, the lone avocado plant cannot survive, almost mirroring how Juana begins to wither away in her northern Virginia apartment by herself, her connections to El Salvador (her annual trips, her regular phone calls to her sister, the memories of her people and country, and elements of her identity) all severed. In due time, the avocado plant dies in Juana's Virginia garden. The avocado, Bencastro writes, "wasn't just another plant; for Juana, it was a symbol of identity. It was a constant and crisp reminder of her beloved faraway native country" (180). Like Juana, the plant could not take root in the new environment without the full incorporation of its Afro-Indigenous identities. The story, thus, seems to suggest that the typical, mestizo-coded Salvadoranness is incomplete without its Blackness and Indigeneity; it cannot take root in new soil and survive in new environments (182). At the end of the story, Juana calls her sister to tell her the sad news of the *aguacate*'s death and to inform her of her decision not to visit El Salvador the following summer. With the avocado's passing, Juana appears to give up her illusion of (mestizo) Salvadoran identity and her avocado dream of returning to El Salvador. The "immigrant bargain" (Louie) that she made in exchange for her children's success did not reward her. The loss of her illusions, as illustrated by the grimace on the face of Rodas's migrant woman crossing over, represents, perhaps, the final outcome of transnational life. Although migrants may cross over, they must often pay a heavy price for their American Dream.

Conclusion

An allegory of sorts, Bencastro's story "Juana's Dreams," like the work of other D.C. Salvadoran poets, artists, and musicians discussed in this chapter, grounds readers in the reality of Salvadoran migration and transnational life, caught in the limbo of migratory status, family separation, economic disparities, and racial ideologies. The texts discussed here question notions of home, belonging, and diasporic ethnoracial identity in transnational sites. For many Salvadorans, their complicated migratory status, financial conditions, and family separation mean that there are no easy returns to the homeland, nor easy cultural translocations, transplantations, and transculturations in new home- or host lands. Capturing the moment of passing into D.C., Avilés, Bencastro, Larios, and Rodas, in their respective narratives, explore the process of becoming "Wachintonian Salvadoran" and the remaking of *aguacatero* (hybrid) identities in other soils.

3

SALVATRUCAS/OS

Finding Voice and Voz/s in the District

In his bilingual poem "Canción para un Salvatruco" (Song for a Salvatruco), Quique Avilés pays homage to Salvadoran immigrants who, like Mario Bencastro's protagonist Juana in "Juana's Dreams," toil daily in the nation's capital. In the *Diccionario de salvadoreñismos,* Matías Romero defines *salvatruco/a* and, by extension, *salvatrucha* (figure 12) as "Salvadoreño" or Salvadoran, that is, as someone from El Salvador or of Salvadoran heritage (314). These colloquial monikers, however, have been weaponized by mainstream culture in and outside of El Salvador and deployed to signal affiliation or association with the transnational gang La Mara Salvatrucha (MS-13). While the media, popular culture, and political discourse have rendered these terms synonymous with hemispheric illegality, crime, violence, and fear, Avilés, in his poem, resignifies and uses the terms to refer to people who "prevail," persevere, and persist despite experiencing great injustices, exploitations, indignities, and injuries, and as such have valuable lessons to teach us. In the poem, the speaker, who identifies as *salvatruco,* alternates between stanzas in Spanish and in English to tell the story of *salvatrucas/os* in the District of Columbia. Cryptically, the speaker glosses over images of Salvadoran life: "Bleak or bright / Rise and shine / Gun or knife / And yet we prevail"; "In the midst of poison or blight / Spit or spite / Black or white / And yet we prevail"; "14th or 16th / Clean this or clean that Mother fucker what? / And yet we prevail." These lines allude to daily acts of abuse, violence, and racism experienced by many working Salvadoran residents of D.C. and the DMV, who, regardless of the hour, peril, or job as "white baby nanny / hot dogs and tamale [street vendors] / busboy or scholar," face daily challenges with the same drive to prevail, overcome, and resist. To make this point, almost every line of the poems ends with the chorus, "And yet we prevail" or "Aquí estamos" (We are here), attesting to the ingenuity, resilience, and significant presence and contributions of Salvadorans in the diaspora.

Through a study of D.C.-based performance texts by Avilés, Culture Clash, and Lilo González and Los de la Mount Pleasant, this chapter examines Salvadoran ethnoracial, cultural identity construction as shaped by processes of transmigration, translanguaging, and transculturation in the Washington, D.C. metropolitan area and the DMV. In particular, I focus on the use of the term *salvatruco/a* or *salvatrucha* to resignify national identity in the diaspora, and on the deployment of the colloquial Salvadoran speech act of *vosear* (the informal second-person singular pronoun) in the production of Salvadoran American *voces* (voices) and the hybridization of U.S. Salvadoran identities. Prompted by a set of cultural interrogatives, I ask: where and how are Salvadoran *voces* and *voices* articulated in the multiple diasporic translocations that Salvadorans occupy? In the context of the Washington, D.C. metropolitan area and local creatives like Avilés, this chapter further explores the artistic production and worldmaking of vibrant Salvadoran communities that are no longer strictly Salvadoran, but rather hybrid *aguacatera/o* and *salvatruca/o* cultural formations, translocated across extranational sites.

At a distance, apart, and in their own right, diasporic Salvadorans, thus, produce *vos* and *voz* (subjectivities and discourses) through transmigration, transculturation, and translanguaging in translocal sites. In situ, they build and deploy what Ofelia García and other sociolinguists have called translanguaging—full linguistic and cultural repertoires drawing from multiple languages, cultures, and experiences, produced in contact and in diaspora. In diaspora, Salvadorans cannot be thought of as singularly, monolithically, or unilaterally national subjects; rather, they are interpellated by multiple and various experiences, histories, cultures, languages, identifications, and ethnoracial formations, among other things, remaking their subjectivities in diasporic locations. Thinking about the production of diasporic identities in different translocal sites through the lens of translanguaging and raciolinguistics allows us to decenter the notion of

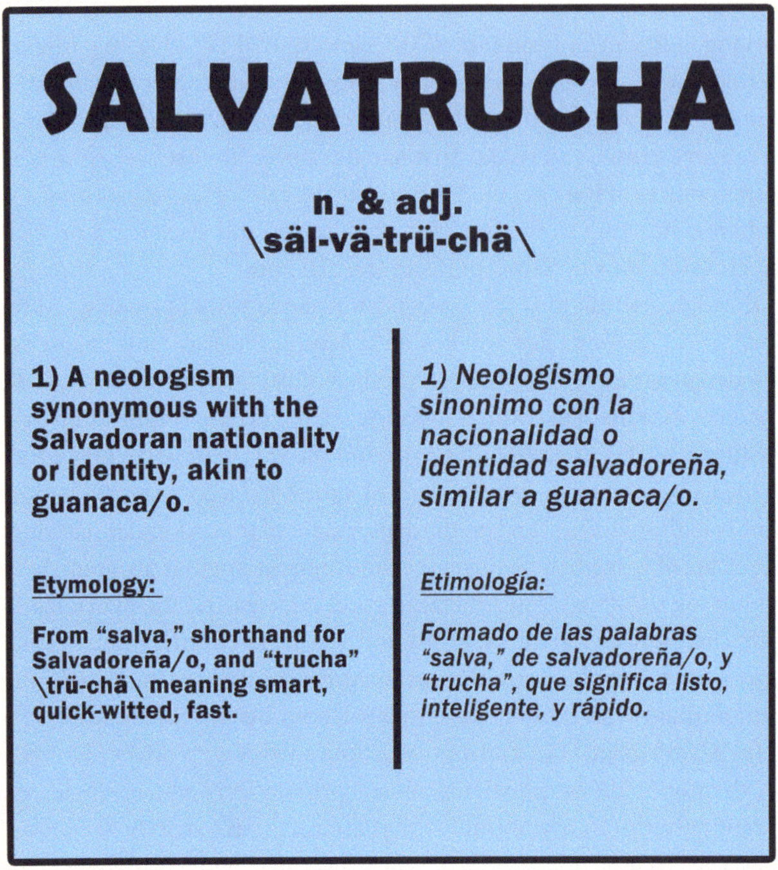

SALVATRUCHA

n. & adj.
\säl-vä-trü-chä\

1) A neologism synonymous with the Salvadoran nationality or identity, akin to guanaca/o.

Etymology:

From "salva," shorthand for Salvadoreña/o, and "trucha" \trü-chä\ meaning smart, quick-witted, fast.

1) Neologismo sinonimo con la nacionalidad o identidad salvadoreña, similar a guanaca/o.

Etimología:

Formado de las palabras "salva," de salvadoreña/o, y "trucha", que significa listo, inteligente, y rápido.

FIGURE 12. "Salvatrucha," by Víctor H. Interiano (Dichos de un bicho), 2020. Courtesy of Víctor H. Interiano.

a monolithic, essentialized Salvadoran national identity in diaspora, in favor of a focus on the production of ever-evolving and expanding Salvadoreñidades and their sociocultural expressions and markings across diasporic geographic contexts and historical moments.

Salvatrucas/os in Washington, D.C.

For the most part, discussions to date about the Salvadoran diaspora in the United States have focused on the transnational movement of migrants from

El Salvador to particular locations in the United States (Baker-Cristales; Hamilton and Chinchilla; Mahler, *American Dreaming*; Mahler, *Salvadorans*; Menjívar; Molina-Tamacas; Repak; Sánchez Molina, *Mandar*; Sánchez Molina, *Proceso*). Salvadoran labor migration and the production of material and cultural capital associated with it have been routinely traced from El Salvador to divergent locations, and from these sites back to El Salvador (Mahler, "Migration"). Along these transnational routes, people, money, media, communications, and various material and cultural goods seem to travel between determined points of departure and arrival (Anastario). In this schema, there are sending and receiving cities, poles of expulsion and attraction, and sites of dislocation and relocation in places such as Arlandria-Chirilagua, a housing complex (à la Salvadoran *colonia*) in Alexandria, Virginia, duly named after the town of Chirilagua in eastern El Salvador; and streets in Intipucá City, El Salvador, renamed after streets in Washington, D.C. (Moon; Pedersen, "States"; Pedersen, "Storm"). There are *hermanos/as lejanos/as*, or distant Salvadoran immigrant brothers and sisters, who not only populate the imagined diasporic province called Department 15, extending across the world, but also infuse the Salvadoran economy with regular remittances and migratory flows (see Baker-Cristales; Rodríguez, "Departamento 15"). These are the *salvatruchas* and *salvatrucas/os* who are the subject of this chapter.

As Avilés recounts in his 2003 poem "El Salvador At-a-Glance," "El Salvador's major cities [are presently]: San Salvador / San Miguel / Santa Ana / Los Angeles / San Wachinton, D.C." Avilés's cultural geography of the Salvadoran nation widens to include and recognize the Salvadoran diaspora, residing outside the geopolitical borders of the country yet within its extended geocultural reaches. In "El Salvador At-a-Glance," Avilés explores the reconfiguration of El Salvador according to a transnational logic and global economic system, by which El Salvador's "major exports" include "coffee, sugar, city builders, busboys, waiters, poets." In this logic, immigrants are both producers and products, generating socioeconomic and cultural remittances that greatly transform and (re)make El Salvador and Salvadoran society as a whole, and that mark translocations of the diaspora throughout the world. Both used by and using the transnational economy for the purposes of producing remittances, as Avilés claims, diasporic Salvadorans feel El Salvador just beneath the skin, like a "little question mark that begins to itch" and to ask why Salvadorans across the diaspora are only cast or seen as laborers who "were supposed to clean carpets / not ask for time out and dialogue." Implicitly, Avilés's poem interrogates the predominant stereotypes ascribed to Salvadorans. It asks: what is it really like to be Salvadoran in Washington, D.C., "in the strangest moments / in the strangest cities / under the strangest circumstances"?

Culture Clash in the District

Like Avilés, the renowned Los Angeles–based Chicano/Latino theater troupe Culture Clash was drawn to the enigma that is the Salvadoran community in Washington, D.C. Known for its socially conscious theatrical productions, a groundbreaking comedy variety TV show in the 1980s, and site-specific plays such as *Mission Magic Mystery Tour* (San Francisco), *Chavez Ravine* (Los Angeles), *Nuyorican Stories* (New York City), and *Radio Mambo* (Miami), Culture Clash was commissioned by the Arena Stage, in 2000, to produce a piece about D.C.'s multiethnic and multiracial communities. Based on interviews with local community members, officials, and artists like Avilés, Culture Clash produced and performed *Anthems: Culture Clash in the District* in fall 2002, at the Arena Stage in southwest Washington, D.C.[1] A collage of sorts, *Anthems* sought to represent the "multicultural story" of an often culturally, racially, and socioeconomically stratified city, as well as the transnational story of Salvadorans in the district in the post-9/11 context.

According to Molly Smith, artistic director of the Arena Stage, *Anthems* gave "us an entirely unofficial and unauthorized tour of the city—shot through the lens of Culture Clash's wild comic imagination" (155). In an effort to write "anthems," or narratives of a city that is at once the nation's capital and home to local residents, the main character and narrator of the metafictional play (a writer, performed by Richard Montoya) walked in and out of the lives of loosely disguised personality figures of the district. Culture Clash represented famous politicians and socialites, Black and white "native Washingtonians," and people from diverse local communities, including Muslim refugees and Salvadoran immigrants. Even Tian Tian, the émigré panda in residence at the National Zoo at that time, makes several cameo appearances (again played by Montoya), offering meta-reflections on the city, as when he says: "D.C. can be a real jungle and you people can be animals sometimes." On point, Tian Tian comments on the racial divides that mark the district and the DMV: "Look at me I'm a black-and-white panda bear in a mostly black-and-white town. . . . Black patches, white patches, together, apart, slightly segregated, but in the same general area" (Culture Clash 158, 159). Indeed, Culture Clash critically represented D.C.'s hidden faces, facets, and issues. As Smith claims, in Culture Clash's *Anthems*, "we see some familiar faces and places, but mostly we encounter ordinary, everyday people we rarely see or hear on stage" (155).

In Culture Clash's montage of the Washington, D.C. metropolitan area and the DMV, the audience also catches fleeting glimpses of immigrant Salvadoran life. In one brief scene, "The Ballad of Douglas Martínez," Ric Salinas—the U.S. Salvadoran member of the Clash team—plays the part of a civil war refugee, pantomiming his movements from La Unión, El Salvador, in 1984, as he flees the violence that resulted in more than seventy-five thousand deaths and countless more people tortured, disappeared, and displaced. Culture Clash's portrayal of Martínez as a campesino from La Unión or Oriente captures a noteworthy feature of Salvadoran migration to the DMV, as a great number of migrants hail from the eastern region of the country, with its distinct language idioms, rural Indigenous experiences, and historically Black racial formations, as discussed in chapter 1. And yet, the myth that "*nunca llegaron negros*," no Black people ever inhabited El Salvador—as observed by Virginia-raised, Afro-Indigenous Salvadoran activist and scholar Danielle Parada in "Learning About My Blackness: Afrodescendencia in El Salvador" (original emphasis)—is widespread. This belief is buttressed by anti-immigration state policies such as Decree no. 65, which was based on U.S. immigration and exclusion acts and adopted before the Maximiliano Hernández Martínez regime in 1930 (National Legislative Assembly). Through research and reflection, Parada finds that

> Our African history is not only present, but more deeply rooted than I expected. Culinary roots from Africa can be found in many dishes (especially in eastern El Salvador) such as sopa de pata and horchata, or in traditional dances such as El Baile de La Negra Sebastiana, or even in our dialect with words such as cachimba or mucama. To my surprise, I also learned that in 1821, 95% of people in my parent's [*sic*] hometown of San Miguel identified as afrodescendant or mulatto. Africans were forced to work in haciendas

and plantations due to the agricultural and textile industry found in eastern El Salvador (including San Miguel).

A composite of the Salvadoran community that settled in the D.C. metropolitan area and throughout the DMV, Douglas Martínez, in *Anthems*, embodies not only the deep-set war traumas of the Salvadoran diaspora fleeing Oriente in the 1980s, but also the anti-Blackness in the Salvadoran nation, which elevated *mestizaje* as its racial ideology. From all indications, Martínez is coded mestizo in *Anthems*, although he comes from an Afro-Indigenous region of El Salvador.

As embodied by Salinas in several scenes, Martínez is shown in mesmerizing, silent, slow-motion moves, dodging bullets in his country, running across the U.S.-Mexico border, and crossing the Potomac River in a symbolic reenactment of George Washington's crossing of the Delaware River, all the while searching for his final destination—the Lincoln Memorial, "a dream com[e] true" for him (Culture Clash 200). Upon reaching D.C., Martínez is again shown caught in a silent scene of cross fire and fighting. This time, however, it is not the Salvadoran civil war (1980–92), but rather the Mount Pleasant uprising, which broke out in the Salvadoran/Latinx neighborhood of Mount Pleasant on May 5, 1991 (see chapters 1 and 2 on this uprising). At the end of the scene, Martínez is seen silently dying in a shoot-out in the streets of Prince George's County, Maryland, having been hit while walking home from work one evening. In a voice-over, a D.C. news telecast announces: "The first reported Black-on-Latino murder occurred tonight in Prince George's County" (200). The silent representation of Martínez's death on the street is chilling, for it brings to center stage the plight of many Salvadoran immigrants in the nation's capital: rendered nearly invisible and silent by what cultural critic Lauren Berlant calls the "national culture industry" (185), built in part on the U.S. interventions and economic aid that helped produce the Salvadoran diaspora. For the most part, this history of U.S. interventions in Central America remains opaque even to this day, as Andrew Friedman suggests in his book *Covert Capital: Landscapes of Denial and the Making of U.S. Empire in the Suburbs of Northern Virginia*, and as Mario Bencastro portrays so well in the short story "Juana's Dreams," as discussed in chapter 2. Along with these texts and others, *Anthems* breaks the silence of Salvadoran migration and amplifies Salvadoran stories in the Washington, D.C. metropolitan area.

It is telling that throughout all the scenes in which Martínez appears, he is represented in silent action, whether fleeing his country, crossing borders, arriving in Washington, or simply going about his business in the DMV. Culture Clash's silent mimicry of the history of violence and displacement that mark the Salvadoran diaspora magnifies the traumatic dimensions of the war-induced dispersion. The silence or silencing of Martínez suggests the layers of trauma that underpin the diaspora, which Leisy J. Abrego so brilliantly describes in "On Silences: Salvadoran Refugees Then and Now." As Abrego explains for her own family and other Salvadorans who fled the violence of the civil war, their history is "inextricably woven into a national and regional history of multiple layers of state and gendered violence that most humans would prefer to forget" (74). This migration story is obscured by the "deafening silence" about U.S. covert interventions (75), which caused such unspeakable suffering and enduring intergenerational trauma in survivors, some of whom migrated to the DMV and other translocations of the Salvadoran diaspora. As Abrego explains,

> There is the silence that is the large void in generations of children of Salvadoran immigrants growing up in the US being denied access to our own histories. [. . .] There is the silence that was filled by others who did not know how to understand us and so used stereotypes and imposed their own experiences to make sense of who we are. And we continue to reproduce the silences when we do not know, cannot locate, have never been told of the structural, political, and economic sources of our collective pain, or of our collective resilience. (76)

Almost in step, the silent narration of Douglas Martínez's story in *Anthems* mirrors what Abrego calls "the silenced history of the region" and invites spectators to fill the deep void and chasm of memory with knowledge of the histories denied to Salvadorans by power structures in El Salvador and the United States (83). Although we can only imagine Martínez's personal story in El Salvador and in Maryland, where he is killed, we know that his and other Salvadoran stories must be told if we are to "correct the official version of our history" (83).

In other words, through the telling of Martínez's (silenced) story, Culture Clash not only brings to light the presence of Salvadoran migrants in D.C.

and the DMV, but also challenges the narrative of coming to America, or the so-called American Dream, which in Bencastro's story "Juana's Dreams" was shown to be but a false illusion. In *Anthems*, we are told that Martínez's dream was to see and stand before the Lincoln Memorial, the national symbol of freedom, emancipation, and citizenship. To live in Washington would be Martínez's "dream [that] comes true," except that he is killed walking home from work one night in "Prince George's County, Ward 9," and is accompanied back to El Salvador by the phantom panda Tian Tian in a final requiem scene (200). As *Anthems* shows with the death of Martínez, the American Dream is fleeting, denied not only to certain foreigners but also to "native citizens," residents, and immigrants, alike, as is discussed in the next section.

Salvadorans Go to Washington, D.C.

In *The Queen of America Goes to Washington City: Essays on Sex and Citizenship*, Lauren Berlant calls attention to a "national culture industry" engaged in the production, commodification, and consumption of narratives of acceptable "native citizens," as well as unacceptable noncitizens, undocumented immigrants, and others in the U.S. cultural imaginary (175–220). Through readings of various mass media texts, including an issue of *Time* magazine, Berlant identifies normative "native citizens" as "implicitly native-born, white, [heterosexual] male salaried citizens," and "infantilized citizens" as those necessarily made "anesthetized, complacent, unimaginative" by a hegemonic ethos and politics (193, 199). Subject to, unquestioning of, and often supportive of a U.S. world order, the ideal citizens of the United States, according to Berlant, embody an "infantile citizenship" shaped by patriotism, individualism, and (almost blind) "faith in the nation" and "the state's commitment to representing the best interests of ordinary people" (27–28). This citizen ideal looms over ethnoracialized, would-be citizens at large, including foreigners, immigrants, minorities, and other unincorporated, marginalized, and excluded subjects (185), who are called to have "faith in the nation" in order to assume their place in U.S. society. As Berlant explains, for all their negative and ambivalent representation by the "national culture industry," immigrants not only revitalize the United States with their labor and cultural contributions, but also serve as "symbolic evidence for the ongoing power of American democratic ideals" (195). In their desire for incorporation into the U.S. nation-state, immigrants, to various degrees, partake in the "faith in the nation" assumed to be held by "native citizens."

In the education of immigrants, Berlant underscores the role of the "national culture industry [which] seeks to stipulate that only certain kinds of people, practices, and property that are, at core, 'American,' deserve juridical and social legitimation" (185). Films and mass media texts of various genres—such as *Forrest Gump, The Pelican Brief, Mr. Smith Goes to Washington,* and the parodic *The Simpsons* episode "Mr. Lisa Goes to Washington"—serve, in Berlant's analysis, to highlight how the figure of the "infantile citizen" and the trope of the pilgrimage to Washington reproduce the monumental yet empty signifiers of American patriotism. These texts reify modes of inclusion and exclusion in the nation, especially for immigrants. On the significance of immigrants' narratives, Berlant writes, "Their [immigrant portraits' and stories'] importance is in the ways they express how completely generic immigrant hopes and dreams might unfold from particular bodies, and they tell a secret story about a specific migrant's odds for survival—by which *Time* means successful Americanization" (197).

Living in the shadow of monumental signifiers and experiencing "citizenship" on more disenfranchised terms, Salvadoran and other immigrant communities of color in the greater Washington, D.C. metropolitan area offer significant revisions to the vacuous citizenship narrative, albeit through symbolic and cultural rather than legal and political means. A great number of Salvadoran immigrants in the region, after all, remain marginalized and disenfranchised labor citizens of the metropolitan area, working and living without legal residency and in precarious conditions, with no access to political representation. Along with Berlant and other critics of an exclusive "national culture industry," I seek to understand how Salvadoran immigrants, nonetheless, inscribe themselves into national and local narratives of Washington, D.C., while at the same time producing new modes of cultural citizenship.

In *Latino Cultural Citizenship: Claiming Identity, Space, and Rights,* William V. Flores and Rina Benmayor suggest that for many Latinos/as in the United States, cultural citizenship embodies a significant set of social practices. They explain: "In this way, immigrants who might not be citizens in the legal sense or who might not even be in this country legally, but who labor and contribute to the economic and cultural wealth of the country, would be recognized as legitimate political subjects claiming rights for themselves and their children, and in that sense as citizens" (11). The terminology and practices of "cultural citizenship" are particularly significant for Central Americans and Salvadorans, who have been historically and indiscriminately denied legal immigrant and resident status in the United States. In the geopolitical context of the 1980s, people fleeing the armed conflict in the isthmus were generally classified as economic rather than political refugees, and many were deported to their deaths in El Salvador and Guatemala. In more recent times, Salvadoran and Central American migrants have been subject to politically ambiguous and restrictive conditions produced by their migratory Temporary Protected Status (TPS), which makes it possible for undocumented immigrants to work indefinitely in the United States without being afforded the security of legal residency and full-scale political representation. For many undocumented Salvadoran migrants, living in a prolonged state of legal indeterminacy creates a sense of instability and disempowerment. While many may continue to struggle to acquire full legal and political citizenship status in the United States, "cultural citizenship" might provide a venue for sociopolitical action and agency through other modes of sociocultural representation, especially when their prolonged TPS and undocumented condition threaten to foreclose on possibilities of political organizing.

Where Are the Americans?

In *Anthems*, Culture Clash tapped into the nearly invisible narrative of the transmigration of Salvadorans and their ambiguous sociopolitical status in the D.C. region, which in itself is a highly dynamic contact zone of diverse racial, ethnic, and inter/national groups, as discussed in chapter 1. In this context, U.S. Salvadoran cultural, social, and ethnoracial identities are transformed and shaped in proximity to and in contact with white, Latinx, Black, and other identities, and Salvadorans are called on to question our biases and center Blackness in our own identities and communities. In a telling *Anthems* scene, "Salvadoran Jungle Fever / Fiebre de la Selva," Noe Ramírez, a fortysomething, Salvadoran immigrant father, lays bare the anti-Blackness in Salvadoran communities, opening a space of meta-reflection for the audience. In a monologue, Ramírez recalls the shock that he and his newly arrived family experienced when they resettled in D.C. in the 1980s. He explains that neither U.S.-made TV programs broadcast in El Salvador nor U.S. imperialist goodwill messengers (all part of an exported U.S. "national culture industry" consumed in Latin America) had prepared the family for what they would encounter in Washington, D.C. He says: "We came to Washington, D.C., in 1984, and landed on 14th and Irving. I said 'Puta! This look more like *Good Times*.' We didn't know the capital of the United States was Africa! Puta! Where were the gringos? Where were the tall, blond, blue-eyed guys from the Peace Corps that I met in El Salvador?" (Culture Clash 201). Ramírez had been unprepared to face his own anti-Blackness and to engage with the multiracial, multi-ethnic, and multilingual realities of the United States. Looking back, he describes Salvadorans' machete-armed fights with Black youths in high school, a story that Quique Avilés and other D.C. Salvadoran immigrants likewise acknowledge as part of their own life experiences and that partially provides the ethnographic basis for Culture Clash's representation in this scene. Ramírez explains:

> We were the new immigrants on the block, it was tough. . . . There was a lot of violence, people getting stabbed. And so, we started to fight back: "La ley del machete." We would take machetes to school. Los Negros started getting hurt, people getting cut. It was nasty. Then word got out, "Don't mess with the Salvadorans, the 'migos,' cause they got the big knives." We had to fight or die—survival. Finally, the black community said, "OK, these people are here to stay, so we're gonna have to deal with them." (201)

Through the character of Noe Ramírez, Culture Clash exposes, thus, the internalized racism, anti-Blackness, and conflicted race relations of the Salvadoran community in the District of Columbia. Indeed, the question of how Latinxs, particularly Salvadorans, dismantle racism and form more equitable alliances and coalitions, is posed in *Anthems*.

Calling the District of Columbia home as his family acculturates to their new surroundings, Ramírez is shocked one day to find that his U.S.-raised Salvadoran son has become a "stranger in my house" (201). His son no longer speaks Spanish like a Salvadoran, but rather speaks a translanguaged mix of homemade, heritage-brand Spanish and African American English. When Ramírez tells, or rather orders, Enrique to, "Hey, speak English! . . . Hablá Inglés . . . [*vos*]" (202), he uses an imperative speech act, *hablá*, in the informal *voseo*, which Enrique apparently neither uses nor understands. Enrique and his father are separated not only by a generation gap but also by cultural, linguistic, and ethnoracial fissures. While Ramírez attempts to speak in Salvadoran Spanish to his son, Enrique appears unable to *vosear*, manifesting a sociolinguistic adaptation that might be taken as a breach or break with his Salvadoran national identity. Instead, Enrique answers in a translanguage beyond his father's comprehension: "I'm speaking English, doggy-dog" (202). To his father's dismay, Enrique has adopted African American English and culture. To Ramírez's greater surprise, it is Enrique's African American girlfriend, Lashanda, who greets him in Spanish: "How you doing, Mr. Ramirez? Oh—como estas?" (no accent marks, 202). And Mr. Ramírez responds in Spanish to his son's Spanish-speaking Black girlfriend, "gracias, Lashanda, mucho gusto," bringing to life the greater transculturations in the DMV (202).

In this contact zone of sorts, Salvadoran Americans and Black Americans not only mix, date, and live in proximity but also produce transculturated, inter-ethnoracial identities, or what Montoya, in his afterword to *Anthems*, calls "mixed and remixed living histories." According to Montoya, Latinxs at this intersection have the opportunity to acknowledge their "Negritude," dismantle their racisms, align with the struggles of Black Americans, and build wider coalitions outside of their communities to fight against systemic oppressions (Culture Clash 224). In his monologue, Ramírez reveals what is perhaps his greatest lesson learned from living in D.C., when he says: "There are no black people in El Salvador, so we never knew any, we never had contact. Salvadorans are very prejudiced people. But we [Salvadorans and African Americans] have a lot in common. Oh si, we're both jinchos, country folk, we are both family-oriented, go to church, we work side by side, we like greasy-ass food, we like to swear a lot, por la gran puta—we're in the same boat" (201). Alluding to Salvadorans' often uninterrogated biases, blatant and sometimes polite racisms, and internalized colonialisms, *papá* Ramírez inadvertently reflects on the often-unspoken anti-Blackness among Salvadorans, and suggests the possibility of building alliances, solidarities, and interracial and interethnic coalitions, especially with Black Americans in the district, based on shared experiences of exclusion, culture, and values: "we're both jinchos, country folk" and can "work side by side." The key here is understanding that many Salvadoran immigrants and Black Americans share common Afro-Indigenous origins and experiences.

Thus, *papá* Ramírez acknowledges that Salvadoran and Black residents of the District of Columbia "[are] in the same boat," experiencing systemic oppressions (if to different degrees) and living side by side in neighborhoods like Mount Pleasant, Columbia Heights, Petworth, and Anacostia. Moreover, Ramírez suggests that Latinxs and Black Americans share larger histories of exclusion, injustice, and racism in the United States. Among groups with shared disenfranchised histories and social positions, alliances could be built around issues of equity across living wages, affordable housing, proper health care, access to education, and other rights. These are issues that affect a great number of marginalized communities—including Black Americans and Latinxs—in the District of Columbia and elsewhere, as manifested in the Black Lives Matter and immigrant struggles in the United States.

Along these lines, D.C. Salvadoran singer, composer, and community activist Lilo González suggests the possibilities of transnational coalition-building among Latinxs, Central Americans, Salvadorans, and Black Americans in his song "Las historias prohibidas de Pedro y Tyrone" (The Forbidden Tales of Pedro and Tyrone) from his 1994 CD *A quien corresponda . . .*[2] Invoking the Salvadoran poet Roque Dalton's *Las historias prohibidas del pulgarcito* (The Prohibited Stories of Tom Thumb [a reference to El Salvador, for its small geographic territory]), González and his musical group, Los de la Mount Pleasant, chronicle the life of Pedro in D.C.: his separation from his parents, search for employment, drug addiction, and disenfranchisement as a noncitizen of the United States. Pedro's exclusion from the "native citizenry," as Berlant posits, is mirrored in the parallel telling of Tyrone's life in Washington. As González tells us, Pedro and Tyrone live in the "shadow of the White House," amid social, economic, and racial violence. In the 1991 Mount Pleasant uprising, Latinxs and African Americans (personified in the song by, respectively, Pedro and Tyrone) rose up against systemic oppressions and social disenfranchisement in their communities. Like in many U.S. cities, Black American and Latino/a/x youths in the District of Columbia live in neighborhoods adversely affected by lack of access to employment, education, housing, and opportunities (Jennings and Lusane). Set to reggae, a revolutionary musical genre, González's song tells of "Negro matando a negro, / negro matando a Latino, / Latino matando a negro, / Latino matando a Latino" (Black killing Black, / Black killing Latino, / Latino killing Black, / Latino killing Latino). The song, however, suggests that this narrative of "uncommon" ground must be transformed and rewritten with other endings.

A product of the 1980s migration of Salvadorans to the area, Pedro is orphaned, homeless, and addicted to crack. At six years of age, he emigrated from his war-torn country, but in D.C. he has lost hope: "Llegó buscando a estas tierras, / la estatua de la libertad, / pero ella estaba muy alta, / me dijo, no la pude yo alcanzar" (He came to this land in search of, / the Statue of Liberty, / but she was much too high, / he told me, I wasn't able to reach her). The Statue of Liberty, symbolizing opportunity, freedom, and justice in the United States, does not extend her hand to new immigrants from Central America. Instead, the statue represents the denial of (unalienable) refugee rights to a people fleeing the fallout of U.S. imperialism, the Cold War, globalization, neoliberal regimes, and now climate destruction in their homelands. Against these insurmountable forces, Pedro learns to think and live in the present and to survive by his own wits: "siempre piensa en el presente / suspira por el pasado, / conociendo nuestra historia, / Pedro, el futuro es tu regalo" (He always thinks of the present, / he always longs for the past, / but if you know your own history, / Pedro, the future shall be your reward). Pedro's counterpart, Tyrone, also lives in the margins, in the shadow of the White House, subject to the workings of power, poverty, and oppression.

Underscoring the parallels in Pedro and Tyrone's lives, González's song leads to the conclusion that Pedro and Tyrone equally lack access to opportunities, education, employment, safety, and affirmation of their human potential. Both are overcome by a sense of entrapment, alienation, and disenfranchisement, and, contorted into "infantile citizens," both are denied the ideals of the American Dream. Both youths, the song suggests, have internalized the capitalist imperative and consumption narrative, "que ser y tener, es igual" (that what you have is what you are). And if you have nothing, then you are nothing. The lyrics to the song, however, challenge the materialist American ideals so heavily tied to free enterprise, consumption, and commodification, asserting to Pedro and Tyrone that "tu vales . . . no importa que carro manejés" (you are . . . no matter what car you drive). In its final appeal, the song calls on the youths to engage in creative intervention and coalition-building, despite their experiences of civil and urban warfare. In an indictment of Tyrone and Pedro's disenfranchisement (what Berlant calls "infantilizing") by greater economic and material forces, González's song imagines the possibility of forging alliances among ethnic, racial, and diasporic communities: "¿Por qué no se ponen en onda, / luchando por el pueblo de Sudáfrica, / ¿por qué no se ponen en onda, / luchando por la paz en América?" (Why don't you get high, / supporting the people of South Africa, / why don't you get high, / struggling for peace in America?).

Ultimately, Lilo González and Los de la Mount Pleasant produce an *himno* (anthem), one that is highly critical of the racial, ethnic, and classed order that structures and divides Latinxs, Black Americans, and other ethnoracial groups from one another, and that "infantilizes," disciplines, and denies basic rights to its citizenry. Moreover, González and Los de la Mount Pleasant sketch a narrative of the highly neglected and excluded Salvadoran immigrant citizenry, as Pedro struggles to survive in the streets of D.C., always reaching for memories, dreams, and prospects. "Sí se puede" (Yes, we can), the song seems to say, plaintively calling out to the Pedros and Tyrones of D.C.: "Why don't you get high, / struggling for peace in America?" America, in this case, is the *Américas*, produced in the contact zones of urban interethnic and interracial communities cohabitating in the Washington, D.C. metropolitan area and the DMV. It bears commenting that the meme in figure 12 interrogates the construction of Salvadoreñidades in diaspora and the maligning of migrants (especially youths) through the use of weaponized, racialized terms such as *salvatruco/a* and *salvatrucha*, to which we turn in the next section.

What Languages Does Your Salvadoreñidad Speak?

It is to this transmigrated, transculturated, and translanguaging Salvadoreñidad that Quique Avilés turns in his poetry collection *The Immigrant Museum*. Avilés reminds us that the Washington, D.C. metropolitan area is now home to "Wachintonian Salvadorans" ("El Salvador At-a-Glance"), with their intersectional subjectivities and mixed voices. The sociolinguist John M. Lipski duly notes that

> In the ensuing quarter century [after the civil war], the Salvadoran community has become established in cities [such as Washington, D.C.], and a generation [and more] of U.S.-born Salvadorans has altered the language mix of this rapidly evolving group. Not only is the use of English and contact with other dialects of Spanish imprinting the patrimonial Salvadoran speech forms, but innovative combinations are emerging, to set this speech community apart from other Spanish-speaking Americans. (*Varieties* 161)

In his poem "Latinhood," Avilés explores D.C. Latinhood as sensed, shaped, and heard in the streets through Latinx speech acts, particularly through Salvadoran Spanish's contact with other variants and with African American English. The echoes of Salvadoran Latinidades elicit from the poet a poignant line of questioning, when he asks, "What does it feel like inside? / what color is this latinhood? / how does it do what it does? . . . What language does it like to speak? / cachitquel / spanish / nahuatl / creole / or english" (8). What does this Salvadoran Latinidad speak when the Salvadoran diaspora is spread widely across the United States, Mexico, Europe, Asia, and Australia, among other places? "How do you know that you are a latin? / that you are not / a russian impostor with a peruvian accent" (9), asks Avilés of those who would argue that the key identifier of Latino/a/x identities is the Spanish language (see García Bedolla). Instead, in the same poem, Avilés suggests that U.S. Salvadoran identity has more to do with the ability to masticate, domesticate, and interpellate multiple languages into new hybrid articulations or translanguaging practices, such as those performed by Chicano, Nuyorican, and other U.S. Latino/a/x communities. For Avilés, a local Latinhood, Latinidad, or Salvadoreñidad is "the simple ability / to swallow the world at birth / keeping it / learning to chew at it / letting it grow / letting it grow inside" (9), invariably incorporating local histories, experiences, and languages and speaking in creative mixes that have been more technically defined as linguistic and cultural code-switching (Tseng, *Empanadas*).

What Avilés, González and Los de la Mount Pleasant, Culture Clash, and other U.S. Salvadoran cultural producers, such as the California-based writers' collective featured in the groundbreaking anthology *Izote Vos: A Collection of Salvadoran American Writing and Visual Art* (Kim et al.), have in common, I suggest here, is the articulation of U.S.-made Salvadoran hybridized *salvatruco/a* and *salvatrucha* identities, or Salvadoreñidades made in the United States. In speaking local variants of Spanish—whether California Chicano Spanish, "Wachintonian" African American English, or Salvadoran translanguaging and code-meshing (Tseng, *Empanadas*; V. A. Young et al.)—U.S.-raised Salvadorans articulate their own homebred experiences, transnational migration histories, translocal settlement patterns, and generational identity shifts in transcreative languages (Flores and Yúdice). In his poem "bilingual education," Avilés, for example, illustrates the creative code-meshings that happen when two subaltern languages meet, with groups jamming in poetry and speaking in tune. Made up of a series of two-line, one- or two-word stanzas, the poem uses the literary strategy of enjambment, by which lines and meaning blend from or run on from one poetic line to the next, seemingly re-creating the flow of casual conversation between two subjects and the distilled exchange of two words: *what up* and *que pasa* (no accent marks).[3]

Understanding is reached with the repetition of the word *aight*, from African American English, which becomes part of the common language of Avilés's Black and Brown speakers in his poem:

What up? / que ondas
aight / Ya vas
what up? / al suave
aight / y?
what up? / Que rola
aight / vaya broder
what up? / Te wacho
aight / janguiando
aight / sale vacile
what up? / Que dice carnal
aight / simon loquillo
what up? / vergon
aight / chingon
what up? / aight
que pasa / que pasa?

A lesson in "bilingual education," the poem illustrates bilingualisms in the making in the streets, among peers, and amid the differences and hyperdiversity of the Washington, D.C. metropolitan area. These greater sociocultural and ethnoracial transformations are encoded in the mixed languages spoken especially by new generations of Black American and Salvadoran (Brown-identified) American youths—"Salvis," as some California youths call themselves, or "Wachintonians," as Avilés calls fellow Salvadorans in the Washington, D.C. metropolitan region. Using and mixing African American English and Spanglish, Salvis and African Americans engage in creative code-meshing, bringing together complex communities, peoples, and histories into new worldmakings.

On the other hand, U.S.-born and U.S.-raised Salvadorans also experiment with Spanish heritage idioms. For example, when they play with the informal second-person singular pronoun *vos*, a most significant speech act and dis/claiming of cultural identity is in progress. As sociolinguists explain, the use of *vos*, *tú*, and *usted* in Latin American Spanish variants represents markers, interplays, and intersections of solidarity, intimacy, distance or deference, and power, among other things (Quesada Pacheco; Vaquero de Ramírez). But, moreover, in one-and-a-half and successive generations of Salvis, *vos* is often used as an intentional sign of Salvadoranness in inhospitable diasporic contexts. Indeed, Lipski notes, contrary to what some Salvis claim, "currently, young Salvadorans born in the United States who have never lived in El Salvador rarely use *voseo* verb forms or other markedly Salvadoran morphosyntactic traits. However, many add the tag *vos* to questions and affirmations, much as is done in Central America, as an explicit affirmation of their Salvadoran identity" (*Varieties* 163). The celebration of *voseo* is most vividly exemplified in the anthology *Izote Vos* (Kim et al.), which compiles the writings of a group of Salvis upon their first-time, eye-opening return to El Salvador in 1999. As co-editors Katherine Cowy Kim and Alfonso Serrano F. write in their introduction to that historic text:

> Almost all of the writers [ages fifteen to twenty-nine, most in high school or in college] were born in El Salvador; some came to the United States as infants, others as young children and some even as teenagers. *Izote Vos* dedicates a section to each writer, so that a portrait of each person is captured through their own words and images. [. . .] Even the title, *Izote Vos*, was a joint effort. [. . .] The *izote* is El Salvador's national flower, its fruit found in many native dishes. But the flower also flourishes in parts

> of California. *Vos* in Salvadoran Spanish means "you," but also conjures images of "*voz* . . . voice." (2)

According to sociolinguists, the *voseo* is not used in most of Mexico and the Spanish-speaking Caribbean, but is used widely in Argentina, Uruguay, and Paraguay; parts of Bolivia, Peru, Ecuador, Venezuela, and the states of Chiapas and Tabasco, Mexico; and almost all of Central America, with the exception of Panama (Quesada Pacheco 86–89; Stewart 123–24). But as Miranda Stewart, citing the work of John M. Lipski (*Latin American* 259), explains, "In El Salvador a three-way system appears to be developing amongst the educated urban classes [. . .] where *vos* and *Vd.* [*usted*] occupy the extremes of intimacy on the one hand and respect on the other, with *tú* occupying an intermediate position, signifying familiarity but not intimacy" (126). Indeed, as Lipski, one of the first sociolinguists outside of the country to examine Salvadoran Spanish, insists, "*Vos* remains the pronoun of maximum familiarity and solidarity, while *usted* expresses distance and respect" (*Varieties* 158).

To speak in *vos* or to *vosear*, hence, is to claim an intimate colloquial subjectivity, for the *voseo* in El Salvador (and most of Central America) is used in daily communications, in informal and intimate relationships and cultural exchanges among equals and loved ones, and in the formation of a popular national idiom and imaginary, herein identified with being Salvadoran *aguacatera/o*. It is worth emphasizing that as Stewart explains, *tú* in El Salvador signifies "familiarity but not intimacy," while *vos* implies intimacy and belonging. As Salvadorans, Central Americans, and others of the *voseo* linguistic region absorb the media-generated global or standard Spanish of the United States, they may substitute *tú* for *vos*, or eliminate the use of *vos* altogether. The negotiation of the intimate colloquial *vos* is worthy of note because it may signify a breach or distance from (or on the other hand, a desire for) Salvadoran culture, traditions, and community, among other things. Fully aware of the signifying power and potential of *vos/voz*, the editors of *Izote Vos* explain that the title of their anthology refers not only to the *flor de izote*, the edible national flower of El Salvador, but also to something greater. In their introduction, they write: "*Vos* in Salvadoran Spanish means 'you,' but also conjures images of 'voz . . . voice'" (Kim et al. 2). For Salvadorans, to speak in *voseo*, then, is a marker of cultural identity, belonging, community, and *aguacateridad*, even across their transnational migrations to the United States and elsewhere.

The use or disuse of *voseo* in Salvadoran American cultures may be read, consequently, as a desire for and sign of belonging to (or, conversely, of no longer strictly and exclusively identifying with) the national group because of migration, distance, or transculturation processes. When used by Salvadoran Americans, the *voseo* often serves as a badge of cultural and linguistic belonging and Indigeneity, or a reclaiming of Salvadoran cultural identity. In *Anthems*, Noe Ramírez commands his son to speak at least a proper form of English (read: non-Black) since he appears not to speak Salvadoran Spanish: "Hablá inglés [*vos*]." *Voseando* to this son, Ramírez implicitly hopes that Enrique will identify and understand Salvadoran idiomatic and cultural nuances (202). *Papá* Ramírez's appeal, however, is lost on Enrique, who has apparently lost the ability (or refuses) to *vosear*, speak in the colloquial register of Salvadoran Spanish, and identify and connect with his father. Indeed, many one-and-half, second, and successive generations of Salvadoran Americans negotiate their use of the *vos*, signifying thus the production of more hybridized translanguages and transcultural identities in the United States (Portes and Rumbaut). Growing up in the United States among English speakers and Spanish speakers from nations where the form *tú* or *usted* predominates, or in families where *tú* and *usted* are used to express respect, some Salvadoran Americans have little opportunity to use the *vos* form and to conjugate verbs for that familiar second-person singular pronoun. The loss or disuse of *vos* is particular to the experience of Salvadorans and other Central Americans and, perhaps, some South Americans growing up in the United States.

In my Salvadoran family, for example, children always address their parents and elders in the respectful *usted*. Communication in Spanish with other Latino/a/x peers, especially Mexicans, usually requires the use of *tú*. Thus, my siblings and I, like other one-and-half and successive generations of U.S. Salvadorans, did not learn to *vosear* in our daily communication. In this context, I ponder whether the disuse of the Central American *vos* signifies a loss of Salvadoran identity, culture, language, and homeland sensibilities and solidarity, as some would claim. Does the disuse of *vos* mean that we are no longer *salvatrucas/os* and *salvatruchas*, but rather U.S. Salvadorans who are losing the most essential markers of Salvadoran identity, including idioms, customs, traditions, and other forms of national identification? Or, does it signify the transnationalization and translocation of Salvadoran cultural identities into U.S. Latino/a/x identities, or what Juan Flores and George Yúdice call the transcreation of Latino/a languages and identities in the U.S. context? Further, does the negotiation of *vos/z* announce the construction of hybridized Salvadoran identities made possible outside of the national territory of El Salvador? In conclusion, we can now ask: why must this creative process of producing new Salvadoreñidades in translocal sites outside of El Salvador be branded as a loss, rather than as a gain for U.S. Salvadorans?

Conclusion: "Wachintonian" Salvadoran Bilingual Arts

Indeed, for some time, Latino/a/x scholars have argued that Spanish language maintenance under the weight of U.S. hegemonic culture and the uneasy transculturation of Spanish and English have generated some of the most creative practices in the cultural history of Latinxs in the United States. Amelia Tseng (*Empanadas*), Jonathan Rosa, Nelson Flores, Ed Morales, Ana Celia Zentella, Rosaura Sánchez, Fernando Peñalosa, and other scholars of translanguaging have posited that the hybridized and racialized Spanish spoken in the United States breaks with linguistic rules and confines, and in its many forms expresses a range of hybrid Latinidades. U.S. Latino/a writing that comes out of this space of cultural contact has produced what Doris Sommer, in her book *Bilingual Games: Some Literary Investigations,* has called the "art of code-switching" by bilingual artists and writers "overloaded" and overflowing with linguistic and cultural codes (1). Latino/a/x cultural producers like Tato Laviera (*AmeRícan; Mixturao*), the artists affiliated with the Nuyorican Poets Café and the Central American EpiCentro spoken word movement (see Chinchilla and Alvarado), and Chicana writers like Gloria Anzaldúa and Margarita Cota-Cárdenas have expressed themselves in the mixed language of Latino/a/x *AmeRíca,* the greater *borderlands,* and the transnationalized world.

Speaking further about the use of Spanish in his own U.S. Latina/o/x writings, the U.S.-Guatemalan writer Francisco Goldman points out that the Spanish language may not be the primary marker of Latino/a/x identity, especially for those living in between languages, cultures, and traditions.

He notes that "Spanish mixed with English is for many of us the language of our homes, of our most exuberant and eloquent friendships and loves, the language of the streets and many workplaces—not a separatist conceit, but like it or not, a living, breathing, ever-evolving new American vernacular" ("State"). Along these lines, Goldman, Avilés, and others (including this writer) question whether speaking Spanish, or not, makes one any more or less Latino/a/x in the United States. Who is Latino/a/x, and what languages do Latinxs speak? I would further ask: how do we go beyond classification systems that reductively identify Latinxs as "Spanish-speaking communities" or as extensions of "Spanish-speaking countries," as official demographic discourse stipulates in the United States? Finally, I must ask, somewhat tongue in cheek, whether Spanish is the de facto language and essential marker of U.S. Latinxs, be they of Dominican, Guatemalan, Uruguayan, Salvadoran, Garifuna, Maya, or Aymara descent? Or is Spanish just one of the many possible languages spoken by Salvadorans and other Latinxs in translocal sites such as Washington, D.C.?

In closing, D.C. *salvatruco* poet Quique Avilés, in his poem "Spanglish Morongon," amplifies Wachintonian *espanglish voces* that reverberate across D.C. and the DMV. In the figurative mobile space of a bus (the location of enunciation of his poem), we hear the distended internal monologues of people who are thinking aloud, reflecting on their day, and mulling over their health insurance, employment, laundry, family, school, and the Saturday night date. One bus rider ruminates, "Me subi en el bus que va para downtown / pedi un transfer / sonrei con el bus driver / me sente all the way in the back / el pinche bus iba full / lleno de gente llendo al part time / medio mundo hablando sobre insurance / los complaints y el medicaid" (I got on the bus that goes downtown / asked for a transfer / smiled with the bus driver / sat all the way in the back / the fucking bus was full / full of people going to their part-time [jobs] / half the world talking about insurance / the complaints and Medicaid) (notice the code-switching, the lack of accent marks, and the spelling of the gerund *yendo* as *llendo [going]*). The in-transit and transient bus serves as a metaphor for the transnational and hyperdiverse city filled with uniquely "Wachintonian" Salvadoran voices and identities produced outside of El Salvador and in translocal sites across the United States and elsewhere. This is the American anthem (*himno*) of *salvatrucas/os* and *salvatruchas* in Washington, D.C.

4

CHOLERAS/OS

Documenting Histories in Wachinton

The year 2010 marked a number of high-profile anniversaries in Latin America, including the bicentennial of the wars of independence in a number of countries, the centennial of the Mexican Revolution, and the thirtieth anniversary of the official start of the Salvadoran civil war. The violence of the armed struggle in the 1980s brought the Cold War into the homes of Salvadorans and forced many to flee the country, many never to return. In 2010, however, there were few acts of remembrance of the Salvadoran civil war in the Washington, D.C. metropolitan area to commemorate the so-called lost decade of El Salvador and its displaced people now living in the region. With the exception of commemorative events sponsored by organizations affiliated with the Farabundo Martí National Liberation Front (FMLN), solidarity and nonprofit immigrant-serving organizations like the Central American Resource Center (CARECEN) and the Committee in Solidarity with the People of El Salvador (CISPES), and other community-based groups, the Salvadoran Embassy and diasporic communities throughout the DMV virtually avoided recognition of the civil war on its thirtieth anniversary. Despite the Washington, D.C. metropolitan area being home to one of the largest (if least politically represented) Salvadoran communities in the United States, the date came and went with little fanfare.

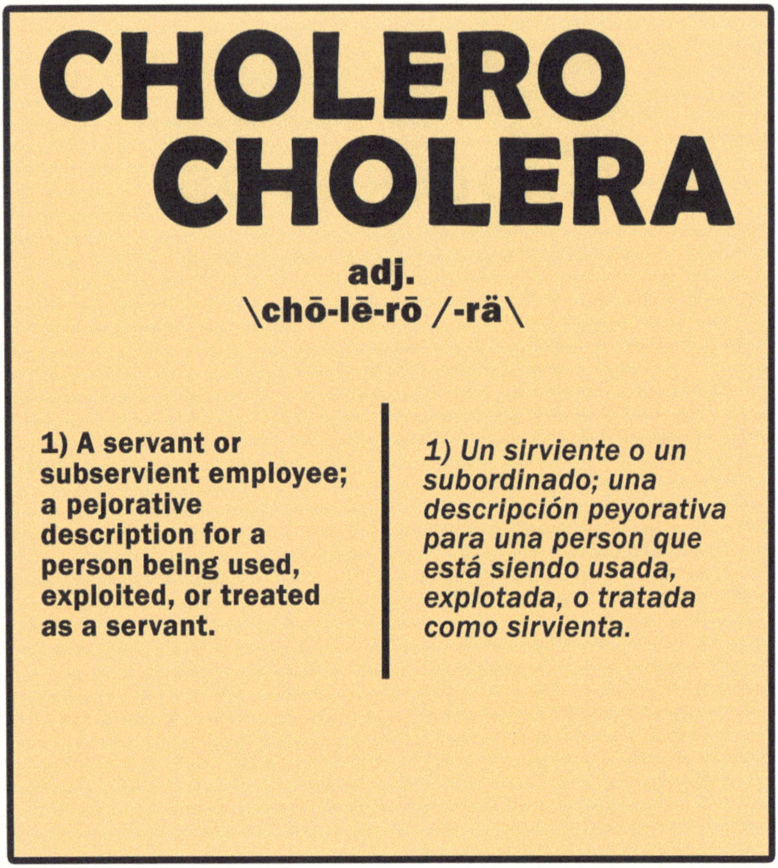

CHOLERO
CHOLERA

adj.
\chō-lē-rō /-rä

1) A servant or subservient employee; a pejorative description for a person being used, exploited, or treated as a servant.

1) Un sirviente o un subordinado; una descripción peyorativa para una person que está siendo usada, explotada, o tratada como sirvienta.

FIGURE 13. "Cholero/Cholera," by Víctor H. Interiano (Dichos de un bicho), 2020. Courtesy of Víctor H. Interiano.

This chapter opens with two terms of note: Los Treinta, referring to the thirty years of Salvadoran migration to the Washington, D.C. metropolitan area, as of 2010, and *cholero/a*, signifying classed and ethnoracialized notions of Salvadoranness. Both terms require some unpacking. The term *cholero/a* is used pejoratively both within and outside of El Salvador to stigmatize Salvadoran people as manual, exploitable, and cheap labor. In the *Diccionario de salvadoreñismos*, Matías Romero defines the term as follows: "Nombre despectivo dado al sirviente o al que trabaja para otro en oficicios humildes" (Name given to a servant or someone who works for another doing humble jobs) (149). The term carries the same negative connotations parodied by Roque Dalton in his poem "Poema de amor" (Love Poem), when he describes Salvadoreñas and Salvadoreños as "los guanacos hijos de la gran puta" (the *guanacos,* the sons of whores), and refers to them as a generic unknown and unknowable (illegible) entity: "los eternos indocumentados, / los hacelotodo, los vendelotodo, los comelotodo" (the eternal undocumented / the do-everything, the sell-everything, the eat-anything). They are the ones capable of *hacelotodo,* that is, of doing almost any task, meeting any challenge, or taking all the risks, in order to persevere, persist, survive, and prevail, as Quique Avilés posits in his poem "Canción para un Salvatruco" (Song for a Salvatruco), examined in chapter 3.

As the meme in figure 13 notes, the term *cholero/a* emphasizes the maligning of Salvadoran working people because of their association with exploitable (and often racialized and criminalized) labor, whether it be with their hands, bodies, or minds. On the flip side, the exploitation, extraction, and appropriation of Salvadoran labor has generated and sustained the myth of the ever-ready-to-work-at-anything *trabajador arrecho* (hard worker), remittance-sending *hermano/a lejana* (distant brother/sister), and model resilient employee, who will take any job and do it well, despite being exploited. D.C.-based Salvadoran troubadours Lilo González and Los de la Mount Pleasant pay tribute to these hardworking Salvadoran migrants in their song "La Mount Pleasant," in which they sing the praises of "los que limpian las ventanas, / Ay! Dios mío como iguanas, / Los mejores vendedores, / . . . Panaderos, cocineros, / Artesanos, carpinteros, / Los arrechos pa'l trabajo" (Those who clean windows, / Ay! My God, they're like iguanas, / the best vendors, / . . . Bakers, cooks, / Artisans, carpenters, / Always ready to work). In 2010, seeking to tell the collective story of these Salvadoran migrants and working people in the Washington, D.C. metropolitan area, Avilés wrote, produced, and performed his theatrical piece *Los Treinta.* In it, he embodied the quintessential Salvadoran immigrant story, that of his own family and the Salvadoran migrant community at large, who had fled en masse to the Washington, D.C. metropolitan area and the DMV in the 1980s.

In this chapter, Los Treinta refers, thus, to the period of war and postwar, from 1980 to 2010, marking three decades of the Salvadoran diaspora reterritorialized across the world, but particularly in the D.C. and DMV region. It also refers to Avilés's performative piece *Los Treinta,* commemorating the officially recognized thirty years of Salvadoran migration to the region. In spring 2010, in an effort to fill the notable void in the commemoration of this diaspora, my students at the University of Maryland and I collaborated with Avilés to produce a community-based oral history and performance project (figure 14).[1] Funded by a small grant from the

FIGURE 14. Flyer for *Los Treinta* at the University of Maryland, College Park, 2010. Courtesy of author.

D.C. Humanities Council on its own thirtieth anniversary of public art service in the city, Avilés and his production team, my students from two classes in the Department of Spanish and Portuguese and the U.S. Latina/o Studies Program, and I set out to document the Salvadoran diaspora in the region through the collection of oral histories of Salvadoran immigrants and Salvadoran-adjacent members of communities who had witnessed the arrival and settlement of Salvadorans in the district. Our goal was not only to interview and collect stories of migration, but also to make visible the long-standing presence of Salvadorans in the DMV and to contribute to what performance scholar Diana Taylor, in *The Archive and the Repertoire: Performing Cultural Memory in the Americas*, calls the "repertoire of resistance"—the *testimonios*, popular anecdotes, oral narratives, and resistance literature—associated with Salvadoran migration in the 1980s.

Los Treinta sought to challenge the official and unofficial archives that so often disappear Central Americans and Salvadorans from the historical record, or represent them simply as compliant, hardworking *choleros* and *choleras*, and to bring Salvadoran stories to life in Avilés's "embodied performances," as Taylor would have it. Together, we collected and transcribed more than sixty oral histories and wrote narratives that were then incorporated into Avilés's performance of *Los Treinta*, covering the more than thirty years of the Salvadoran migration to the nation's capital. Hence, the phrase Los Treinta in this chapter also refers to the collaborative, intergenerational, and community-based artistic work of collecting and writing local diasporic narratives undertaken by my students and me, which Dorinne Kondo, in her book *Worldmaking: Race, Performance, and the Work of Creativity*, theorizes as "a way to remake worlds through engaged participation" (8).

The Lost Decade of the 1980s

The 1980s in El Salvador were marked by prolonged and inconceivable bloodshed, beginning with the assassination of Archbishop (San) Óscar A. Romero on March 24, 1980; the massacre of approximately six hundred women, men, and children by Salvadoran and Honduran military forces as they attempted to cross the Sumpul River into Honduras on May 14, 1980, so well documented in Claribel Alegría's collection of poetry *Woman of the River*; the consolidation of five leftist-politico-military organizations under the umbrella of the Farabundo Martí National Liberation Front on October 10, 1980; and the ambush, rape, and killing of three U.S. Maryknoll and Ursuline nuns (Maura Clarke, Ita Ford, and Dorothy Kazel) and a lay church worker (Jean Donovan) on December 2, 1980. These events of 1980 were followed in succession by the massacre at El Mozote and its surrounding *cantones* (villages) on December 11, 1981, and other mass and singular killings across the country, as well as the exodus of countless Salvadorans to safer grounds. By the end of the decade, more than seventy-five thousand Salvadorans had been killed, and countless more disappeared and tortured. Over 20 percent of the population had been displaced internally and externally, as recorded by human rights organizations. The escalating violence would end in ceasefire a decade after it began, with the signing of the Peace Accords on January 16, 1992, in Chapultepec, Mexico. For Central Americans, especially those who experienced the wars in El Salvador, Guatemala, and Nicaragua, the 1980s represent an era of "terrible miseria" (terrible misery) (González Mejía 11), during which military and state violence, foreign intervention ($6 billion in total from the United States to El Salvador), growing external debt, loss of lives and livelihoods, and other global and local crises permeated the isthmus.

According to Mario Lungo Uclés, in *El Salvador in the Eighties: Counterinsurgency and Revolution*, the displaced populations in El Salvador fled the war zones into other parts of the country, Central America, Mexico, and the world. Salvadorans sought refuge particularly in the United States, settling in places such as Los Angeles, San Francisco, Long Island, Houston, and Washington, D.C. (see also Rodríguez, "Departamento 15"; Rodríguez, *Dividing*; Rodríguez, "Refugees"). As the scholar Edelberto Torres-Rivas puts it,

> Ha sido esta década, 1979–1991, infame para el destino de la inmensa mayoría de la población centroamericana. La región no había experimentado nunca ni guerras civiles tan sangrientas ni una crisis económica tan profunda y prolongada. Habituados en todos estos años a vivir los ominosos signos de la crisis: la violencia, el miedo, la pobreza de masas, estos rasgos adversos hoy nos parecen inadvertidas formas habituales de vida, aunque al mismo tiempo ahora constituyan los mayores problemas de esta época. (11)

> (The decade, 1979–1991, has been critical to the destiny of the majority of Central Americans. Up to then, the region had not experienced such bloody civil wars, or such profound and prolonged economic crisis. [With us] having become accustomed during those years to live amid the ominous sign of crisis—violence, fear, massive poverty—these adverse effects seem to be part of our daily lives now, although they constitute the greatest of our current problems.)

In this context, El Salvador became a nation seeking political asylum largely denied by the U.S. legal system, as noted by the immigration legal scholar Susan Bibler Coutin (*Legalizing Moves*; *Nation*). By the 1990s, the deleterious effects of the war had extended into the postwar period, and the Salvadoran exile experience had given way to a veritable diasporic community spread out across the world—a transnational phenomenon that I have elsewhere analyzed as "Departamento 15" (Rodríguez, "Departamento 15"; Rodríguez, *Dividing*).

While Salvadoran and Central American migration to the Washington, D.C. metropolitan area and the DMV dates back to the late nineteenth and early twentieth centuries, migration to the region reached a feverish pitch in the 1980s (see chapters 2 and 3 for a telling of this history). Living testament of the 1980s Salvadoran great migration, Avilés left El Salvador at the age of fifteen years and arrived in the Mount Pleasant neighborhood of Washington, D.C., or what he calls the epicenter of the Salvadoran migration to the District of Columbia. Since then, he has been at the forefront of writing about Salvadoran cultural experiences in the region. In the late 1980s, he cofounded and directed the theater collective LatiNegro, which recruited local Latino and African American youths to perform in theaters, schools, prisons, universities, and communities. In 1999, he cofounded Sol & Soul, a nonprofit arts organization that continued the work of LatiNegro in conducting workshops with young performers in D.C., collaborating with community groups, and organizing theater events in the district for local and visiting artists and performers. To this day, Avilés continues to perform his mixed-media work onstage, in schools and theaters, and on the streets and plazas of D.C. Addressing issues of race, class, gender, gentrification, labor, migration, and hybrid identity, among other things, his performance pieces and poetry often incorporate the stories, voices, and experiences of Latinx immigrants and everyday folks from local neighborhoods.

In 2003, Avilés published *The Immigrant Museum,* which includes poems such as "El Salvador At-a-Glance," "My Tongue Is Divided into 2," and "Latinhood," many of which he reads, performs, and repurposes in his solo monologues. As discussed in previous chapters, in one of his most cited poems, "Latinhood," Avilés explores the nuances of Salvadoran Latinidad, repeatedly asking "What does it feel like inside? / what color is this latinhood? / how does it do what it does? . . . Is it mexican latin / salvatrucan latin / patagonian latin / latin with an american passport? . . . How do you know that you are a latin? / that you are not / a russian impostor with a peruvian accent?" (8–9). With this line of questioning, Avilés, along with other practitioners and scholars of performance, suggests that identity is *performative,* scripted, cited, reconverted, and negotiated in daily exchanges within and among subjects (Christian). In "El Salvador At-a-Glance," he further ponders his relationship with his native country: "El Salvador, / there are questions in the air about your character / they say you've dared to do the impossible / you've challenged the tiger to a wrestling match / you've decided that bullets hold the answers / El Salvador, / little question mark / . . . Little question mark that begins to itch" (10). Throughout the poem, Avilés reflects on his homeland, reimagining and reconstituting it to include its missing diasporic elements: "city builders, busboys, waiters, poets" (10); major cities San Salvador, Los Angeles, and "San Wachinton, D.C." (11); and "El Salvador in Wachinton," where people are "forever Wachintonian Salvadorean" (11), no less Salvadoran for living in the capital of another country.

Meanwhile, in his multiple-character performance *Caminata,* Avilés interrogates essentialist notions of Salvadoran national identity by exploring the kaleidoscopic intersections of diasporas in Washington. Drawing on ethnographic interviews with D.C. residents, Avilés brings to life the character of Demetrio, a Salvadoran-Chicano searching for meaning in the United States. On the sparse stage, set with just a few props—a handmade *carreta* (cart), a box to sit on, and a few pieces of clothing—Demetrio recounts the stories of the people he meets on his voyage of discovery. In the process, Demetrio becomes, or rather embodies and performs, the characters he meets. Yombo, from the Central African Republic, is a division director at the Latin American Youth Center on Columbia Road in northwest Washington. Upon arriving in the United States, Yombo studied English with Latinos/as, married a Dominican woman and "becomes part of them," and adopted U.S. citizenship—only to realize that he "might have to defend this nation, bear arms . . . kill somebody" (14). Olga is a Jewish refugee from Saint Petersburg, Russia, by way of Indianapolis; she "speaks Spanish better than English" after having had a love affair with her Spanish teacher and having lived in an apartment with nine people, some of whom are Latinx. Although she "can pass for white," she identifies as an immigrant and "not American" (16). Then there is Rahman, a Catholic-raised, Iraqi refugee camp survivor, migrant laborer, dishwasher, pizza deliveryman, and car repairman, now working in Washington with an Iraqi refugee organization. At the end of his monologue, Rahman-Demetrio-Avilés says, "since Sept. 11th, I am the enemy" on the streets of D.C. (24), despite wearing a "R*dsk*ns" (now Washington Commanders) hat, changing his hair color, and sporting an earring.

Perhaps Avilés's most iconic character in *Caminata* is doña Rosita. His performance of her makes full reference to the clichés and stereotypes of Salvadoran femininity: she is a hardworking, good-natured mother, informal food vendor peddling mangoes and tamales at La Clinica del Pueblo (the People's Clinic), and undocumented border-crosser turned legal resident, who religiously sends remittances home (much like Juana in Mario Bencastro's story "Juana's Dreams"). In her monologue, Rosita gives testimony of her life in war-torn El Salvador, from which she fled seeking refuge in "los Yunais Estates." Rosita says, "Yo soy de Ciudad Delgado, San Salvador. I am from El Salvador. I came here because of the situation. The father of my children, he got killed. We never knew if it was the guerrillas or the national guard. A bullet through his head. After that, I knew I had to leave" (8). On the streets of D.C., Rosita sees "sad and depressed" people who reflect her pain back at her, but she wards this off with humor and work, making, as she says, "illegal tamales, wetback tamales, legal resident pupusas and . . . citizen enchiladas." She reminds the audience that "if you laugh, you can talk" (10). Through the characters of Rosita, Rahman, Demetrio, and the others, Avilés brings to life adjacent, intersecting diasporic experiences mirroring his own *caminata* (journey) through Washington, D.C.

On the thirtieth anniversary of the migration of Salvadoran *pioneras* (pioneers) like doña Rosita, Avilés conceptualized his new performance piece, *Los Treinta*, for, by, and with the participation of communities who identified as Salvadoran and as allies of the Salvadoran diaspora in D.C. For that endeavor, he recruited students in my classes, and me, to collect oral histories to be put on full display through public performances at the University of Maryland, College Park, the GALA Hispanic Theatre, the DC Arts Center in Adams Morgan, and other venues across the United States, as he took the show on the road by invitation. As a group, we interviewed and wrote the oral histories of Salvadorans and others who came to the D.C. metropolitan area or who bore witness to that migration. We gathered a wide array of stories, from those of long-standing Black residents of the Chocolate City to those of more recently arrived Salvadoran migrants and their families. We reflected on three decades of a people's history, by now forgotten by many, but embodied by the Salvadorans who continue to immigrate to the region. Thus, in spring 2010, we studied not only the 1980s in Central American history as a point of departure for the Salvadoran diaspora, but also the present-day U.S. context as a point of arrival amid growing anti-immigrant sentiment and legislation enacted across the country. Spring 2010 served as our backdrop for understanding the migration of Salvadorans over the previous thirty years, in the context of the passing of the controversial anti-immigration Senate Bill 1070 in Arizona, the banning of social service provisions to undocumented immigrants, and the pro-immigrant marches that took place in D.C. that spring. We also studied the newly approved Texas social studies curriculum, which excised discussions about Archbishop Romero, Harriet Tubman, and Black enslavement from textbooks in the state, a situation replicated more recently with book bans and curricular restrictions as of 2023.

Los Treinta reckoned with the decade of the 1980s as it affected the collective life of the Salvadoran diaspora in the Washington, D.C. metropolitan area. The performance (re)historized and grounded the lived experience of narrators of oral histories in the larger material and economic transformations of late capitalism (Jameson; Nealon). On the one hand, the 1980s are remembered as the decade of Ronald Reagan's war on communism and the meteoric rise of the neoliberal economy, as Argentine journalist José Ricardo Eliaschev describes in his account of the ascent of the United States into a global power in his book *Reagan, U.S.A.: Los años ochenta* (Reagan, U.S.A.: The Eighties). On the other hand, for many people, displaced by the violence and impact of neoliberalism across Latin America and the Caribbean, the decade is also known as "the lost decade of Latin America." Among the capital losses of Central America were the thousands of casualties of war, the ever-increasing economic and political subjection to U.S. power, and the mass exodus of its people. Avilés's project *Los Treinta* walked a fine line, telling the story of the Salvadorans disappeared in their country and their reemergence as an invisible presence in the same country that manufactured their war. Tellingly, in his opening line of *Los Treinta*, Avilés says that Salvadoran immigrants in the 1980s were like a hurled "human grenade" that landed in D.C. For my students, many of them born in the 1990s, of Latinx or Salvadoran descent and the first generation in their families to attend college, this history of the 1980s was all but a void, which the project sought to fill with community history, history from below, and oral histories or *testimonios*.

In 2010, although it seemed that the Salvadoran civil war was old news, its afterlife persisted in collective traumas, silences, and social harms, displayed in violence, generalized poverty, ongoing displacement and migration, and historical amnesia institutionalized across the isthmus and the diaspora. To tell the story of the Salvadoran diaspora in the Washington, D.C. metropolitan area would require not only recasting and retelling the stories of the 1980s, but also recognizing the United States as an imperial power and the cause of much violence, displacement, and migration in the Americas. It would mean reading El Salvador into the historiography of the Americas and unleashing the repressed and occult history of U.S. Cold War interventions that designated El Salvador as part and parcel of the "Vietnam syndrome." As Christian Smith so well explains in *Resisting Reagan: The U.S. Central America Peace Movement*, Reagan and his cabinet set out to make an example of El Salvador, announcing to the world in million-dollar military aid packages that "the national security of all the Americas is at stake in Central America. If we cannot defend ourselves there . . . the safety of our homeland would be put in jeopardy" (18). In the post-9/11 context, the so-called Salvador Option—counterinsurgency warfare involving the use of death squads like those trained by the U.S. military in El Salvador during the 1980s—was proposed for implementation in Iraq. For most people, the central place of El Salvador in Cold War and 9/11 war ideologies remains an unclear and covert episode in history. Even today, El Salvador's methods of securitization and policing are presented as viable responses to organized transnational narcotrafficking, crime, and gangs. Cold War tactics and rhetoric as deployed in El Salvador in the 1980s have been retooled for the war on terrorism and international narcotrafficking in the twenty-first century. How, then, would we re/tell the story of the 1980s and the Salvadoran diaspora in the nation's capital, where such consensus was manufactured and where a critical mass of Salvadorans and their children now reside?

The Power of Community Oral Histories

In what follows, this chapter ponders how we might document the nearly invisiblized presence of Salvadorans in the DMV and speculates with Diana Taylor on how to draw alternatively from ephemeral sources like Avilés's performances, oral histories, anecdotes, and other unofficially archived texts to produce grounded histories about the Salvadoran diaspora. To tell the story of the extensive Salvadoran diaspora, as Taylor claims in *The Archive and the Repertoire,* would entail drawing from the "nonarchival system of transfer of stories" (xvii)—that is, from a repertoire of performances texts such as Avilés's *Los Treinta* and the oral histories that my students and I undertook. To that end, I developed an assignment for my students that required them to work closely with Avilés on research questions and methods to excavate the history of Salvadoran and Latinx migration to the Washington, D.C. metropolitan area. Students interviewed people, gathered oral histories, and wrote up and presented their findings. Avilés incorporated their findings and oral history narratives into his performance. And, finally, *Los Treinta* was presented to the general public, with performances at the University of Maryland, College Park; the GALA Hispanic Theatre in Washington, D.C.; the DC Arts Center in the heart of Adams Morgan, once part of the Latinx/Salvadoran barrio; and other venues across the United States. In essence, my students and I engaged in public scholarship and brought public humanities to various spaces, contributing not only to the production of Avilés's piece but also to the recovery and archiving of Salvadoran stories of migration to the Washington, D.C. metropolitan area. The student projects were evaluated on their use of oral history methodologies and protocols; their collection and composition of oral histories; and their presentation of materials.[2]

In preparation for the project, Dr. Olivia Cadaval, folklorist and curator for the Smithsonian Center for Folklife and Cultural Heritage and longtime Avilés collaborator on projects dating back to his days with LatiNegro and Sol & Soul, was brought in to train my students in interview methodologies and the production of oral histories. Avilés also came to my classes to perform his poetry and describe his vision for the project, which would take various forms. Using community-based theories and practices (Strand et al.), my vision for the project was, first and foremost, to involve students in researching the 1980s in Central America; interviewing subjects associated with or witness to the Salvadoran migration in the 1980s; and writing oral histories that could serve as archives for the repertoire that Avilés was building.

The student oral histories gathered for *Los Treinta* ranged from personal family histories of migration to exposés of key figures, places, and events related to the migration of Salvadorans to the DMV in the 1980s. Students learned about apartment complexes, employment sites, organizations, clinics, youth centers, theaters, churches, restaurants, grocery stores, clubs, street festivals, and even bus lines, where the community came into contact, established ties, and thrived. They heard about places in the barrio that only exist now in the memories of the people they interviewed—the Ontario Theater on Columbia Road, El Tazumal Restaurant on Eighteenth Street, and the fruit stands on Mount Pleasant Street, all in Ward 1, in northwest D.C. In one oral history written in my class for *Los Treinta,* José Alfredo Centeno-Meléndez, who is now an oral historian at the Smithsonian Institution, interviewed a man who came as a child in the 1970s, the early wave of Salvadoran migration. His mother, a *pionera,* "sent for him while she had a stable job in Washington, D.C.," as Terry A. Repak writes about such *pioneras* (77). Centeno-Meléndez writes that his narrator, only twelve years old when he arrived in the DMV, recollected:

> We first arrived in the United States back in 1975. We came from Morazan, which is one of the states from El Salvador. We came from a small little town called El Divisadero. The reason we came to the United States was because my mom had already migrated here in 1969, 1970 I believe. And of course, she wanted us to be with her. When we first arrived, we arrived in a town called Accokeek, Maryland. That's near Ft. Washington. We were there for . . . we weren't there for long. We were there for about

> 4 to 5 months, and then we moved into the Latino community, 18th and Columbia Rd. 6 months later. ("Los 30" 1)

The family would then move to D.C., which, for the newcomer, was "like a whole different world to me and it was something very different because of the culture, the language"; its "people look[ed different] from the country that we came from. You know, tall . . . blonde . . . not like . . . different. That's what I remember seeing, how different people looked"; "it was like a culture shock" (1–2). The narrator goes on to tell Centeno-Meléndez that

> Moving into DC was a little better than living in Accokeek, Maryland because when we arrived there, there was a Salvadoran community already in Columbia Rd. It was mostly based of Puerto Ricans and Salvadorans back in those days. There were a few Spanish stores, not like there are now, but there were a few . . . and you could communicate because there were more Latino people there than in Ft. Washington. There's no monuments [at] 18th and Columbia Rd. There was a lot of what you may call "El barrio." It was Latinos . . . Puerto Ricans, Salvadorans, Bolivians, and it was sort of like, it gave me a little comfort because it reminded me of back home a little bit. (3)

Almost in tune with the research on the burgeoning Salvadoran community arriving in the Washington, D.C. metropolitan area in the 1970s and '80s, Centeno-Meléndez's narrator describes the Latinx/Salvadoran barrio as a haven for migrants, refugees, and asylum seekers, who could rent a room or apartment, find employment in construction, housecleaning, caretaking, or other jobs, buy products from their countries, and speak in Spanish in the neighborhood, providing them with a degree of security, if not all the comforts of home. As the narrator tells it:

> Back in those days [the '70s], the Salvadoran community was known, and still is, as hardworking people, working in restaurants . . . working in the construction field, and being hard workers, and family oriented, and that's about it—that I remember. Mostly the Salvadorans worked at restaurants, carry-outs, construction jobs, and still up to this day, they still . . . that's where most of the Salvadorans still work. Restaurants, hotels, and construction sights. Back in those days we were known as a hardworking peo-

> ple . . . people that came here because of the civil war. We were running from the war . . . even though we [my brothers and I] were not because we came here before the war. But I remember when the civil war was going on in El Salvador, people were coming here to try to get away from the war. We were seen as hardworking people, and basically, you know, that's all I can remember . . . being judged as hardworking people. (4)

Almost echoing the words of Roque Dalton, the narrator describes Salvadoran migrants as hardworking people, *los hacelotodo*, willing to do anything and everything to persist and prevail, as Avilés also recognizes in his poem "Canción para un Salvatruco." Indeed, Centeno-Meléndez captures in his oral history the story of most Salvadoreños and Salvadoreñas who came to the DMV to work as *choleros/as* and, in the process, built thriving communities and enclaves; laid the cornerstone for subsequent waves of Salvadoran and Central American migrations; and, in some cases, like Centeno-Meléndez's narrator, grew to count themselves among "the Salvadorans that made it in the United States" ("Los 30" 5).

Like Centeno-Meléndez's oral history, the texts produced by my other students for *Los Treinta* documented the presence of Latino and Salvadoran communities once living in the now-gentrified neighborhoods of Adams Morgan, Columbia Heights, and Mount Pleasant. The stories illustrated in great part the scholarly literature that we read in class (Cadaval, *Creating*; Repak). By interviewing and listening to the people who had lived in those neighborhoods, we learned firsthand of the labor of the so-called *choleros/choleras* who, in great part, have made D.C. and the DMV a thriving, hyperdiverse region. We also bore witness to the losses of the community. Gone today from the gentrified neighborhoods are the vendors selling *queso duro* (hard cheese) out of suitcases, cassette tapes on makeshift tables, and *micas* (false green cards) on the street corners and in the parks of the barrio. In fact, most Salvadoran families are now gone, but they return to Adams Morgan, Columbia Heights, and Mount Pleasant to do business, go to church, eat at *pupuserias*, and remember the old times. The past is memorialized in their personal photo albums and memorabilia, the People's Archive at the Martin Luther King Jr. Memorial Library, and the occasional performances of artists like Avilés, as well as research projects sometimes conducted by local students and community members on their own or through the DC History Center, the Smithsonian Institution, local universities, and other organizations.

Los Treinta in the District

Avilés's original intention in producing *Los Treinta* was to tell his own story of migration to the Washington, D.C. metropolitan area, his witnessing of the mass exodus from El Salvador that would become the Salvadoran diaspora in the region, and his gathering of stories to be retold. In *Los Treinta,* characters from his previous pieces would be restaged: doña Rosita, the food vendor in Mount Pleasant; Ms. Huntington, a white woman gentrifier angered by the influx of Spanish-speaking children at her daughter Vivian's school; Nico, a young U.S.-born Salvadoran who helps his mother sell bootleg cassette tapes on Columbia Road NW; and Yombo, the son of diplomats from the Central African Republic, who works at the Latin American Youth Center, is married to a woman from the Dominican Republic, and mentors Salvadoran youths. Based on composites from previous interviews or contacts made by Avilés, these fictionalized characters represented D.C. as a contact zone of historically racialized communities, multiple, intersecting diasporas and migrations, and hyperdiverse demographics, as defined by Amelia Tseng ("Advancing"), as well as a hyperlayering of cultures, languages, practices, and memories. In *Los Treinta,* Avilés also performed and played tribute to his *pionera* mother, who left El Salvador amid the growing violence to work in Washington and send money back for Quique and his siblings, thus, recalling the classic narrative of the pioneer immigrant women "waiting on Washington," as scholars have so well documented (Cadaval, *Creating*; Cadaval, "Latino Community"; Repak; Sánchez Molina, *Mandar*; Scallen, *Bombs*).

Amid the many stories gathered in his embodied performances, Avilés produced a space for meta-reflection as he broke the fourth wall, speaking in his voice while meditating on the generations of people who have lived in the Mount Pleasant neighborhood. For this, he drew excerpts from interviews with Salvadoran immigrants and others conducted by my students and himself. During the performance of *Los Treinta,* voiceovers from the interviews could be heard from backstage as images of migrants were projected on a screen. Additionally, he interpolated poems from his chapbooks and collections, which have become favorites among his readers, like “El Salvador At-a-Glance,” a manifesto of sorts that maps out the Salvadoran diaspora from San Salvador and San Miguel to Santa Ana, Los Angeles, and “Wachinton, D.C.” The pièce de résistance—or climax of the entire performance—however, was Avilés’s reading of a poem, “Notes on How They Lied About Your Existence (a poem for my Afro-American brothers and sisters),” which dates back to his writings in the 1980s. In the poem, Avilés (meta)reflects on the exclusion of people of color from primetime TV when he was growing up in El Salvador and later when he migrated to Washington. The poem underscores how Black Americans, Central Americans, Salvadorans, and others were not only “disappeared” from mainstream television screens in the 1980s but also expunged from the archives and official records. To question these erasures and omissions, Avilés asks:

> Where did they put you?
> what did they do with you?
> all that time you were not on prime time?
> Were you on vacation in California?
> Without a number to be reached?
> Were you too busy being happy?
> Were you in other T.V. programs?
> with street scenes
> white dogs biting black skin?
> White firemen being nice to you giving you a free shower?
> Getting your hair done with police clubs?
> What did they do to you when you were not on prime time?
> Were you wearing white robes
> burning crosses?
> Lynching your own?
> Were you looking for a toilet with the proper sign?
> were you sinning
> Trying to love a white man/white woman
> under the darkness of the land of the free?
> What did they do with you
> when you were not on Prime Time T.V.?

In the absence of inclusion and representation of people of color on television—an absence that serves as a metonym for systemic racism as a whole—Avilés zeroes in on the erasure of histories of racial violence in the United States, the very "darkness of the land of the free." He alludes to searing images of lynchings, burning crosses, police beatings, dogs biting Black skins, white-robed figures, and other signs of racism hidden by the camera. Using biting satire, he comments on systemic and institutionalized oppression, segregation, exclusion, and the invisibilization of people of color, as he asks, "What did they do with you / when you were not on Prime Time T.V.?" In the larger narrative of *Los Treinta*, spectators might also ask: What did they do with (and to) you when you were not included in the history, the archives, and the stories told? Seeking to challenge those invisibilizing images, tropes, and practices of documentation, *Los Treinta* was conceived as embodied performance, drawing from the oral histories of Salvadoran people who have lived in the region since the 1980s, if not earlier.

Indeed, the official archives on the violence in Central American, especially in El Salvador, make poor historical records of the 1980s and its aftermath. In the absence of reliable official sources, *Los Treinta* recovered people's everyday stories, anecdotes, and memories of the civil war and their migration to the DMV. As testimonies of migrant experiences in the 1980s, the oral histories gathered by my students varied in recollection, giving proof that memory is ephemeral and storytelling is creative, inventive, and amorphous, always subject to change, for there is no one truth in storytelling, only many stories (Adichie). The controversy surrounding Rigoberta Menchú's *testimonio* in the 1980s and '90s demonstrates well how there can never be just one story, one truth, and one source (Arias, *Rigoberta Menchú*), only many stories and sources. In their work for *Los Treinta*, my students were tasked with collecting and processing oral histories of the Salvadoran diaspora, without the intention of eventually producing one narrative. Instead, we gathered pieces, impressions, and recollections, contributing to a repertoire of voices and a larger collage of transnational and translocal hi/stories of the Salvadoran diaspora. As Diana Taylor suggests, we went beyond the archive (the official record) and traditional performance formats, adding to "the repertoire of embodied performances, transmit[ting] . . . its own particular history" (267). My students and I uncovered/recovered and made visible and audible multiple stories, memories, and struggles of the Salvadoran diaspora in the DMV. We contributed to the growing public scholarship on the Salvadoran diaspora (see Bencastro, *Odyssey*; Cadaval, *Creating*; L. González and Los de la Mount Pleasant; Modan; Pedersen, "States"; Repak; Sánchez Molina, *Mandar*), as well as to Avilés's expansive spoken word and performance repertoire, which extends from his early works like *Caminata* to our production of *Los Treinta*, and beyond.

So it was that on April 26, 2010, the first reading of *Los Treinta* as a work in progress was performed at the University of Maryland, College Park, as well as live streamed in Los Angeles and El Salvador with the collaboration of Dr. Beatriz Cortez, then chair of the Central American Studies Program at California State University, Northridge, the first (and, to date, only) program awarding a bachelor of arts in Central American studies in the United States. Using virtual media and live streaming technology, we linked up two of most important sites of the Salvadoran diaspora—the Washington, D.C. metropolitan area and Los Angeles—with El Salvador, no longer serving as an originating site, but now representing another translocal site of Salvadorans across the world, as Avilés claims in his poem "El Salvador At-a-Glance." Leading up to April 26, students from the University of Maryland's only Latinx newspaper, *La Voz Latina*, published a feature story on Avilés in the Spring 2010 edition. As a final project, a Latino/a studies student, Marissa Lang, now a leading journalist for the *Washington Post*, produced a ten-minute film, *"Los Treinta": Documenting the Undocumented.* On April 26, University of Maryland students, families, friends, and the community gathered for a night of Salvadoran storytelling, at which Avilés, Lilo González, Lilito González (son of Lilo), and longtime collaborator and educator Mark Perkins performed *Los Treinta* before the live and virtual transnational audience. We had accomplished our objective of making visible the stories of Salvadoran migration in the Washington, D.C. metropolitan area.

Conclusion

With *Los Treinta*, multifold in design, production, and collaboration, Avilés breathed life into the narrative of the Salvadoran diaspora in the Washington, D.C. metropolitan area. He told of the lifeblood and lifeline of Salvadoran communities in D.C., which today are newly experiencing displacement and migration as gentrification pushes them to the outskirts of the city and the suburbs of the DMV, and draconian immigration policies in 2025 threaten to deport them to their homelands and other "third" countries. No stranger to community activism, Avilés sought with this performance piece to reembody and reinvigorate what he called the Salvadoran heart, lungs, and aorta of the Latino/a/x communities in the Washington, D.C. metropolitan area, symbolically located, for Avilés, at Irving and Sixteenth Streets NW. Rather than being invisible as Arias argues, the Salvadoran diaspora in the Washington, D.C. metropolitan area brought life to the post-1968 blighted neighborhoods of D.C., which had been abandoned in the 1960s, '70s, and '80s. Through their *cholero* and *cholera* labor, Salvadorans have energized Adams Morgan, Mount Pleasant, Columbia Heights, and other neighborhoods, contributing economically, politically, and culturally. It is the Salvadoran *cholero/a* work ethic, labor, entrepreneurship, community-building, solidarity, activism, artivism, and cultural production that continue to sustain many neighborhoods of the Washington, D.C. metropolitan area and the DMV.

In *Los Treinta*, all who were involved had the opportunity to challenge the invisibility myth of Salvadorans in the D.C. metropolitan area and to produce a repertoire of stories that might fill the void of representation of Salvadorans in the United States. For those who participated in its creation, *Los Treinta* also pointed to a need to create spaces for self-reflection on how we critically produce community narratives and other types of archives, for, as Taylor reminds us, making visible invisible populations also "give[s] rise to an industry of 'experts' needed to approach and interpret them: language experts, scientists, ethicists, ethnographers, and cartographers" (64). *Los Treinta* invited us to interrogate and situate our own scholarly work documenting the Salvadoran diaspora in the Washington, D.C. metropolitan area, and reminded us to be ever vigilant about our own complicity in (re)producing archives that might silence and erase the more ephemeral repertoires. In the end, *Los Treinta* also called on us to create more critical and engaged stories.

EPILOGUE

CACHIMBONXS

Curating Cultural Resistances for a New Era

In *Create Dangerously: The Immigrant Artist at Work,* U.S. Haitian writer and cultural critic Edwidge Danticat states that in her work she tries "to write the things that have always haunted and obsessed those who came before [her]" (13). Thus, she writes about Haitian history, genocide, and intergenerational trauma, and about migration and solidarity as acts of remembrance and resistance. She explains that diasporas have "creation myths—that haunt and obsess [us]" (5). For the Salvadoran diaspora, the civil war in the 1980s figures as a "creation myth," one that we must "unforget" (remember) (Lovato), unsilence (Abrego, "On Silences"), and reimagine dangerously and courageously (Danticat). This epilogue offers a reflection on the work of *cachimbon/a/x* (courageous and prevailing) Salvadoran creatives, artists, and writers born or raised in diaspora in the DMV, who, through their artwork, challenge the invisibilizing, silencing, disciplining, and victimizing of Central Americans across the isthmus and beyond. As defined in the meme in figure 15, these *cachimbonx* artists create new narratives for and about the Salvadoran diaspora. According to Matías Romero, in the *Diccionario de salvadoreñismos,* a person who is a *cachimbón, cachimbona,* or *cachimbonx* is "un individuo valiente que no se raja ante las adversidades, capaz de cumplir cualquier compromiso, aun a costa de su propia vida" (a courageous individual who never succumbs to adversities, capable of fulfilling all commitments, even if they cost her/his life) (91). Being *aguacateras/os, salvatrucas/os, choleras/os,* and *cachimbonxs,* everywhere all at once, across the translocalities of the diaspora, Salvadorans are indeed exemplary people (if I do say so myself)—adaptable, proud, courageous, persistent, prevailing, and resistant. This epilogue looks at various diasporic narratives curated in the intergenerational work of *cachimbon/a/x* artists of the DMV, including the artist Rafael Rodríguez Molina; the poet Claudia Rojas; the

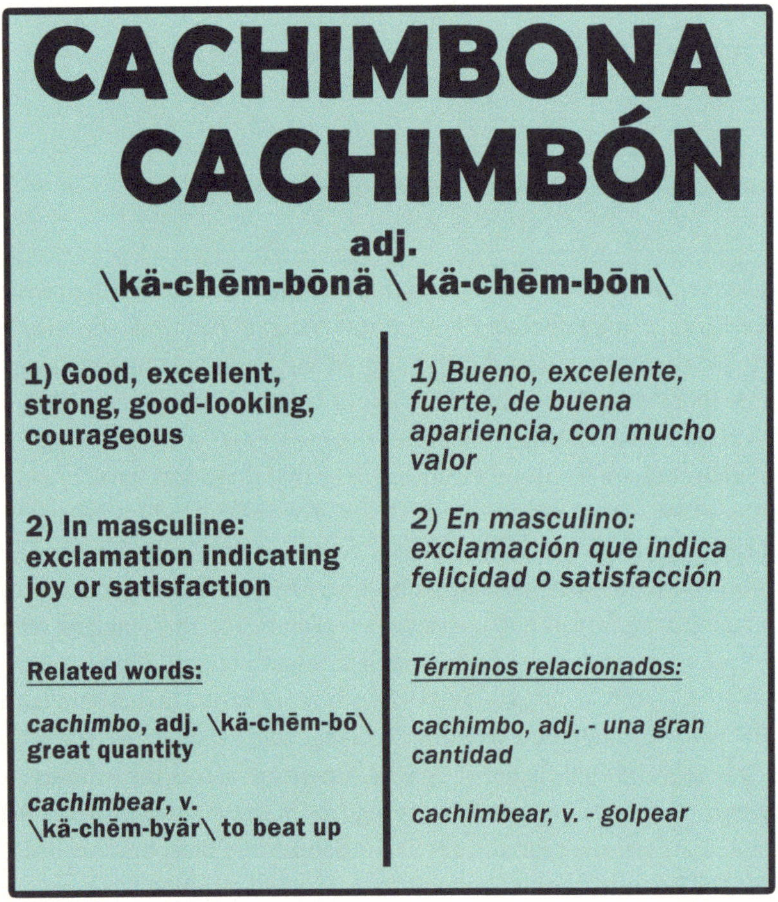

FIGURE 15. "Cachimbona/Cachimbón," by Víctor H. Interiano (Dichos de un bicho), 2020. Courtesy of Víctor H. Interiano.

creatives Veronica Meléndez and Kimberly Benavides, co-editors of the multivolume *La Horchata Zine*; and the artists featured in the 2020 exhibition *Connected Diaspora: Central American Visuality in the Age of Social Media*, curated by Meléndez. It also surveys the public humanities and community-engaged work conducted by my students and myself throughout the years. Through these projects involving artists, artivists, students, organizations, and community members, we have created a Salvadoran people's archive in and for the Washington, D.C. metropolitan area and the DMV.

Entre Mundos, *Home Stories*, and the Art of Public Humanities and Community-Engaged Work

I begin this epilogue by reflecting on my student-centered and student-created digital storytelling projects, *Entre Mundos / Between Worlds* and *Home Stories* (see Rodríguez, "Entre Mundos"). At the time of this writing, this digital storytelling archive comprises almost one hundred short videos representing various aspects of the Latinx, Central American, and Salvadoran diasporas in the Washington, D.C. metropolitan area and the DMV. Produced with students and community members, *Home Stories* and *Entre Mundos / Between Worlds* capture, memorialize, and elevate through the art of digital storytelling what I call, following the work of Sami Miranda, the art of everyday *we-is-placemaking* in the lives of migrants, neighborhoods, and communities in the DMV (Lambert and Hessler). I conceived the projects *Entre Mundos / Between Worlds* and *Home Stories* as a way to represent *aguacateros/as* like Juana from Mario Bencastro's short story "Las Ilusiones de Juana" / "Juana's Dreams," which, truth be told, inspired the writing of this book, *Avocado Dreams*. Examples of digital stories produced by my students at different points of the projects include "Amor a la distancia" (Ashley Escobar, 2018); "La Mount Pleasant" (Sheyla Alpach, Julia Blindon, and Caroline Nugent, 2015); and "Los 30" (Marissa Lang, 2010), all of which revisit the stories of Salvadoran, Central American, and Latinx immigrants in the DMV; capture the sounds, visuals, and foodscapes of the Mount Pleasant barrio being lost to gentrification; and engage the voices of poets and artivists like Quique Avilés, Frida Larios, Lilo González, and others documenting the long-standing presence of Salvadorans and Latinxs in the district, while official narratives continue to invisibilize them even today, as Arturo Arias so rightly claimed in his initial analysis of Central Americans in the United States (*Taking Their Word*).

Entre Mundos / Between Worlds and *Home Stories* consist of individual and group digital stories produced by students in a number of my classes at the University of Maryland, College Park. Based on particular topics covered in class, and particular interests through the years, student have produced digital stories of two to three minutes, including voice-overs, sound effects, music, and bilingual scripts. These stories focus on a wide array of topics about Latinx, Central American, and Salvadoran transnational migration, including: (1) personal narratives of family, home, and community; (2) im/migration processes; (3) immigrant service providers and organizations; (4) immigrant spaces such as restaurants, supermarkets, indoor soccer fields, and neighborhoods; (5) local transportation, businesses, and communication networks; (6) foodways and markets, including the ubiquitous pupusas, *queso duro* (hard cheese), and other nostalgic comestible products; (7) remittances; (8) violence, security, and sanctuary; (9) citizenship and (non)belonging in the United States; (10) family, gender, and motherhood.

All the digital stories use original material or Creative Commons assets to represent the local context of Salvadoran and Latinx transnational migration, and are recorded or captioned bilingually in Spanish and English. They were created using various technological formats, software, applications, and platforms. The production of each of the stories required multiple drafts, editing, and consultations with me (either face-to-face or electronically) to arrive at the final narrative captured in digital form. Videos have included tributes to parents; first-generation college graduations; homeland visits; infomercials with instructions on how to apply for asylum or Temporary Protected Status (TPS), or how to enroll in public schools; and shopping trips to local Latinx markets. Perhaps one of the most compelling digital stories is "The Life Line / El celular" (Chaska Hansen, 2014), representing a student's daily encounters in her dorm's stairwell with a Salvadoran housekeeper who every day at the same time takes her break on the stairs and calls her daughter in El Salvador, using her cell phone. In the story, the student reflects poignantly and critically on the material, symbolic, and affective ties mediated by the cell phone as the housekeeper calls her daughter. In another exemplary digital story, "The Salvadoran 7–11 / El 7–11 salvadoreño" (Ana R. Ventura-Molina, 2014), a student shows the impact of the Salvadoran demographic in northern Virginia as pupusas, *pan dulce* (sweet bread), and other Salvadoran products become staple items for sale at her local 7-Eleven. In "The Traveling Cheese / El queso viajero" (Madaí Berrios, 2014), another student recalls how her family eagerly awaits the return of her grandparents from El Salvador with the much-coveted *queso duro*, giving them a taste of home. In "The Hummingbird: Peace and Violence / El colibrí: La paz y la violencia" (Daniela Nevo, 2014), a student ponders the systemic and gendered violence of the civil war, which pushes a family friend into exile in the United States. Finally, in "Amor a la distancia," a student recounts the love story of her parents, who met in El Salvador as children during the civil war and after a long separation reconnected and married in the DMV. Through the years, many students have created visual stories about the Latinx and Salvadoran neighborhoods of Mount Pleasant and Langley Park (just outside of the University of Maryland), one of the most densely populated immigrant neighborhoods in the United States and home to many Latinx and Salvadoran students and their families. These are only a few examples of the critical digital stories produced by my students in *Entre Mundos / Between Worlds*, most of which are available for viewing online. Some of these digital stories also received a public screening on May 3, 2014, on the main stage of the Rasmuson Theater at the Smithsonian Institution's National Museum of the American Indian (figure 16).

Produced as final projects for my Spring 2014 class on Salvadoran transmigration, the students' collaborative digital stories presented at the Smithsonian covered a range of topics on Salvadoran migration history, neighborhoods, remittance-sending practices, hometown associations, education, and racial identity. The group digital stories included: "Digital Stories of Transnationalism and Transmigration: El Salvador to D.C. / Historias digitales del transnacionalismo y de la transmigración de El Salvador a D.C." (Ryan Amstrong, Leandra Bitterfeld, Elise Marengo, and Ana R. Ventura-Molina), a behind-the-scenes student-produced documentary on the making of *Entre Mundos / Between Worlds*; "Vignettes of Salvadoran Transmigration / Viñetas de la transmigración salvadoreña" (Yenia Cardozo Gómez, Chaska Hansen, and Alex Moyer), an overview of Salvadoran migration to the United States from the nineteenth century

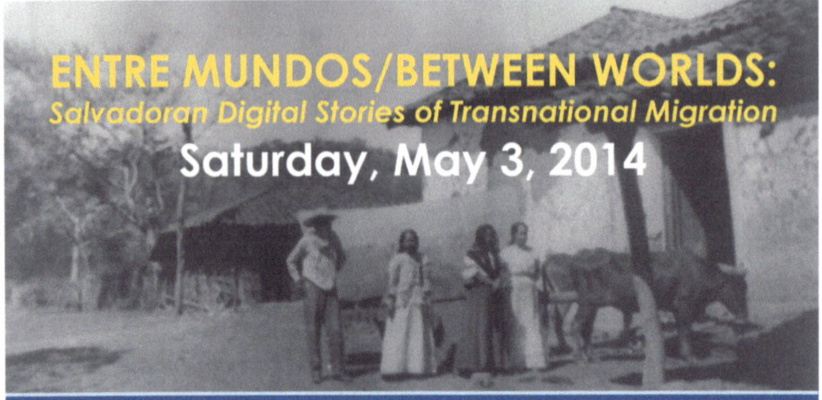

3 p.m.-4:30 p.m., Rasmuson Theater
National Museum of the American Indian
4th Street & Independence Avenue, S.W.

Join the Smithsonian Latino Center and the University of Maryland for a student-led program that combines digital media with live performance to share stories from the third-largest Latino community in the United States—Salvadoran Americans. Organized with Professor Ana Patricia Rodríguez, student presentations will bring to life the history and context of Salvadoran migrations since the 19th century into the present. Theater doors will open at 2:30 p.m. First come, first seated. This FREE program will be webcast live!

View it here:
http://latino.si.edu/newsevents/webcasts.htm

The nearest Metro station is L'Enfant Plaza (Orange, Blue, Green, and Yellow Lines). For more information call (202) 633-0925 or email woodamanr@si.edu. Image courtesy of the Library of Congress.

FIGURE 16. Flyer for the public presentation of *Entre Mundos / Between Worlds* at the National Museum of the American Indian, Smithsonian Institution, 2014. Courtesy of author.

to the present through fictionalized vignettes; "In Search of Security: Salvadoran Immigration and Its Transnational Routes / En búsqueda de seguridad: La inmigración salvadoreña y sus rutas transnacionales" (Rebecca Dixon, Gerardo González-Vasquez, and Daniela Nevo), an exposé of the migratory routes taken by Salvadoran transmigrants as they travel to the United States by train, plane, and foot; "The Salvador Flavor of Mount Pleasant / El sabor salvadoreño de la Mount Pleasant" (Katie Clark, Marcela de Campos, and Sandra Shaker), a virtual tour of Mount Pleasant, the historical epicenter of Salvadoran migration to the Washington, D.C. metropolitan area, and its ever-changing character as it undergoes gentrification; "The Kings of Remittances: Salvadorans in the Washington, D.C. Area / Los reyes de las remesas: Salvadoreños en el área de Washington, D.C." (Astrid Díaz, Edwin González, and Alexandra Reyes), a close-up look at remittances, the transnational economic pillar of Salvadoran communities in the United States and El Salvador; "Transnational Foundations: Destination El Salvador / Fundaciones transnacionales: Destino El Salvador" (Julia Navarro, Jasmine Rivas, and Rocio Rosa), a reflection on how Salvadoran immigrants maintain ties with their hometowns, particularly Santa Teresa and Mogotillo; "Empty Desk: The Process of Registering International Students / Pupitre vacío: El proceso de matricular estudiantes internacionales" (Madaí Berrios, José Granados, and Andrea Knowles), a fictional account that exposes the difficulties of enrolling newcomer immigrant students in the Prince George's County Public Schools, Maryland; and "Trigueña/o: Culture of Three / Trigueña/o: Cultura de tres" (Nataly Cruz-Castillo, Kimberly Hall, and Sharon Pérez Ferreras), an exploration of racial identity in El Salvador and Latin America through a reflection on the word *trigueña/o*, an ethnoracial category erasing Blackness and Indigeneity.

With these digital stories, my students and I sought to understand the workings of transnationalism in the form of "real," material, affective, and symbolic practices, and to ponder critical questions on what it means to live in between nations, territories, cultures, and languages. We wanted to observe and represent local examples of Salvadoran transnational migration and translocation. Ultimately, our mission was to work with community partners to produce original research on Salvadoran transnational migration, particularly in our local area—in other words, to counter the invisibility of Salvadorans with visual media. At the public presentation at the Smithsonian, students not only presented their digital stories but also participated in a Q and A session, capably responding to questions from the audience regarding their work and experience producing the digital stories. In their own right, my students became producers (and not merely consumers) of digital media, knowledge, and public scholarship about the Latinx, Central American, and Salvadoran diasporas in the DMV.

Following various models of digital storytelling, *Entre Mundos / Between Worlds* developed a virtual space for the collecting, representing, digitizing, and archiving of stories of Salvadoran transnational migration. This project has gone on to take different iterations in other classes, including the *Home Stories* project, for which we were awarded a National Endowment for the Humanities Access Grant in 2016. These projects have yielded almost one hundred digital stories on the formation, practices, and processes of the Salvadoran and Central American transnational migration, diaspora, and home/land in the Washington, D.C. metropolitan area, most of which are available for viewing at the class Vimeo site by any parties interested in transnational migration.

Connected Diasporas and *La Horchata Zine*

In fall 2020, amid the COVID-19 pandemic, I also co-organized and coordinated the *Connected Diaspora: Central American Visuality in the Age of Social Media* art exhibition at the Stamp Gallery of the University of Maryland, College Park (figure 17). Curated by Veronica Meléndez, the exhibition featured the work of sixteen U.S. Central American artists, some from the DMV. Featured artists included Eddy Leonel Aldana, Kimberly Benavides, Erick Antonio Benitez, Jessy DeSantis, Xiomara Garay, Galileo Gonzalez, Celea Guevara, Kimberly LaVonne, Glenda Lissette, Kiara Aileen Machado, Juan Madrid, Julia Mata, Veronica Meléndez, Dennissé Carlota Nieto Zelaya, Elizabeth Fernanda Rodríguez, and Johanna Toruño. The exhibition showcased "pieces in different mediums, styles, and materials that ranged from delicate ceramic sculptures to large scale paintings to digital art and explored images of displacement, war, and trauma, as well as everyday life, nature, and joy" (Meléndez, *Connected Diaspora* proposal). Along with the exhibition, we offered a series of online keynote and artist talks by Salvadoran art historians and practitioners Mauricio E. Ramírez, Beatriz Cortez, and Muriel Hasbun, as well as an online *La Horchata* zine-making workshop led by Meléndez. For the opening of the exhibition, we held an outdoor, public event with a DJ dance party in Lamont Plaza NW in the Mount Pleasant neighborhood, which was also live streamed via Zoom.

Meléndez and Benavides also co-edit *La Horchata Zine*, self-described as "an arts publication featuring creatives from the Central American

FIGURE 17. *Connected Diaspora* exhibition, featuring *Centro* by Kiara Aileen Machado, 2019, and work by other artists. University of Maryland, College Park, September 22–December 12, 2020. Photo courtesy of author.

diaspora and from Central America, self-published in Washington, D.C. and Troy, NY." Named after the famed drink of ground morro seeds and milk that appears on all the covers of the zine, the DIY-fashioned publication features photography, graphic design, paintings, engravings, woodcuts, poetry, prose, vignettes, oral histories, interviews, reflections, *testimonios*, video QR codes, and mixed-media art inspired by Central American lived experiences, identities, traditions, heritage, history, and imagery. Articles, too, cover such topics as migration, family, memory, intergenerational trauma, colorism, (internalized) racism, and other intersectional oppressions bearing down on Central American diasporas. According to Raquel Reichard of *Remezcla*, "just as there are several variations of horchata, the popular Latin American beverage the publication is named after, the duo believe Central American artists bring different experiences, histories, cultures, identities, and talents that deserve to live and be seen in art spaces."

Reviews of the zine praise it for creating a much-needed culturally affirming platform to showcase Central American artists' work (Reichard); entering "the wider conversation of Latin American art," which tends to exclude all things Central American (Díaz-Hurtado and Contreras); and pushing back against stereotypes, "making space outside of traditional publishing for Latinx people to express their sexualities, struggles, autonomy, and triumphs in all the complexity that they deserve—by telling their stories on their own terms" (De la Luz). The viewing and making of zines can also be therapeutic, as when, during the COVID-19 pandemic lockdown, I invited Meléndez to one of my online U.S. Central American literature and culture classes to talk about her work and lead us through a zine-making session on Zoom. Materials in hand, the students and I engaged Meléndez in an hour of reflection on placemaking and home. Not only did my students learn firsthand about the art of making zines from Meléndez, but they were also able to engage zines as a creative practice and "form of therapy" (De la Luz).

Flipping through the issues of *La Horchata Zine* (ten in total as of 2024), readers find images, stories, and *testimonios*, which conjure memories and reflections through colors, words, and objects of places near and far, familiar and unfamiliar, realistic and abstract. In *La Horchata en los tiempos de cuarentena* (Horchata in Times of Quarantine), issue 8 (2020–21), the scholar and oral historian José Alfredo Centeno-Meléndez poignantly contributes a visual snapshot of doña Vásquez, a domestic worker residing in Langley Park, who, at 3:05 p.m. on Thursday, May 7, 2020, was at work cleaning buildings as COVID-19 spread all around her. Capturing a moment in time, Centeno-Meléndez captioned the photo: "193 new cases in Washington, D.C.; 1,213 in Maryland; 1,314 in Virginia" ("Thursday"). In a brief *testimonio* accompanied by a QR code with more information, doña Rosa, another essential worker interviewed by Centeno-Meléndez, says: "Estamos lejos de nuestro país. Tenemos nuestra familia que, quiérase o no, tenemos que salir adelante con pandemia o sin pandemia. Entonces tenemos que ir a esos lugares de trabajo por nuestras familias y por nosotros mismos" (We are far from our country. We have family and, whether we like it or not, we have to go on, with or without the pandemic. So, we have to go to those places to work for our families and for ourselves).

La Horchata Zine, with contributions from Centeno-Meléndez and other creatives from the DMV and the wider Central American diaspora in the United States, opens a space for mourning, remembrance, and reflection for the many Salvadorans who day in and day out went to work and kept their city and society functioning, *haciendo de todo* (doing everything) to survive, persist, and prevail during the pandemic, as they have done for so many decades. Featured work in *La Horchata Zine* and the *Connected Diaspora* exhibition paid homage to these unsung heroes, who especially during the COVID-19 pandemic were *cachimbonxs,* working tirelessly to keep the DMV running safely for the general population. During the lockdown, it was primarily African American, Latinx, and Central American (including Salvadoran) essential workers who kept local economies going, despite great risks to themselves and their communities (Olivo et al.). Without them, cities like Washington would have simply come to a standstill, as portrayed in the 2004 film *A Day Without a Mexican,* directed by Sergio Arau. This book recognizes that Central Americans and Salvadorans in the United States are central to the economy, body politic, and well-being of the DMV, the United States, and the Americas. Shining a light on their communities, Meléndez and Benavides, with *La Horchata Zine,* represent a new generation of *cachimbonxs,* young creatives who dare to create dangerously, as Danticat would have it, by working with new media and forms, telling new diasporic stories, and courageously making visible Central American and Salvadoran life and culture in the Washington, D.C. metropolitan area. Like the other artists discussed throughout this book, they produce an art of unforgetting, unsilencing, and prevailing (Avilés, "Canción"), and create experimental narrative and aesthetic spaces that push the boundaries of traditional representations of the Salvadoran diaspora. These creatives demonstrate the true *cachimbonx* spirit, courage, and resilience, as Matías Romero defines it in the *Diccionario de salvadoreñismos.*

Cachimbonx Poetics and Visuality in the DMV

Along similar lines, northern Virginia–based Salvadoran Claudia Rojas writes as a *poeta* and community advocate for immigrant rights. Born in El Salvador and raised in the Washington, D.C. metropolitan area as a TPS recipient, she has published her work online and in various literary journals and magazines (Rojas, artist website). Her poem "Family Detention Center" imagines an immigrant mother as "she presses her round face between the metal bars" in a detention center to watch her son march to school under the watchful eye of an immigration officer. The mother in

Rojas's poem ponders, "this place / could / be / like / home, / almost. / Nevermind / the food tastes the same / or the son who has stopped playing / the same. / The son, / a child growing up in a prison." Many of Rojas's poems reflect on the trope of illegality ascribed to Salvadoran migrants (Padilla, *From Threatening Guerrillas*), bringing that condition back to her own personal experience as a tenuous TPS recipient. In "Temporary," perhaps recalling her own border-crossing as a child, she writes about "things my body doesn't remember now: / sardine cans. / eating a man's last tangerine. / shrubs and weeds. / asking to catch a bunny for dinner. / a bridge at dusk. / another night, still not there."

In her online poem "Residence," Rojas creates a concrete, visual poem (à la E. E. Cummings), using letters and words to form the image of the flag of the United States. For the flagpole, she vertically aligns letters and words in one column, a single word or letter on each row: "(We) We (are) are (so) so (like) like (A) A (M) M (E) E (R) R (I) I (C) C (A) A (no) no (one) one (sees) sees ( ) us." This vertical line challenges Western (imperialist?) modes of reading from left to right, creating an echo chamber of letters and hiding the meaning of the line. Rojas challenges readers to see that the *we* that is the subject of the poem—perhaps immigrants and Salvadorans—exists (hides) in plain sight because no one attempts to see them. To the right of this vertical line, additional words are arranged in the shape of the stars and stripes of the flag, but with the space of the white stars representing the fifty states replaced by a blank, empty space, perhaps calling attention to the vacuous nature of U.S. nationalist and nativist ideologies. Where the American flag has thirteen stripes (seven red, six white), there are seven lines of text, double-spaced so as to also form the white stripes. Each line documents the disappearance of migrants: "DMV centers will see and take less of us. . . . The postage office will see less of us. . . . Immigration services will not eat up our savings. . . . Daughters and sons won't fight out-of-state-tuition in their home state." The poetic voice seems to say that as the needs and rights of immigrants are invisibilized, left unattended, or outright abolished, the United States loses its cherished foundational values and diminishes in stature. In yet another poem, "My Bones Said 'Write This Poem,'" Rojas writes of the "morning after / Election Day [2016] and I can't name this feeling," for fear of what is to come, because, as she tells us, "Today I know nothing / bad ever happens to the bad."

Like Rojas, the Maryland-based Salvadoran artist and painter Rafael Rodríguez Molina is part of the great migration wave of accompanied and unaccompanied child migrants in the twenty-first century (Briggs). Also, like Pedro in Lilo González's song "Las historias prohibidas de Pedro y Tyrone," discussed in chapter 3, Rodríguez Molina migrated unaccompanied as a teenager from El Salvador and resides in Prince George's County, where he graduated from high school and began to develop as an artist (M. González).[1] According to the artist statement at his website, "The art that he creates not only reflects his life as an individual but also the struggles of many other immigrants in this country who work hard towards their dreams." His work is representative of what I call a DMV *cachimbonx* aesthetics—representing different stages of his life, his peers, his family, and members of his community, using various expressive, artistic genres from painting to performance art, as we shall see. He has produced works in various forms, styles, and media, including oil, acrylic, sculpture, pencil drawing, and sketches. A series of oil paintings, for example, represent his own migration journey, detention in the infamous *hieleras* (iceboxes), and immigration court proceedings and hearings. A constant theme in his work is his migratory passage through Mexico and the labyrinthine court system that migrants must navigate for a chance to gain legal resident status in the United States. In his self-portrait *My Decade in a Mugshot* (2023; oil on collaged canvas, 40 × 30 inches), he captures an image of his younger self surrounded by scraps of documents, forms, letters, money order receipts, and confirmation slips from U.S. Citizenship and Immigration Services communications. The collage of documents creates an entangling paper trail of his time in the immigration court system and represents the criminalization of migrants as they seek asylum, to which the title of the image painfully alludes (figure 18).

Indeed, according to Rodríguez Molina's artist statement:

> My artwork explores the criminalization of undocumented immigrants, which is mostly based on my own experiences as an undocumented immigrant. Most of my ideas for my artwork come from a combination of memories of my journey when I came to the United States and the emotions that I feel while facing present obstacles. My artwork narrates the stories of many other immigrants with similar experiences. We face many challenges starting the day that we decide to leave everything behind to

go to an unknown land and immerse ourselves in a different culture. We leave our beloved homes in search of a life where we can at least have basic human needs. Once we arrive at the "land of dreams," we are criminalized and the system names us as "Illegal Aliens," as if we are from another planet. Moving from one place to another to look for a better life should be a fundamental human right. However, the system is designed to keep us out, but we are here and we have always been here.

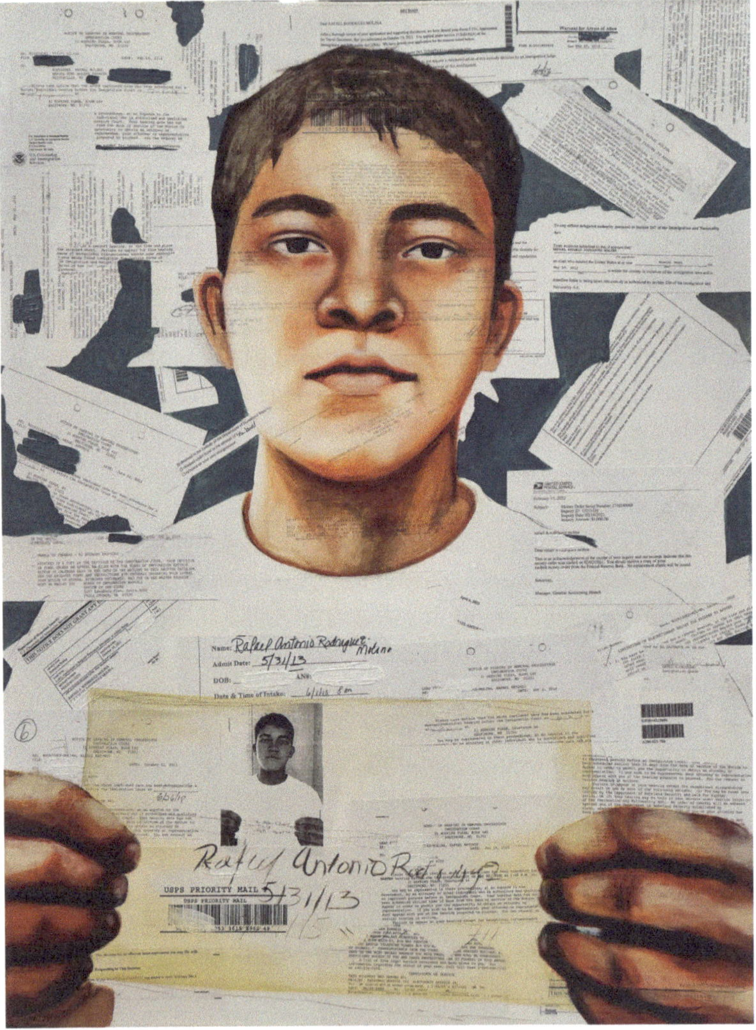

FIGURE 18. *My Decade in a Mugshot*, by Rafael Rodríguez Molina, 2023. Courtesy of Rafael Rodríguez Molina.

In a poignant image of contemporary family migration and the search for "a better life" and safe haven, Rodríguez Molina's painting *Madre Inmigrante / Immigrant Mother* (2018; acrylic on canvas, 5 × 3 feet) represents a mother holding a child in her arms while standing in the middle of the desert, surrounded by what could be saguaros and brush under a cloudy blue sky (figure 19).

Evoking the naturalistic realism of Italian Renaissance landscape paintings, with their human figures in the foreground against a background that produces a semblance of depth (think of the *Mona Lisa* by Leonardo da Vinci), Rodríguez Molina's *Madre Inmigrante* seems to recall classical images of the Madonna and Child. In Rodríguez Molina's rendition, the immigrant mother tightly clasps her barely clad son with one arm and raises the other arm with open palm in the air as if in prayer. She looks up to the sky, while her toddler son looks directly out of the painting at an unseen spectator. Mother and son are alone and unaccompanied in the desert. Wearing an oxidated-green robe in the desert, the immigrant mother also conjures up the image of the Statue of Liberty, with her raised torch, as represented in González's "Pedro and Tyrone." While González's song notes that the torch was "much too high" for Pedro to reach, Rodríguez Molina's painting suspends the mother's arm/torch high in the air. If the mother is to reach her destination with her child, she will do so with her own strength, will, and, perhaps, prayers. So too, are this immigrant Madonna and son courageous *cachimbonxs*, facing adversities and risking their lives crossing the desert (M. Romero 91). Indeed, in the twenty-first century, migrants, asylum seekers, and refugees fleeing deadly conditions in order to have a chance at life are the model of *cachimbón* survivance. Read in this light, Rodríguez Molina's painting may signify the migrant search for refuge and freedom, the lasting bond between im/migrant mothers and children, the reunification of separated families, and the resilient spirit of migrants crossing (and surviving) the desert and border. At the same time, following Lauren Berlant's trope of the infantilization of immigrants in the American Dream narrative, the image of the child migrant in Rodríguez Molina's painting may also allude to the scapegoating of migrants as potential public charges, anchor babies, and "illegal" and illegible subjects, lacking voice, visibility, and, thus, citizenship in the national imaginary (Padilla, *From Threatening Guerrillas*).

Following Renaissance iconography, the image could also be read as recalling the Assumption of Mary—that is, the im/migrant mother and

FIGURE 19. *Madre Inmigrante / Immigrant Mother*, by Rafael Rodríguez Molina, 2018. Courtesy of Rafael Rodríguez Molina.

her son, having died in the desert, are being lifted into heaven. The significance of the polysemic image of mother and child is left, thus, to the beholder to interpret. The painting seems to ask: Will the im/migrant mother and child live or die? How will they survive? What can be done to ensure their safe passage? What immigration policies would make that possible? There is no doubt that Rodríguez Molina's *Madre Inmigrante* calls on us to think deeply about the suffering endured by migrant families and children who attempt to cross multiple borders from the South, seeking safe haven in northern countries. The painting produces an empathetic space for spectators to question the reasons why people cross deserts by foot, atop trains, and in caravans to reach the North, pushing their human limits, risking their lives, and sometimes even dying in the process. The painting invites viewers to envision the conditions that force people to migrate and to ponder humane solutions for displacement and migration in the twenty-first century. Indeed, Rodríguez Molina hopes that his artwork "change[s] the perspective of Latinos or Salvadorans in general, about the way we see ourselves as undocumented immigrants in the U.S." (M. González).

In a breakout performance on April 10, 2024, at the University of Maryland, College Park, where, at the time, he was a student completing a bachelor's degree with honors in studio art (2025), Rodríguez Molina courageously proposed a solution to the chains of undocumented immigration. Once an undocumented immigrant himself, he sought in this performance piece to embody and shatter the internalized oppressions that living undocumented in the United States signifies for many. In his written statement for the performance, he explained: "This performance intends to express the frustration created by the systemic criminalization of people. The themes of resistance and struggle with oppression can resonate with multiple marginalized communities. In this case, the piece aims to reflect the criminalization of immigrants, with a focus on undocumented people living in the United States. The performance is an expression toward a system that dehumanizes others." For the public performance, he constructed a large block of cement with embedded chains that he locked to his ankles. Over the course of an entire day, from 10:00 a.m. to past sundown, he chipped away at the cement block with a hammer. He ate nothing and drank very little water as the midday sun bore down on him and his exhaustion depleted his energies. In the late afternoon, his brother (a construction worker), a family friend, and a professor and student colleagues helped him hammer away at the block. In the mode of Archbishop (San) Óscar A. Romero's practice of accompaniment, whereby witnesses are called to stand and walk with the oppressed, a group of us spectators accompanied him, watching, sitting, and standing vigilantly throughout the day in case he needed assistance. Finally, at approximately 9:00 p.m., with the help of his brother and family friend, he was able to break free, only to go home in pain, exhaustion, and shock, not to sleep that night. In conversation months after the event, Rodríguez Molina explained that breaking himself from the cement block was a way to deal with the lingering trauma of migrating unaccompanied at a young age, for which art has been healing, expressive, and communal (figures 20 and 21).

Just as on the day of his performance spectators accompanied Rodríguez Molina, so, too, he recognizes that in all of his work he accompanies others like himself who have been and are migrants in the United States. In his work, he pays special homage to the migrants, but in particular the Central American and Salvadoran *choleros* and *choleras*, who work hard in their country and in diaspora and, by default, have always been *cachimbonx*, people willing to rise to challenges, meet adversities, and risk their lives in order to survive, much like himself and his family. As testament to this *cachimbón* spirit of survivance, Rodríguez Molina pays tribute to his eldest brother in another painting, *Portrait of José Rodríguez* (2024; oil on canvas, 7 × 4 feet; faces are blurred by the author to protect the identity of the subject). José helped him immigrate to the United States and has supported him through the years, providing him with shelter and the means to pursue his dream of an education. Rodríguez Molina produced the larger-than-life-size painting for the *Midpoint Exhibition* at the University of Maryland in December 2024, as part of his honors notation in studio art. In the caption, he describes his brother as a construction worker and titan of the Salvadoran migration (figure 22).

The artist goes on to say that "the painting seeks to honor the contributions of the workers, especially immigrants, to the U.S. economy. These workers are often unrecognized and deemed less important. The dimensions of this painting are intended to . . . [give] my brother the space he deserves." It is not an exaggeration to say that José Rodríguez, like so many immigrant workers throughout the DMV, Maryland, and the entire United States, is a titan of labor, standing tall despite an industry that often mistreats, undervalues, and erases them. I hope that someday Rafael

FIGURE 20. *Block and Figure 1,* by Rafael Rodríguez Molina, 2018. Courtesy of Rafael Rodríguez Molina, 2024.

FIGURE 21. Rafael Rodríguez Molina breaks out of block of oppression at the University of Maryland, College Park, April 10, 2024. Photo courtesy of author.

FIGURE 22. *Portrait of José Rodríguez,* by Rafael Rodríguez Molina. University of Maryland, College Park, December 6, 2024. Photo courtesy of author.

Rodríguez Molina will paint many such portraits and create a gallery of titans, honoring not just the labor but the lives of migrants dispersed across the Americas and beyond.

Closing Words

In examining the work of Rafael Rodríguez Molina, Claudia Rojas, Kimberly Benavides and Veronica Meléndez, Quique Avilés, Mario Bencastro, Culture Clash, Lilo González, Frida Larios, and so many other writers, artists, and creatives, including my own students, I hope to have shown how Salvadorans remake their lives and leave their creative mark across the Washington, D.C. metropolitan area and the DMV. While discourses of Central American and Salvadoran invisibility have reified the erasure of Central Americans in the United States, or presented them as disparaged *salvatrucos/as, choleros/as,* and *aguacateros/as* from s*hole countries, we need to find other means and methods to make visible the material, social, and cultural value of the Central American and Salvadoran diasporas in the United States through acts of visual disobedience and decolonization, as the *cachimbona* Salvi art historian Kency Cornejo so valiantly proposes.

As highlighted in this epilogue, the brave (read: *cachimbonx*) cultural imaginary associated with the artists of the Central American and Salvadoran diasporas, exemplified by the *Connected Diaspora* exhibition, *La Horchata Zine* collective, and the work of the artists mentioned here, serves as a living archive of the struggles for representation, memory, voice, and visibility of the Central American and Salvadoran diasporas. This artwork, literature, and artivism should make us question why Central American children, women, and men are driven out of their homelands into perilous migrations, and how art can "create dangerously," represent courageously, and remake the world with art. Ultimately, this creative work attempts to build a space for greater critical understanding and cognitive empathy for Central Americans facing great precarity in their homelands and even greater harm and injury migrating through vast territories. While unaccompaniment (migrating alone and without supports) has become a way of life for many, we are called, in the words and practice of the slain archbishop Romero, to accompany and bear witness to the root causes of migration in Central America—or, as he put it, to "estar presente en este campo de la realida" (remain present in people's reality) (169). Now, more than ever, art must be present in people's lived realities and must be recognized as a worldmaking endeavor. Indeed, Rojas, Rodríguez Molina, *La Horchata Zine* collective, and others whose work is examined here might be said to "create dangerously," courageously, and purposefully. Not only do they provide insights into the Central American and Salvadoran diasporas in the DMV, but they also create new ways of being Central American and Salvadoran in diaspora.

NOTES

INTRODUCTION

1. I am indebted to Paul Gilroy (1993) for giving us the language to talk about the roots and routes of diasporas.
2. The terms Latino, Latina, and Latinx are used interchangeably throughout this book. When referring to or citing the work of scholars, I use their terms. I do not use the term Hispanic.
3. Except where otherwise indicated, the translations from Spanish to English in this book are my own. I am grateful to the Los Angeles–based Salvi creative Víctor H. Interiano (known online as Dichos de un Bicho) for producing a meme based on the quote from Argueta's novel, which captures the essence of my own avocado dreams, or dreams of a homeland, peppered with images from La Palma. Interiano also kindly provided images of Salvadoran idiomatic expressions from his *Salvi Dictionary*, which are used to organize ideas, raciolinguistic concepts, and cultural tropes throughout this book.
4. At the time of this writing, Central American families and children continue to migrate en masse to the United States and areas like the DMV from the so-called Northern Triangle (El Salvador, Guatemala, and Honduras), due to violence, state repression, insecurity, scarcity, climate change, and overall inhospitable living conditions in their home countries. In their 2015 book *Centroamérica en la mira: La migración en su relación con el desarrollo y las oportunidades para el cambio* (*Confronting the Challenges of Migration and Development in Central America*), Manuel Orozco and Julia Yansura of the Washington-based organization Inter-American Dialogue attribute mass migration from the region to the ever-increasing levels of social and political violence; the rise in organized and state crime; high levels of socioeconomic and political insecurity; lack of employment and educational opportunities, especially for the youth; demand

for labor in places like the United States; and, to some extent, the desire for family reunification (*Centroamérica en la mira* 48). While migrants seek material well-being for themselves and their extended families, they also conceive of the American Dream as a promise of survival, security, and family reunification.

5. In *Visual Disobedience: Art and Decoloniality in Central America*, the U.S. Salvadoran art historian Kency Cornejo examines the Salvadoran artist Catalina del Cid's 2012 multimedia installation *Electrodomésticos + Regalos = Amor* (Electrical appliances + gifts = love). In the piece, the artist reproduces a humble home entertainment media center with shelving filled with gifts sent by family members who have migrated. Almost a shrine to the remittance senders, the stand showcases gifts of TVs, electronics, brand-name sneakers, and fancy toys, among other items. Taken as signs of love and emotional support, the material goods, however, cannot fill the emotional gaps produced by the distance and absence of loved ones. As Cornejo explains, the installation represents "the emotional traumas between separated families and their struggles to maintain loving connections despite the distance brought on by forced migration" (162–63).
6. Here, and whenever I use the word *dirt* in this book, I am making reference to Jeanine Cummins's 2020 novel *American Dirt*, which has caused great harm to Central American migrants and allies; readers, scholars, and sympathizers of Central American migration; and U.S. Central American studies as a whole. While *American Dirt* purports to tell the story of Mexican and Central American migration, it has been heavily critiqued for its appropriation of other writers' texts; lack of rigorous contextualization; exploitation of migrant narratives; and deployment of what Latinx writer Myriam Gurba calls "trauma porn." Cummins's novel triggered the social movement #DignidadLiteraria (Literary Dignity), which challenged stereotypical representations in the novel and exposed racial inequities in mainstream publishing.
7. Note the use of Náhuat when I refer to the Mesoamerican language spoken or under revitalization in parts of El Salvador and beyond, and Nawat in reference to people and communities, as in Nawat people. The appellation Náhua-Pipil is no longer used by Indigenous communities in El Salvador. Most Nawat people or speakers of the Náhuat language identify by the geographic areas, towns, or *cantones* in which they reside. I am indebted to Dr. Karina Zelaya (2023), a Náhuat language learner, for clarifying these terms.
8. Avilés is a local Salvadoran poet, performance artist, and community activist who emigrated from El Salvador to Washington in 1980, at the age of fifteen. In the late 1980s, Avilés cofounded and directed the theater collective LatiNegro, which recruited local Latino and African American youths to perform in theaters, schools, prisons, universities, and communities. In 1999, he cofounded Sol & Soul, a nonprofit arts organization, which continued the work of LatiNegro in conducting workshops with young performers in the District of Columbia, collaborating with community groups and organizing theater events in the district for local and visiting actors. Avilés continues to perform his mixed-media work

on- and offstage, writing, producing, and acting in pieces like *Caminata* (2003, 2004), a travel narrative about the immigrant life of Salvadorans, Russians, Africans, Iraqis, and others whose lives intersect in Washington, D.C. Addressing issues of race, class, gender, and identity, among other things, his performance pieces and poetry often incorporate life narratives, voices, and experiences of immigrants and everyday folks from local neighborhoods. His story is told in two groundbreaking films about Salvadorans in the DMV: *La Manplesa* (2021) and *Las muertes más bellas del mundo* (2024).

9. In short, the Zero Tolerance Policy, initiated by the Trump administration, criminalized undocumented entry into the United States; the Public Charge Rule restricted authorized immigrants receiving public assistance from seeking permanent resident status, readjusting their status, or simply gaining entry to the United States; the Remain in Mexico Plan or MPP forced migrants to remain in border towns in Mexico while they waited for asylum court hearings; the revocation of 1997 *Flores* settlement would lift the twenty-day limit for holding migrant children in detention centers and rescind other minimal protections; and the rescission of TPS for Salvadorans, Hondurans, and others would force migrants to return to their countries of origin.

CHAPTER 1

1. These figures do not account for the large number of undocumented Latina/o/x immigrants (many of whom are Central Americans, especially Salvadorans) residing in the region.
2. Parada was born and raised in Virginia and has roots in San Miguel, El Salvador. She has worked as a statistician for the Office of Child Care in the Administration for Children and Families in the state of Virginia. She is also a community advocate for *canton* El Brazo, a rural Indigenous community in San Miguel, where she raises support for medical, educational, and housing needs for community members.
3. The ethnoracial terms *ladina* or *ladino* in El Salvador refer to westernized persons of predominantly mixed Spanish and Indigenous descent. The category is almost synonymous with *mestizo/a*, but carries more assimilationist connotations.
4. This poem is an excerpt from Quique Avilés's earlier monologue *The Return of Loco Culebra / Crazy Snake*, which he performed in March 2019 at GALA Hispanic Theatre in Washington, D.C.

CHAPTER 2

1. In "Domestication and Significance of *Persea americana*, the Avocado, in Mesoamerica," Amanda J. Landon asserts that the avocado was of great importance in Maya horticulture, cosmology, and symbology. The avocado glyph K'ank'in' represents the fourteenth Classic Maya month and is also associated with great

cities like Quiriguá in Honduras and Pusilhá in present-day Belize (74). Used as early as 8000–7000 BCE and domesticated around 5000 BCE (Galindo-Tovar et al. 325), the *ahuacatl*, which in Náhuatl means testicle, was thought to "transfer that strength to whoever eats it" and was an important component of the Mesoamerican diet (Landon 65). Although it seems to have originated in Africa, the avocado migrated to the Americas, acclimatizing well to "the more hospitable habitats of Mesoamerica" (Galindo-Tovar et al. 326). In "The Avocado (*Persea americana*, Lauraceae) Crop in Mesoamerica: 10,000 Years of History," María Elena Galindo-Tovar and colleagues explain that the avocado tree is one of the sacred trees described in the creation story in the *Popul Vuh*. Evidence has been found that the Maya "had used avocado since ancient times" (326–27). The ancestors, like Lady Kanal-Ikal (King Pacal's mother), were believed to be reborn in trees like the avocado; hence, the Maya cultivated avocado and other trees in their gardens and orchards, and over "the graves of relatives" (Landon 64). Using state-of-the-art geographic information system (GIS) visualizations, Alan Farahani and colleagues, in "Identifying 'Plantscapes' at the Classic Maya Village of Joya de Cerén, El Salvador," show that the remains of avocado trees were found at the seventh-century CE site, providing evidence of "everyday food production and consumption" (981); according to them, "the core of Classic Maya plant cultivation and cuisine" included maize, manioc, guava, avocado (*Persea americana Mill.*), and squash (*Cucurbita pepo L.*) (985). Based on these findings and the layout of crops and gardens, they tell the story of a self-sustaining community and their lifestyle at the time when the volcanic caldera erupted. Farahani and colleagues point to "a high concentration of living, unharvested avocado fruit [that] suggests that avocado trees grew there, along with a standing cacao tree" (994), perhaps used to honor their ancestors. Larios's *The Village That Was Buried by an Erupting Volcano* and her pictoglyphs draw from rich archaeological and horticultural research in the Joya de Cerén region.

2. In much U.S. Central American literature, there is no representation of Blackness, and, if there is mention of Indigeneity, it is most likely from the positionality of Indigenismo. There is little critique of the absence or erasure of Blackness and Indigeneity, to which Paul Joseph López Oro alerts readers ("Refashioning").

CHAPTER 3

1. To the best of my knowledge, the play has not been produced and performed in its entirety outside of this Washington production, which featured Culture Clash members Richard Montoya and Ric Salinas (without fellow member and Salvadoran Chicano Herbert Sigüenza).
2. Lilo González and Los de la Mount Pleasant compose and perform songs that chronicle the lives and events of Latinos/as in the Mount Pleasant neighborhood

of Washington, D.C. Born in Armenia, El Salvador, González immigrated to the United States in 1981, arriving in the Washington area—or, to be more exact, the Columbia Heights and Mount Pleasant neighborhoods, after which the group is named. González and his musical group work with the Latino community in Washington, D.C., playing a mix of folk music, cumbia, salsa, tango, and reggae at local fundraising events in the United States and El Salvador.

3. Avilés's work is radical in that it rejects, resists, and pushes against normative, prescriptive grammar structures in Spanish. He especially rejects the use of accent marks in translanguaging.

CHAPTER 4

1. Avilés's spoken word and performance repertoire includes *Salvatrucans*, *The Other Two* (*Los otros dos*), *Latinhood* (*Latinez*), *Chaos Standing* (*El caos de pie*), *Caminata: A Walk Through Immigrant America* (*Caminata: Pasos a través de la América inmigrante*), *Rehab*, *El canuto del rock* (The Rock Joint), *The Children of Latinia* (*Los hijos de Latinia*), and *Los Treinta* (Thirty Years), among others.
2. The assignment for the oral history project, titled "Los Treinta / Thirty Years of Salvadoran/Latin@ Migration to Washington, D.C.," included the following instructions and prompts:

> Following the interview protocols outlined in the *Oral History Manual* and the oral history methodologies presented by Dr. Olivia Cadaval (the Center for Folklife and Cultural Heritage, Smithsonian Institution), students will identify a subject/narrator to interview; conduct background research to prepare for the interview; design a set of questions for the interview (based on a template of questions provided); conduct an interview with subject; record the interview using appropriate technology (e.g., iPod, tape recorder, Flip Camera, computer, etc.); transcribe interview; and compose (write) an oral history of that subject.
>
> Students must get signed permission from the subject to interview, record, and write an oral history. You must provide your subject with the proper "Oral History Donor Form" or a version of it (in Spanish if necessary) granting you permission by the subject to conduct and use the interview for the purposes of this project. You must explain what the "Los Treinta / Thirty Years" project is about.
>
> - The written oral history must provide background historical information on the group with whom the subject/narrator identifies (e.g., Salvadoran, Ecuadorian, Peruvian, etc.) and/or the group the subject talks about (e.g., Latinos in D.C., Salvadorans, etc.).
> - The written oral history will be presented and handed in class on Wed. March 31, 2010.

- All oral histories must be 3–4 pages (DS, Times New Roman, 12 pt.). Interview questions and "Oral History Donor Form" (permission form signed by subject/narrator/donor) must accompany your written Oral History on due date. After the professor has read and returned oral histories, students must edit their Oral Histories / Interviews and post them to Discussion Board. We will provide Avilés with the edited oral histories. **See below for more specific instructions.

The Interview: Specifics

- The questions below are suggested questions for your interview with a person whom you have selected. You can choose from the questions below and add your own questions. If you are adventurous and would like to interview a person from a list that Quique Avilés has drawn up, please let Prof. Rodríguez know. She will give you the contact information.
- Your interview should be in person, should be recorded on a machine (e.g., iPod, computer, tape recorder), or filmed if the person gives you permission (e.g., Flip Camera). We will make it possible for you to turn in the recording through some appropriate technology.
- You must ask your subject/interviewee for permission to interview her/him, to record her/him, and to use her/his story to write an oral history. You must explain the purpose of the interview and project, "Los Treinta / Thirty Years." You must ask your subject/interviewee to sign an "Oral History Donor Form" (i.e., you may use the standard form given in class, or you may modify it stating that permission is granted. I will provide a Spanish translation for you to use in case your donor speaks Spanish only).
- You must transcribe your interview. In other words, you must write the script of your interview. Your transcription does not have to be word-for-word, but it must provide the text of the interview in written form.
- Lastly, you must compose the interview into an "oral history." Look over your notes from the methodologies training session in class with Dr. Olivia Cadaval. Your oral history must give some historical/background context on the person or place from which the person comes or the context of Washington, D.C. in the years in question (e.g., 1970s, 1980s, or 1990s). You may decide to start your oral history with this background. You must decide how to tell the person's story, how to narrate it, in other words, how to organize her/his responses to your questions into a "narrative" of her/his life.

EPILOGUE

1. According to the U.N. Refugee Agency, in summer 2014, approximately sixty-five thousand Central American migrant youths, in many cases unaccompanied by adults—or unaccompanied alien children (UAC)—arrived at the U.S.-Mexico border, an event that was identified as nothing short of a humanitarian crisis by the Obama administration, the media, human rights organizations, immigration scholars, border journalists, and literary and cultural critics. Because the Washington, D.C. metropolitan area and the DMV were already home to a sizable Central American population, particularly Salvadoran, the region was the destination for many child migrants in 2014 and thereafter. In 2014–15, Maryland and Virginia each received almost five thousand unaccompanied minors and the District of Columbia almost four hundred, figures that do not account for the youths who arrived alone and undetected by immigration services. Given the long-standing population of Central Americans who have resided and built enclaves in neighborhoods such as Langley Park and Riverdale in Maryland, many of these newcomers sought to reunite with their families, relatives, or friends in the region. See "Children"; Kandel; Krogstad and González-Barrera; Soboroff.

WORKS CITED

Abrego, Leisy J. "On Silences: Salvadoran Refugees Then and Now." *Latino Studies*, vol. 15, no. 1, Spring 2017, pp. 73–85.

Abrego, Leisy J. *Sacrificing Families: Navigating Laws, Labor, and Love Across Borders*. Stanford UP, 2014.

Abrego, Leisy J., and Alejandro Villalpando. "Racialization of Central Americans in the United States." *Precarity and Belonging: Labor, Migration, and Noncitizenship*, edited by Catherine S. Ramírez et al., Rutgers UP, 2021, pp. 51–65.

Adichie, Chimamanda Ngozi. "The Danger of a Single Story." *TEDGlobal*, July 2009, www.ted.com/talks/chimamanda_ngozi_adichie_the_danger_of_a_single_story.

AFROOS (Fundación Afrodescendientes Organizados Salvadoreños). Facebook page. www.facebook.com/AfroosSv/. Accessed 23 May 2025.

Alegría, Claribel. *Woman of the River*. U of Pittsburgh P, 1989.

Alim, H. Samy. "Introducing Raciolinguistics: Racing Language and Languaging Race in Hyperracial Times." *Raciolinguistics: How Language Shapes Our Ideas About Race*, edited by H. Samy Alim et al., Oxford UP, 2016, pp. 1–30.

Alim, H. Samy, et al., editors. *Raciolinguistics: How Language Shapes Our Ideas About Race*. Oxford UP, 2016.

Alvarado, Karina O., et al., editors. *U.S. Central Americans: Reconstructing Memories, Struggles, and Communities of Resistance*. U of Arizona P, 2017.

Ambroggio, Luis Alberto, and Carlos Parada-Ayala, editors. *Al pie de la Casa Blanca: Poetas hispanos de Washington, D.C.* Academia Norteamericana de la Lengua Española, 2010.

Ambroggio, Luis Alberto, et al., editors. *Knocking on the Door of the White House: Latina and Latino Poets in Washington, D.C.* Translated by Deborah Sosobeloff and Burgi Zenhaeusern, Zozobra, 2017.

"American Community Survey Data Tables." *U.S. Census Bureau*. www.census.gov/acs/www/data/data-tables-and-tools/. Accessed 23 May 2025.

Anastario, Mike. *Parcels: Memories of Salvadoran Migration*. Rutgers UP, 2019.

Anderson, Benedict. *Imagined Communities: Reflections on the Origins and Spread of Nationalism*. Verso, 1983.

Anzaldúa, Gloria. *Borderlands/La Frontera: The New Mestiza*. Aunt Lute Books, 1987.

Archdiocese of Guatemala. *Guatemala Never Again! Recovery of Historical Memory Project: The Official Report of the Human Rights Office, Archdiocese of Guatemala (REMHI)*. Translated by Gretta Tovar Siebentrit, Orbis Books, 1998.

Argueta, Manlio. *Cuzcatlán donde bate la mar del sur*. Adelina Editores, 1987.

Argueta, Manlio. *Cuzcatlán: Where the Southern Sea Beats*. Translated by Clark Hansen, Vintage Books, 1987.

Argueta, Manlio, editor. *Poesía de El Salvador*. EDUCA, 1983.

Arias, Arturo. "Central American–Americans: Invisibility, Power and Representation in the US Latino World." *Latino Studies*, vol. 1, no. 1, March 2003, pp. 168–87.

Arias, Arturo, editor. *The Rigoberta Menchú Controversy*. U of Minnesota P, 2001.

Arias, Arturo. *Taking Their Word: Literature and the Signs of Central America*. U of Minnesota P, 2007.

Asch, Chris Myers, and George Derek Musgrove. *Chocolate City: A History of Race and Democracy in the Nation's Capital*. U of North Carolina P, 2017.

Avilés, Quique. "Barrio." *Paper, Fabric, String, and Poetry*. N.p., 1999, unpag.

Avilés, Quique. "bilingual education." *The Immigrant Museum*. PinStudio, 2003, p. 38.

Avilés, Quique. *Caminata: A Walk Through Immigrant Life*. 2002. In the author's possession.

Avilés, Quique. "Canción para un Salvatruco." 1999. In the author's possession.

Avilés, Quique. "El Salvador At-a-Glance." *The Immigrant Museum*. PinStudio, 2003, pp. 10–11.

Avilés, Quique. *The Immigrant Museum*. PinStudio, 2003.

Avilés, Quique, director. *Las muertes más bellas del mundo: A Film About Salvadorean Artists in Washington, D.C.* (trailer). *YouTube*, uploaded by Las Muertes Más Bellas del Mundo Film, 22 Mar. 2023, www.youtube.com/watch?v=OxDweTsk-7U.

Avilés, Quique. "Latinhood." *The Immigrant Museum*. PinStudio, 2003, pp. 8–9.

Avilés, Quique. "Let the Poems Run the Country." *The Immigrant Museum*. PinStudio, 2003, p. 18.

Avilés, Quique. *Paper, Fabric, String, and Poetry*. N.p., 1999.

Avilés, Quique. "Spanglish Morongon." *The Immigrant Museum*. PinStudio, 2003, pp. 16–17.

"B03001: Hispanic or Latino Origin by Specific Origin." *U.S. Census Bureau*. data.census.gov/table?q=B03001. Accessed 23 May 2025.

Baker-Cristales, Beth. *Salvadoran Migration to Southern California: Redefining El Hermano Lejano*. UP of Florida, 2004.

Bárcenas Ortega, Ana Elizabeth. "El aguacate: Luces y sombras en la evolución de un cultivo ancestral." *El pasado del futuro alimentario: Los alimentos ancestrales americanos*, edited by Enriqueta Quiroz and Helena Pradilla Rueda, Instituto de Investigaciones Dr. José María Luis Mora, Consejo Nacional de Ciencia y Tecnología, 2018, pp. 434–52.

Baronian, Marie-Aude, et al., editors. *Diaspora and Memory: Figures of Displacement in Contemporary Literature, Arts, and Politics*. Rodopi, 2007.

Beltrán, Cristina. *The Trouble with Unity: Latino Politics and the Creation of Identity*. Oxford UP, 2010.

Bencastro, Mario. *El vuelo de la alondra*. Ediciones Puerto Santa Lucía, 2018.

Bencastro, Mario. "Juana's Dreams." *Paraíso portátil / Portable Paradise*. Translated by J. Pluecker, Arte Público Press, 2010, pp. 176–83.

Bencastro, Mario. *La Mansión del Olvido*. Ediciones Puerto Santa Lucía, 2015.

Bencastro, Mario. *Odyssey to the North*. Translated by S. G. Rascón, Arte Público Press, 1999.

Bencastro, Mario. *Paraíso portátil / Portable Paradise*. Translated by J. Pluecker, Arte Público Press, 2010.

Bencastro, Mario. *A Promise to Keep*. Arte Público Press, 2005.

Bencastro, Mario. *A Shot in the Cathedral*. Translated by S. G. Rascón, Arte Público Press, 1996.

Bencastro, Mario. *The Tree of Life: Stories of Civil War*. Translated by S. G. Rascón, Arte Público Press, 1997.

Bencastro, Mario. *Vato Guanaco Loco: Rap en Caliche*. Casa de la Cultura El Salvador, 2019.

Berlant, Lauren. *The Queen of America Goes to Washington City: Essays on Sex and Citizenship*. Duke UP, 2002.

Boym, Svetlana. *The Future of Nostalgia*. Basic Books, 2001.

Braziel, Jana Evans, and Anita Mannur, editors. *Theorizing Diaspora*. Blackwell, 2003.

Briggs, Laura. *Taking Children: A History of American Terror*. U of California P, 2020.

Brown, Anna, and Eileen Patten. "Hispanics of Salvadoran Origin, 2011." *Pew Research Center*, 19 June 2013, www.pewresearch.org/hispanic/2013/06/19/hispanics-of-salvadoran.

Cabrera, Yohalmo. "Afrodescendiencias en El Salvador: Participando en su historia y forjándola desde hace 500 años." *Discriminaciones*, Ediciones Boll, 2020, pp. 40–47.

Cadaval, Olivia. *Creating a Latino Identity in the Nation's Capital: The Latino Festival*. Garland, 1998.

Cadaval, Olivia. "The Latino Community: Creating an Identity in the Nation's Capital." *Washington Odyssey: A Multicultural History of the Nation's Capital*, edited by Francine Curro Cary, Smithsonian Books, 1996, pp. 231–49.

Cadaval, Olivia. "My Tongue Is Divided into Two." With Quique Avilés. *Race and Cultural Practice in Popular Culture*, edited by Domino Renee Pérez and Rachel González-Martín, Rutgers UP, 2018, pp. 110–31.

Cañas Dinarte, Carlos. "Esclavos africanos en Sonsonate, en El Salvador." *Elsalvador.com*, 4 Dec. 2016, historico.elsalvador.com/historico/211800/esclavos-africanos-en-sonsonate-en-el-salvador.html.

Cárdenas, Maritza E. *Constituting Central American–Americans: Transnational Identities and the Politics of Dislocation*. Rutgers UP, 2018.

Centeno-Meléndez, José Alfredo. "Los 30 / The Thirty Years." Oral History, Hyattsville, Md., 28 Mar. 2010.

Centeno-Meléndez, José Alfredo. *Placemaking in a City of Nations: Latino Community Formation in Washington, D.C., 1820s–1970s*. 2023. U of Texas at Austin, PhD dissertation.

Centeno-Meléndez, José Alfredo. "Thursday, May 7th, 2020." *La Horchata Zine*, vol. 8, 2020–21, unpag.

Cepeda, María Elena. *Musical ImagiNation: U.S. Colombian Identity and the Latin Music Boom*. New York UP, 2010.

Chacón, Gloria Elizabeth, and Mónica Albizúrez Gil, editors. *Teaching Central American Literature in a Global Context*. Modern Language Association of America, 2022.

Chávez, Leo. *The Latino Threat: Constructing Immigrants, Citizens, and the Nation*. Stanford UP, 2008.

"Children on the Run: Unaccompanied Children Leaving Central America and Mexico and the Need for International Protection." U.N. High Commissioner for Refugees, 2016. www.unhcr.org/en-us/children-on-the-run.html.

Chinchilla, Maya. "Central Americanamerican." *La Revista: Papel Picado / Paper Cuts*, vol. 1, no. 1, Spring 1999, pp. 115–16.

Chinchilla, Maya. *The Cha Cha Files: A Chapina Poética*. Kórima Press, 2014.

Chinchilla, Maya. "Solidarity Baby." *The Cha Cha Files: A Chapina Poética*. Kórima Press, 2014, p. 5.

Chinchilla, Maya, and Karina O. Alvarado, editors. *Desde el Epicentro: An Anthology of U.S. Central American Poetry and Art*. Epicentro, 2007.

Chomsky, Aviva. *Central America's Forgotten History: Revolution, Violence, and the Roots of Migration*. Beacon Press, 2021.

Christian, Karen. *Identity as Performance in U.S. Latina/o Fiction*. U of New Mexico P, 1997.

Cohn, D'Vera, et al. "Remittances to Latin America Recover—But Not to Mexico." *Pew Research Center*, 14 Nov. 2013, www.pewresearch.org/race-and-ethnicity/2013/11/15/remittances-to-latin/.

Cohen, Robin. *Global Diasporas: An Introduction*. 2nd ed., Routledge, 2008.

Córdova, Carlos B. *The Salvadoran Americans*. Greenwood Press, 2005.

Cornejo, Kency. *Visual Disobedience: Art and Decoloniality in Central America*. Duke UP, 2024.

Cortez, Mayamérica. *Nostalgias y soledades*. Editorial Clásicos Roxsil, 1995.

Cota-Cardenas, Margarita. *Puppet: A Chicano Novella*. Relampago Books Press, 1985.

Coutin, Susan Bibler. *Exiled Home: Salvadoran Transnational Youth in the Aftermath of Violence*. Duke UP, 2016.

Coutin, Susan Bibler. *Legalizing Moves: Salvadoran Immigrants' Struggle for U.S. Residency*. U of Michigan P, 2000.

Coutin, Susan Bibler. *Nation of Emigrants: Shifting Boundaries of Citizenship in El Salvador and the United States*. Cornell UP, 2007.

Creet, Julia. "Introduction: The Migration of Memory and Memories of Migration." *Memory and Migration: Multidisciplinary Approaches to Memory Studies*, edited by Julia Creet and Andreas Kitzmann, U of Toronto P, 2011, pp. 3–26.

Culture Clash. *Anthems: Culture Clash in the District. Culture Clash in Americca: Four Plays*, Theatre Communications Group, 2003, pp. 151–221.

Cummins, Jeanine. *American Dirt*. Flatiron Books, 2020.

Dalton, Roque. "The Cops and the Guards." *Poemas clandestinos / Clandestine Poems*, edited by Barbara Paschke and Eric Weaver, translated by Jack Hirschman, Solidarity Educational, 1986, pp. 22–27.

Dalton, Roque. "Poema de amor." *Las historias prohibidas del pulgarcito*, 1974. Universidad Centroamericana José Simeón Cañas Editores, 2000, pp. 199–200.

Danticat, Edwidge. *Create Dangerously: The Immigrant Artist at Work*. Princeton UP, 2010.

De Burgos, Hugo. "Racismo, Símbolos de la Belleza y Autoestima en El Salvador." *Identidades: La Revista de Ciencias Sociales y Humanidades*, vol. 1, no. 1, July–Dec. 2010, pp. 1–21.

"Decreto sobre inmigración." *Leyes y otras disposiciones relativas al servicio exterior de El Salvador*. Talleres gráficos José B. Cisneros e Hijos, 1928.

De la Luz, Rios. "3 Zines Celebrating the Complexity of Being Latinx." *Vice*, 29 May 2018, www.vice.com/en/article/nekey7/latinx-zines-la-horchata-chifladazine-muchacha-fanzine.

DeLugan, Robin Maria. *Reimagining National Belonging: Post–Civil War El Salvador in a Global Context*. U of Arizona P, 2012.

Díaz, Nidia. *Nunca estuve sola*. UCA Editores, 1988.

Díaz-Hurtado, Jessica, and Felix Contreras. "Amidst Political Turmoil, Salvadoran Artists Across the Country Discuss Their Work." *Alt.latino*, NPR, 12 Jan. 2018, www.npr.org/sections/altlatino/2018/01/12/577155260/.

Eliaschev, José Ricardo. *Reagan, U.S.A.: Los años ochenta*. Folios Ediciones, 1981.

Erquicia Cruz, José Heriberto. "'¡Aquí no hay negros!': La negación de la raíz africana en la sociedad salvadoreña." *Revista de Humanidades y Ciencias Sociales*, vol. 2, Jan.–June 2012, pp. 120–51.

Escobar, Gabriel. "Treatment of D.C. Latinos Called 'Appalling' by Panel." *Washington Post*, 6 Feb. 1993.

Farahani, Alan, et al. "Identifying 'Plantscapes' at the Classic Maya Village of Joya de Cerén, El Salvador." *Antiquity*, vol. 91, no. 358, Aug. 2017, pp. 980–97.

Ferris, Elizabeth G. *The Central American Refugees*. Praeger, 1987.

Flores, Juan, and George Yúdice. "Living Borders / Buscando América: Language of Latino Self-Formation." *Social Text*, vol. 8, no. 24, 1990, pp. 57–84.
Flores, William V., and Rina Benmayor, editors. *Latino Cultural Citizenship: Claiming Identity, Space, and Rights.* Beacon Press, 1997.
Freidenberg, Judith Noemí. *Contemporary Conversations on Immigration in the United States: The View from Prince George's County, Maryland.* Lexington Books, 2016.
Friedman, Andrew. *Covert Capital: Landscapes of Denial and the Making of U.S. Empire in the Suburbs of Northern Virginia.* U of California P, 2013.
Galindo-Tovar, María Elena, et al. "The Avocado (*Persea americana*, Lauraceae) Crop in Mesoamerica: 10,000 Years of History." *Harvard Papers in Botany*, vol. 12, no. 2, 2007, pp. 325–34.
Gammage, Sarah. "El Salvador: Despite End to War, Emigration Continues." *Migration Policy Institute*, 26 July 2007, www.migrationpolicy.org/article/el-salvador-despite-end-civil-war-emigration-continues.
García, Edgar. *Signs of the Americas: A Poetics of Pictography, Hieroglyphs, and Khipu.* U of Chicago P, 2020.
García, Ofelia, et al. "Introduction: Language and Society: A Critical Poststructuralist Perspective." *The Oxford Handbook of Language and Society*, edited by Ofelia García et al., Oxford UP, 2016, pp. 1–16.
García Bedolla, Lisa. "The Identity Paradox: Latino Language, Politics and Selective Dissociation." *Latino Studies*, vol. 1, no. 2, July 2003, pp. 264–83.
García Trejo, Carlos, editor. *Ahuácatl: Tesoro verde mexicano.* Coloristas y Asociados, 2011.
Gilroy, Paul. *The Black Atlantic: Modernity and Double Consciousness.* Havard UP, 1993.
Goldman, Francisco. *The Long Night of White Chickens.* Atlantic Monthly Press, 1992.
Goldman, Francisco. "State of the Art: Latino Writers." *Washington Post*, 28 Feb. 1999.
Gómez Menjívar, Jennifer Carolina. *Black in Print: Plotting the Coordinates of Blackness in Central America.* State U of New York P, 2023.
González, Lilo, and Los de la Mount Pleasant. *A quien corresponda . . .* LGP Records, LML-2741, 1994.
González, Milvian. "Rafael Rodríguez Molina." *La Voz Latina*, 1 Dec. 2023, www.lavozlatina.org/post/rafael-rodriguez-molina.
González Mejía, Hernán. *Centroamérica en crisis.* Editorial de la Universidad Nacional, 1992.
Gruesz, Kirsten Silva. *Ambassadors of Culture: The Transamerican Origins of Latino Writing.* Princeton UP, 2002.
Guevara, Tomás, and Hugo Salinas. *Intipucá: 40 años de emigración hacia los Estados Unidos. YouTube*, uploaded by intipucaonline, 6 Nov. 2008, www.youtube.com/watch?v=Rf4B61VFDW0.
Gurba, Myriam. "Pendeja, You Ain't Steinbeck: My Bronca with Fake-Ass Social Justice Literature." Review of *American Dirt*, by Jeanine Cummins. *Tropics of Meta:*

Historiography for the Masses, 12 Dec. 2019, tropicsofmeta.com/2019/12/12/pendeja.

Guzmán, David J. "Población y área, Razas y costumbres." *Obras escogidas: Compilación, edición de texto*, edited by Carlos Castro, Dirección de Publicaciones e Impresos, 2000, pp. 193–97.

Hamilton, Nora, and Norma Stoltz Chinchilla. *Seeking Community in a Global City: Guatemalans and Salvadorans in Los Angeles*. Temple UP, 2001.

Harris, Jeremy, and René Maldonado. "Migrant Wages and Remittances to Latin America and the Caribbean in 2023." *Migration Unpacked, Inter-American Development Bank*, 15 May 2024, blogs.iadb.org/migracion/en/migrant-wages.

"A History of Avocados." *Avocados from Mexico*. avocadosfrommexico.com/avocados/history/. Accessed 1 Feb. 2025.

Interiano, Víctor H. *Salvi Dictionary. Dichos de un Bicho*, dichosdeunbicho.com/salvi-dictionary/. Accessed 23 May 2025.

Jameson, Fredric. "Periodizing the 60s." *Social Text*, vol. 9/10, 1984, pp. 178–209.

Jennings, Keith, and Clarence Lusane. "The State and Future of Black/Latino Relations in Washington, D.C.: A Bridge in Need of Repair." *Blacks, Latinos, and Asians in Urban America: Status and Prospects for Politics and Activism*, edited by James Jennings, Praeger, 1994, pp. 57–77.

Joya, Daniel. *Sueños de un callejero*. Editorial Nuevo Enfoque, 2002.

Kandel, William A. "Unaccompanied Alien Children: An Overview." *Congressional Research Service*, R43599, 5 Sept. 2024.

Karras, Bill J. "José Martí and the Pan American Conference, 1889–1891." *Revista de Historia de América*, no. 77/78, Jan.–Dec. 1974, pp. 77–99.

Kim, Katherine Cowy, et al., editors. *Izote Vos: A Collection of Salvadoran American Writing and Visual Art*. Pacific News Service, 2000.

Kondo, Dorinne. *Worldmaking: Race, Performance, and the Work of Creativity*. Duke UP, 2018.

Krogstad, Jens Manuel, and Ana González-Barrera. "Texas Tops List of States Where This Year's Unaccompanied Child Migrants Ended Up." *Pew Research Center*, 11 Dec. 2014, www.pewresearch.org/fact-tank/2014/12/11/texas.

Lambert, Joe, and Brooke Hessler. *Digital Storytelling: Capturing Lives, Creating Community*. Routledge, 2018.

Landon, Amanda J. "Domestication and Significance of *Persea americana*, the Avocado, in Mesoamerica." *Nebraska Anthropologist*, no. 47, 2009, pp. 62–79.

Lara-Martínez, Rafael. *Indigenismo Salvadoreño*. Editorial Universidad Don Bosco, 2022.

Larios, Frida. *La Aldea que fue sepultada por un volcán en Erupción / The Village That Was Buried by an Erupting Volcano*. Secretaría de Cultura de la Presidencia de El Salvador, 2014.

Larios, Frida. Artist website. fridalarios.com. Accessed 23 May 2025.

Larios, Frida (@fridalarios). "Our Seeds Will Be Millions." *Instagram*, 13 Nov. 2021, www.instagram.com/fridalarios/reel/CWN6G7SMKa7/.

Laviera, Tato. *AmeRícan*. Arte Público Press, 1985.

Laviera, Tato. *Mixturao*. Arte Público Press, 2008.

"Laws and Regulations for the Medical Examination of Aliens." *Immigrant and Refugee Health, U.S. Centers for Disease Control and Prevention*, 15 May 2024, www.cdc.gov/immigrant-refugee-health/laws-regulations.

Lemus, Jorge E. "El sorprendente origen de 'guanaco,' el gentilicio salvadoreño ilegítimo." *Elfaro*, 13 Aug. 2021, elfaro.net/es/202108/ef_academico/25654/.

Lemus, Jorge E. "La palabra pupusa no es pipil." *Elfaro*, 13 Sept. 2016, elfaro.net/es/201609/el_agora/19229/.

"Ley de extranjería: Los árabes equiparados a los chinos." *Leyes y otras disposiciones relativas al servicio exterior de El Salvador*. Talleres gráficos José B. Cisneros e Hijos, 1928.

Limón, Graciela. *In Search of Bernabé*. Arte Público Press, 1993.

Lipski, John M. *Latin American Spanish*. Longman, 1994.

Lipski, John M. *Varieties of Spanish in the United States*. Georgetown UP, 2008.

López Oro, Paul Joseph. "Garifunizando Afrolatinidad: Blackness, Indigeneity, and Latinidad." *Hemispheric Blackness and the Exigencies of Accountability*, edited by Jennifer Carolina Gómez Menjívar and Héctor Nicolás Ramos Flores, U of Pittsburgh P, 2022, pp. 211–25.

López Oro, Paul Joseph. "Refashioning Afro-Latinidad: Garifuna New Yorkers in Diaspora." *Critical Dialogues in Latinx Studies: A Reader*, edited by Ana Y. Ramos-Zayas and Mérida M. Rúa, New York UP, 2021, pp. 223–38.

Louie, Vivian S. *Keeping the Immigrant Bargain: The Costs and Rewards of Success in America*. Russell Sage Foundation, 2012.

Lourentzatos, Rosie. "Avocado Mania: The Rise and Costs of Our Obsession with Avocados." *City U of New York Graduate Center*, Aug. 2021, arcg.is/rvK59.

Lovato, Roberto. *Unforgetting: A Memoir of Family, Migration, Gangs, and Revolution in the Americas*. HarperCollins Books, 2020.

Luna, Ronald. "Latino Presence in the U.S." Lecture, 9 Sept. 2010, U of Maryland, College Park.

Lungo Uclés, Mario. *El Salvador in the Eighties: Counterinsurgency and Revolution*, edited by Arthur Schmidt, translated by Amelia F. Shogan, Temple UP, 1996.

Mahler, Sarah J. *American Dreaming: Immigrant Life on the Margins*. Princeton UP, 1995.

Mahler, Sarah J. "Migration and Transnational Issues: Recent Trends and Prospects for 2020." Working paper, June 2000, Institut für Iberoamerika-Kunde.

Mahler, Sarah J. *Salvadorans in Suburbia: Symbiosis and Conflict*. Allyn and Bacon, 1995.

Marschall, Sabine. "Memory, Migration, and Travel: Introduction." *Memory, Migration, and Travel*, edited by Sabine Marschall, Routledge, 2018, pp. 1–23.

Martin, Simon. "Cacao in Ancient Maya Religion: First Fruit from the Maize Tree and Other Tales from the Underworld." *Chocolate in Mesoamerica: A Cultural History of Cacao*, edited by Cameron L. McNeil, UP of Florida, 2006, pp. 154–83.

Martínez, Demetria. *Mother Tongue*. Bilingual Press/Editorial Bilingüe, 1994.

Martínez Castellón, Javier Alcides. "Algunas características del español salvadoreño / Characteristics of Salvadoran Spanish." *Conocimiento educativo*, vol. 10, Feb. 2023, pp. 139–49.

"Meet the Author: Frida Larios, Antiguo Cuzcatlán, Copán, and Washington." *The Nature of the Cities*, www.thenatureofcities.com/author/fridalarios/. Accessed 23 May 2025.

Meléndez, Veronica, curator. *Connected Diaspora: Central American Visuality in the Age of Social Media*. Exhibit, Stamp Gallery, U of Maryland, College Park, 22 Sept.–12 Dec. 2020, stamp.umd.edu/centers/stamp_gallery/connected_diaspora.

Meléndez, Veronica. *Connected Diaspora: Central American Visuality in the Age of Social Media*. Proposal, 2020. In the author's possession.

Meléndez, Veronica, and Kimberly Benavides, editors. *La Horchata Zine*, vols. 1–9, 2017–22, lahorchatazine.bigcartel.com/.

Menchú, Rigoberta, and Elizabeth Burgos Debray. *I, Rigoberta Menchú: An Indian Woman in Guatemala*. Translated by Ann Wright, Verso, 1984.

Menchú, Rigoberta, and Elizabeth Burgos Debray. *Me llamo Rigoberta Menchú y así me nació la conciencia*. Siglo XXI Editores, 1983.

Meneray, Jennifer. "Mural and Movements." *Columbia Heights Insider*, 23 Aug. 2020, columbiaheightsinsider.com/murals-and-movements/.

Menjívar, Cecilia. *Fragmented Ties: Salvadoran Immigrant Networks in America*. U of California P, 2000.

Miranda, Sami. "Home." *Protection from Erasure*. Jaded Ibis Press, 2023, p. 5.

Miranda, Sami. "ILL Legal." *Protection from Erasure*. Jaded Ibis Press, 2023, pp. 3–4.

Miranda, Sami. "The Waffle Shop." *Protection from Erasure*. Jaded Ibis Press, 2023, pp. 74–75.

Miranda, Sami. "We Is." *We Is*. Zozobra, 2019, pp. 76–77.

Modan, Gabriella Gahlia. *Turf Wars: Discourse, Diversity, and the Politics of Place*. Blackwell, 2007.

Molina-Tamacas, Carmen. *SalviYorkers*. K Ediciones, 2020.

Monge, José Vladimir. *Pasajeros en el Tiempo / Passengers in Time*. CBH Books, 2006.

Monge, José Vladimir. *Voces y huellas*. Editorial Círculo Rojo, 2012.

Moon, Krystyn. "From Arlandria to Chirilagua: The Shifting Demographics of a Northern Virginia Neighborhood." *Metropole*, 11 Feb. 2019, themetropole.blog/2019/02/11/from-arlandria.

Morales, Ed. *Living in Spanglish: The Search for Latino Identity in America*. St. Martin's Press, 2002.

Moslimani, Mohamad, et al. "Facts on Hispanics of Salvadoran Origin in the United States, 2021." *Pew Research Center*, 16 Aug. 2023, www.pewresearch.org/hispanic/fact-sheet/us-hispanics-facts-on-salvadoran-origin-latinos/.

Muñoz, José Esteban. *The Sense of Brown*. Edited by Joshua Chambers-Letson and Tavia Nyong'o, Duke UP, 2020.

National Legislative Assembly of the Republic of El Salvador. "Decree 65." 6 July 1928. *Diario Oficial*, no. 197, 4 Sept. 1930.

Nealon, Jeffrey T. "Periodizing the 80s: The Cultural Logic of Privatization in the United States." *A Leftist Ontology: Beyond Relativism and Identity Politics*, edited by Carsten Strathausen, foreword by William E. Connolly, U of Minnesota P, 2009, pp. 54–79.

Nnamdi, Kojo. "Mt. Pleasant: 20 Years After the Riot." *The Kojo Nnamdi Show*, 5 May 2011, thekojonnamdishow.org/shows/2011-05-05/mt-pleasant-20-years-after-riot/.

Olivo, Antonio, et al. "Crowded Housing and Essential Jobs: Why So Many Latinos Are Getting Coronavirus." *Washington Post*, 26 May 2020.

Orozco, Manuel, and Julia Yansura. *Centroamérica en la mira: La migración en su relación con el desarrollo y las oportunidades por el cambio*. Teseo, 2015.

Orozco, Manuel, and Julia Yansura. *Confronting the Challenges of Migration and Development in Central America*. Inter-American Dialogue, 2015.

Ortiz Jiménez, Macarena. "Stigmatized Linguistic Identities and Spanish Language Teaching." *International Proceedings of Economics Development and Research*, vol. 68, no. 22, 2013, pp. 129–35.

Padilla, Yajaira M. *Changing Women, Changing Nation: Female Agency, Nationhood and Identity in Trans-Salvadoran Narratives*. State U of New York P, 2012.

Padilla, Yajaira M. *From Threatening Guerrillas to Forever Illegals: US Central Americans and the Cultural Politics of Non-Belonging*. U of Texas P, 2022.

Parada, Danielle. "Learning About My Blackness: Afrodescendencia in El Salvador." *Medium*, 31 July 2020, medium.com/@mayraparada92/learning-about-my-blackness-afrodescendencia-in-el-salvador-c491d4e4824b. Article since deleted by creator.

Pedersen, David E. *American Value: Migrants, Money, and Meaning in El Salvador and the United States*. U of Chicago P, 2013.

Pedersen, David E. "States of Memory and Desire: The Meaning of City and Nation for Transnational Migrants in Washington, DC, and El Salvador." *Amerikastudien / American Studies*, vol. 40, no. 3, 1995, pp. 415–42.

Pedersen, David E. "The Storm We Call Dollars: Determining Value and Belief in El Salvador and the United States." *Cultural Anthropology*, vol. 17, no. 3, 2002, pp. 431–59.

Peñalosa, Fernando. "Some Issues in Chicano Sociolinguistics." *Latino Language and Communicative Behavior*, edited by Richard P. Durán, ABLEX, 1981, pp. 3–18.

Peralta, Eyder. "Why a Single Question Decides the Fates of Central American Migrants." *NPR*, 25 Feb. 2016, www.npr.org/2016/02/25/467020627/.

Peterson, Cecilia. "From Sambusas to Pupusas: Washington, D.C. Foodways at the Smithsonian Folklife Festival." *Smithsonian Collection Blog, Smithsonian Institution*, 8 Oct. 2014, si-siris.blogspot.com/2014/10/from-sambusas-to-pupusas-washington-dc.html.

Pineda, Grego. *Centauros ciegos: Verdades evidentes*. Talleres Gráficos UCA, 2003.

Popenoe, Wilson. *The Avocado in Guatemala*. U. S. Department of Agriculture, bulletin 743, 1919. Andesite Press, 2015.

Portes, Alejandro, and Rubén G. Rumbaut. *Legacies: The Story of the Immigrant Second Generation*. U of California P, 2001.

Pratt, Sharon. "Lessons from a D.C. Riot." *Washington Post*, 12 Aug. 2011.

Price, Marie, and Lisa Benton-Short. "Immigrants and World Cities: From the Hyper-Diverse to the Bypassed." *GeoJournal*, vol. 68, no. 2/3, 2007, pp. 103–17.

Quesada Pacheco, Miguel Ángel. *El español de América*. Editorial Tecnológica de Costa Rica, 2000.

"Registro de ciudadanos chinos." *Leyes y otras disposiciones relativas al servicio exterior de El Salvador*. Talleres gráficos José B. Cisneros e Hijos, 1928.

Reichard, Raquel. "La Horchata Zine Is Giving Central Americans a Much-Needed Platform to Showcase Their Art." *Remezcla*, 11 Dec. 2017, remezcla.com/features/culture/central-american-zine/.

Repak, Terry A. *Waiting on Washington: Central American Workers in the Nation's Capital*. Temple UP, 1995.

Rivas, Cecilia. *Salvadoran Imaginaries: Mediated Identities and Cultures of Consumption*. Rutgers UP, 2014.

Rivas, Pedro Geoffroy. *La lengua salvadoreña*. Dirección de Publicaciones e Impresos, 1987.

Rivas Montoya, Melissa. *La diáspora palestina en El Salvador: 1880–2019*. Dirección de Publicaciones e Impresos, 2021.

Rodríguez, Ana Patricia. "Becoming 'Wachintonians': Salvadorans in the Washington, D.C., Metropolitan Area." *Washington History*, vol. 28, no. 2, Fall 2016, pp. 3–12.

Rodríguez, Ana Patricia. "'Departamento 15': Cultural Narratives of Salvadoran Transnational Migration." *Latino Studies*, vol. 3, no. 1, April 2005, pp. 19–41.

Rodríguez, Ana Patricia. *Dividing the Isthmus: Central American Transnational Histories, Literatures, and Cultures*. U of Texas P, 2009.

Rodríguez, Ana Patricia. "¿Dónde estás vos/z? Performing Salvadoreñidades in Washington, D.C." *Imagined Transnationalism: U.S. Latino/a Literature, Culture, and Identity*, edited by Kevin Concannon et al., Palgrave Macmillan, 2009, pp. 201–20.

Rodríguez, Ana Patricia. *Entre Mundos / Between Worlds* and *Home Stories*. Digital storytelling projects, 2014–23. *Vimeo*, vimeo.com/user6833797.

Rodríguez, Ana Patricia. "Entre Mundos / Between Worlds: Digital Stories of Salvadoran Transnational Migration." *Letras Hispanas*, vol. 11, 2015, pp. 326–36.

Rodríguez, Ana Patricia. "The Fiction of Solidarity: Transfronterista Feminisms and Anti-Imperialist Struggles in Central American Transnational Narratives." *Feminist Studies*, vol. 34, nos. 1–2, Spring/Summer 2008, pp. 199–226.

Rodríguez, Ana Patricia. "Refugees of the South: Central Americans in the U.S. Latino Imaginary." *American Literature*, vol. 73, no. 2, June 2001, pp. 386–412.

Rodríguez, Ana Patricia. "Salvadoran Immigrant Acts and Migration to San Francisco (circa 1960s and '70s)." *U.S. Central Americans: Reconstructing Memories, Struggles, and Communities of Resistance*, edited by Karina O. Alvarado et al., U of Arizona P, 2017, pp. 41–59.

Rodríguez, Ana Patricia. "Salvadorean Poetry of Conscience (A Student Term Paper)." *Cipactli*, vol. 1, Fall 1988, pp. 4–7.

Rodríguez, Ana Patricia. "Tan cerca del cielo: El imaginario de guerra, paz y diáspora en la artesanía de La Palma, El Salvador." *Hacia una Historia de las Literaturas Centroamericanas IV—Literatura y compromiso político: Prácticas político-culturales y estéticas de la revolución*, edited by Héctor Leyva et al., F&G Editores, 2018, pp. 317–37.

Rodríguez, Ana Patricia. "Toward a Transisthmian Central American Studies." *Latino Studies*, vol. 15, no. 1, Spring 2017, pp. 104–8.

Rodríguez Molina, Rafael. Artist website. www.rafaelrodriguezart.com/. Accessed 23 May 2025.

Rojas, Claudia. Artist website. claudiapoet.com/. Accessed 23 May 2025.

Rojas, Claudia. "Family Detention Center." *Acentos Review*, May 2017, www.acentosreview.com/May2017/claudia-rojas.html.

Rojas, Claudia. "My Bones Said 'Write This Poem.'" *Brooklyn Poets*, 24–30 Sept. 2018, brooklynpoets.org/community/poet/claudia-rojas.

Rojas, Claudia. "Residence." *Split This Rock*, 13 Apr. 2020, www.splitthisrock.org/poetry-database/poem/residence.

Rojas, Claudia. "Temporary." *Argot*, 9 Feb. 2018, argotmagazine.squarespace.com/poetry-and-fiction/temporary-protected-status.

Romero, Matías. *Diccionario de salvadoreñismos*. Editorial Delgado, 2003.

Romero, Óscar Arnulfo. "Misión de la iglesia en medio de la crisis del país: Cuarta Carta Pastoral de Monseñor Óscar A. Romero, Arzobispo de San Salvador." 6 Aug. 1979. *La voz de los sin voz: La palabra vivía de Monseñor Óscar Arnulfo Romero*, edited by R. Cardenal et al., UCA Editores, 1999, pp. 123–72.

Rosa, Jonathan. *Looking Like a Language, Sounding Like a Race: Raciolinguistic Ideologies and the Learning of Latinidad*. Oxford UP, 2018.

Rosa, Jonathan, and Nelson Flores. "Unsettling Race and Language: Toward a Raciolinguistic Perspective." *Language in Society*, vol. 46, no. 5, Nov. 2017, pp. 621–47.

Salarrué (Salvador Salazar Arrué). *Cuentos de barro*. La Montaña, 1933.

Salarrué (Salvador Salazar Arrué). *Cuentos de cipotes*. 1943. Editorial Universitaria, 1961.

Sánchez, Rosaura. *Chicano Discourse: Socio-Historic Perspectives*. Newbury House, 1983.

Sánchez Molina, Raúl. *"Mandar a Traer": Antropología, migraciones y transnacionalism—Salvadoreños en Washington*. Editorial Universitas, 2005.

Sánchez Molina, Raúl. *Proceso migratorio de una mujer salvadoreña: El viaje de María Reyes a Washington*. Centro de Investigaciones Sociológicas, 2006.

Sánchez Molina, Raúl, and Lucy M. Cohen, editors. *Latinas Crossing Borders and Building Communities in Greater Washington*. Lexington Books, 2016.

Scallen, Patrick Daniel. "1991: Mount Pleasant." *Washington History*, vol. 32, no. 1/2, Fall 2020, pp. 35–37.

Scallen, Patrick Daniel. *"The Bombs That Drop in El Salvador Explode in Mount Pleasant": From Cold War Conflagration to Immigrant Struggles in Washington, DC, 1970–1995*. 2019. Georgetown U, PhD dissertation.

Shapiro, Ellen. "The New Maya Language of Frida Larios." *Print*, 2 July 2014, www.printmag.com/design-inspiration/the-new-maya.

Sheets, Payton D. *Before the Volcano Erupted: The Ancient Cerén Village in Central America*. U of Texas P, 2002.

Singer, Audrey. "At Home in the Nation's Capital: Immigrant Trends in Metropolitan Washington." *Brookings Institution*, 1 June 2003, www.brookings.edu/articles/at-home.

Singer, Audrey, et al. "The World in a Zip Code: Greater Washington, D.C. as a New Region of Immigration." *Brookings Review*, vol. 20, no. 1, Winter 2002, pp. 34–35.

Smith, Christian. *Resisting Reagan: The U.S. Central America Peace Movement*. U of Chicago P, 1996.

Smith, Molly. Introduction to *Anthems: Culture Clash in the District*. *Culture Clash in Americca: Four Plays*, by Culture Clash, Theatre Communications Group, 2003, pp. 153–55.

Soboroff, Jacob. *Separated: Inside an American Tragedy*. Custom House, 2020.

Sommer, Doris. *Bilingual Games: Some Literary Investigations*. Palgrave, 2003.

Stewart, Miranda. *The Spanish Language Today*. Routledge, 1999.

"Story Circle: A Question of Place—Race & Spoken Word in Washington, D.C." *YouTube*, uploaded by Smithsonian Folklife, 22 Oct. 2020, www.youtube.com/watch?v=taASFgqJNoo.

Strand, Kerry, et al. *Community-Based Research and Higher Education*. John Wiley, 2003.

"Student Success Stories—Meet Lilo González." *Carlos Rosario International Public Charter School*, www.carlosrosario.org/meet-lilo-gonzalez/. Accessed 10 Dec. 2024.

Taylor, Diana. *The Archive and the Repertoire: Performing Cultural Memory in the Americas*. Duke UP, 2003.

"Temporary Protected Status." *U.S. Citizenship and Immigration Services*. www.uscis.gov/humanitarian/temporary-protected-status. Accessed 23 May 2025.

Tilley, Virginia Q. *Seeing Indians: A Study of Race, Nation, and Power in El Salvador*. U of New Mexico P, 2005.

Tobar, Héctor. *The Tattooed Soldier*. Penguin Books, 1998.

Torres-Rivas, Edelberto. "Introducción a la década." *Historia General de Centroamérica: Historia Inmediata*, edited by Edelberto Torres-Rivas, Facultad Latinoamericana de Ciencias Sociales, vol. 6, 1993, pp. 11–33.

Tseng, Amelia. "Advancing a Sociolinguistics of Complexity: Spanish-Speaking Identities in Washington, D.C." *The Routledge Handbook of Spanish in the Global City*, edited by Andrew Lynch, Routledge, 2019, pp. 330–54.

Tseng, Amelia. *Empanadas, Pupusas, and Greens on the Side: Language and Latinidad in the Nation's Capital*. Georgetown UP, 2025.

Vaquero de Ramírez, María. *El español de América II: Morfosintaxis y Léxico*. Arco Libros, 1998.

Villalobos Benavides, Mariángel. *Sounding Salvadoran: Popular Music and Postwar Imaginaries of Salvadoran Identity in the Washington, D.C. Metropolitan Area*. 2023. U of Maryland, College Park, PhD dissertation.

Walton, Ellie, director. *La Manplesa: An Uprising Remembered.* Produced by Quique Avilés et al., 2021, www.lamanplesafilm.com/.

Yoon, Howard. "What's in a Name? The Avocado Story." *Kitchen Window, NPR,* 19 July 2006, www.npr.org/templates/story/story.php?storyId=5563805.

Young, Robert J. C. *Colonial Desire: Hybridity in Theory, Culture and Race.* Routledge, 1995.

Young, Vershawn Ashanti, et al. *Other People's English: Code-Meshing, Code-Switching, and African American Literacy.* Parlor Press, 2018.

Yzaguirre, Raúl, and Mari Carmen Aponte. "Willful Neglect: The Smithsonian and U.S. Latinos." *Smithsonian Institution Task Force on Latino Issues,* May 1994.

Zelaya, Karina. "Viñeta Cultural: Nantzin Paula López" (sidebar). "16. Tamachtilis 14. Nitakwa peyna," by Héctor Cárcamo et al., *Achtu Tasksalis: Aprendiendo Náhuat en el siglo 21,* edited by Héctor Cárcamo et al., Open Education University of Alberta, 2023. pressbooks.openeducationalberta.ca/nawatse/chapter/los-pronombres.

Zentella, Ana Celia. *Growing Up Bilingual.* Blackwell, 1997.

Zentmyer, G. A., et al. "Early History of the Avocado During the Time of the Conquistadores." *South African Avocado Growers' Association Yearbook,* vol. 10, 1987, pp. 11–12, www.avocadosource.com/WAC1/WAC1_p011.pdf.

INDEX

ABOUT THE AUTHOR

Ana Patricia Rodríguez is associate professor of U.S. Latina/o and Central American literatures at the University of Maryland, College Park. She is the author of *Dividing the Isthmus: Central American Transnational Histories, Literatures, and Cultures* (University of Texas, 2009) and coeditor of *De la hamaca al trono y al más allá: Lecturas críticas de la obra de Manlio Argueta* (Editorial Universidad Don Bosco, 2016). She is past president of the Latina/o Studies Association (2017–19).

Library of Congress Cataloging-in-Publication Data
Names: Rodríguez, Ana Patricia, 1963– author.
Title: Avocado dreams : remaking Salvadoran life and art in the Washington, D.C. metro area / Ana Patricia Rodríguez.
Description: [Tucson] : University of Arizona Press, 2025. | Includes bibliographical references and index.
Identifiers: LCCN 2025004408 (print) | LCCN 2025004409 (ebook) | ISBN 9780816546435 (hardcover) | ISBN 9780816546428 (paperback) | ISBN 9780816546442 (ebook)
Subjects: LCSH: Salvadorans—Washington (D.C.) | Salvadorans—Ethnic identity. | Washington (D.C.)—Emigration and immigration—Social aspects. | Washington (D.C.)—Emigration and immigration—Economic aspects.
Classification: LCC F205.S26 .R64 2025 (print) | LCC F205.S26 (ebook) | DDC 975.3004968/7284—dc23/eng/20250814
LC record available at https://lccn.loc.gov/2025004408
LC ebook record available at https://lccn.loc.gov/2025004409